AF182984

Competition, Coordination and Diversity

NEW THINKING IN POLITICAL ECONOMY

Series Editor: Peter J. Boettke, *George Mason University, USA*

New Thinking in Political Economy aims to encourage scholarship in the intersection of the disciplines of politics, philosophy and economics. It has the ambitious purpose of reinvigorating political economy as a progressive force for understanding social and economic change.

The series is an important forum for the publication of new work analysing the social world from a multidisciplinary perspective. With increased specialization (and professionalization) within universities, interdisciplinary work has become increasingly uncommon. Indeed, during the twentieth century, the process of disciplinary specialization reduced the intersection between economics, philosophy and politics and impoverished our understanding of society. Modern economics in particular has become increasingly mathematical and largely ignores the role of institutions and the contribution of moral philosophy and politics.

New Thinking in Political Economy will stimulate new work that combines technical knowledge provided by the 'dismal science' and the wisdom gleaned from the serious study of the 'worldly philosophy'. The series will reinvigorate our understanding of the social world by encouraging a multidisciplinary approach to the challenges confronting society in the new century.

Titles in the series include:

Good Governance in the 21st Century
Conflict, Institutional Change, and Development in the Era of Globalization
Edited by Joachim Ahrens, Rolf Caspers and Janina Weingarth

Institutions in Crisis
European Perspectives on the Recession
Edited by David Howden

Constitutional Economics and Public Institutions
Edited by Francisco Cabrillo and Miguel A. Puchades-Navarro

International Aid and Private Schools for the Poor
Smiles, Miracles and Markets
Pauline Dixon

The Rediscovery of Classical Economics
Adaption, Complexity and Growth
David Simpson

Economic Futures of the West
Jan Winiecki

Entrepreneurial Action, Public Policy, and Economic Outcomes
Edited by Robert F. Salvino Jr., Micheal T. Tasto and Gregory M. Randolph

Sweden and the Revival of the Capitalist Welfare State
Andreas Bergh

Competition, Coordination and Diversity
From the Firm to Economic Integration
Pascal Salin

Competition, Coordination and Diversity

From the Firm to Economic Integration

Pascal Salin

Honorary Professor, Université Paris-Dauphine, France

NEW THINKING IN POLITICAL ECONOMY

Edward Elgar
PUBLISHING

Cheltenham, UK • Northampton, MA, USA

© Pascal Salin 2015

All rights reserved. No part of this publication may be reproduced, stored in a retrieval system or transmitted in any form or by any means, electronic, mechanical or photocopying, recording, or otherwise without the prior permission of the publisher.

Published by
Edward Elgar Publishing Limited
The Lypiatts
15 Lansdown Road
Cheltenham
Glos GL50 2JA
UK

Edward Elgar Publishing, Inc.
William Pratt House
9 Dewey Court
Northampton
Massachusetts 01060
USA

A catalogue record for this book
is available from the British Library

Library of Congress Control Number: 2014950858

This book is available electronically in the **Elgar**online
Economics subject collection
DOI 10.4337/9781784710170

MIX
Paper from responsible sources
FSC® C013056

ISBN 978 1 78471 016 3 (cased)
ISBN 978 1 78471 017 0 (eBook)

Typeset by Servis Filmsetting Ltd, Stockport, Cheshire
Printed and bound in Great Britain by T.J. International Ltd, Padstow

For Théodore,
my grandson

Contents

Acknowledgments ix
Introduction xi

PART I FIRMS, MARKETS AND COMPETITION

1 The firm in a free society: following Frédéric Bastiat's insights 3
2 Firm or market: where are the limits? 19
3 Cartels as efficient productive structures 30
4 Property rights, competition and the European Union 44

PART II GLOBALIZATION AND INTERNATIONAL ECONOMIC PROBLEMS

5 Arguing in favor of globalization 57
6 World regulations and harmonization 77
7 International tax problems: between coordination and competition 101
8 The case against "tax harmonization" 127

PART III MONETARY INTEGRATION

9 Monetary union: pleading for another approach 145
10 Can optimum currency areas be determined in Europe? 152
11 A competitive approach to monetary integration 166

PART IV MONEY, FINANCE AND ECONOMIC POLICIES

12 The monetary economics of the Austrian school and the Chicago school 189
13 From the financial crisis to the debt crises 203
14 The future of monetary policies in an online world 221
15 The digital divide: policy or competition 240

PART V FOUNDATIONS OF ECONOMIC THEORY

16 The gap between Austrian economics and the mainstream 263
17 The income effect does not exist 279

References 291
Index 297

Acknowledgments

I am very grateful to the editors and publishers of the following publications who have given me permission to reprint some of the texts used (partially or fully) in the present book:

- *L'actualité économique* (Montréal)
- *The Cato Journal*
- *The Independent Review*
- *Journal des économistes et des études humaines* (De Gruyter, publisher)
- *The Journal of Libertarian Studies*
- *The Review of Austrian Economics*
- *The Wall Street Journal*
- P. Altmiks (ed.) (2011), *Die optimale Währung für Europa? Segen und Fluch des Euro*, Munich, Olzog
- H. Gissurarson (ed.) (2007), *Cutting Taxes to Increase Prosperity*, Reykjavik, Bokafélagio Publishing & RSE
- P. Gonda (ed.) (2007), *In Defense of the Free Market*, Prague, Liberalni Institut, Bratislava, Konzervativny Institut M.R. Stefanika
- M. Gollety (ed.) (2013), *L'art, la gestion et l'Etat – Mélanges en l'honneur de Pierre Gregory*, Paris, Editions Eska
- H. Siebert (ed.) (1990), *Reforming Capital Income Taxation*, Tübingen, J.C.B. Mohr, Institut für Weltwirtschaft an der Universität Kiel
- Centro Italiano Documentazione Azione Studi (CIDAS), Torino

In addition to the editors of the books mentioned above, I also thank the following persons: Robert Garber, Pierre Garello, Harmen Lehment, Tanja Linhardt, Mattia Molari, Lew Rockwell, Gail Saari, Bruce Shearer, Judith Thommesen.

The precise references of the texts are given in the footnotes of the relevant chapters.

Introduction

In any society, in any group of human beings, there is a fundamental problem to be solved: All individuals are different, one from the other – they have different capacities, different goals – and this is a great justification for having an individualistic approach to social and economic problems. But human beings are also social beings and they need links with others in order to fully live or even to survive. But, given their basic differences, how is it possible that a society gets coherence (that is be respectful of individual characteristics) and, meanwhile, makes it possible for individuals to live together and to benefit from their links with others? There is certainly a need for coordination or cooperation between them, but what does it imply? Constructivists are inclined to consider that a centralized process of organization is necessary, whereas others consider that – according to the famous analysis of Friedrich Hayek – a spontaneous order is possible and desirable. In the present book, we explore various aspects of this problem. The need for coordination or cooperation exists at the level of a business or firm as well as at a broader scale, that of a country or the world, and we are exploring the processes that make these all possible.

The present book has been composed from several articles, reports or unpublished papers that have been written by the author in the past. They are different, one from the other, as regards the dates at which they were written or published, their topics or even their level of sophistication. However, in spite of this great diversity, we believe that we could arrange a set of chapters that are coherent because they are founded on an explicit and common foundation. Our aim is to evaluate how coherent social systems can exist in spite of the extreme diversity of its components. This is the reason why we gave to this book the title *Competition, Coordination and Diversity: From the Firm to Economic Integration.*

Integration, unification, economic harmonization, political cooperation: these words are fashionable and they benefit from a positive appreciation. Integration is generally considered without any discussion as a desirable goal and the precise form it takes, for instance in Europe, has been raised to the position of a taboo. However, these concepts are most ambiguous and different people may give them quite opposite meanings.

Quite often misunderstandings and errors about these concepts stem from the fact that one is using arbitrary macroeconomic concepts instead of caring about individual decisions and actions. Using an individualistic and subjective approach provides a better understanding of these concepts and, therefore, policy decisions which better correspond to the real wishes of people.

From a very general point of view, any system – for instance, a human society – can be defined as integrated whenever its different parts are linked together in a coherent way, which means that all contribute to the efficient working of the whole. In other words these parts are not only placed side by side, nor working towards incompatible directions. From this point of view, no one can dispute the idea that societies ought to be integrated: Human beings are not separate atoms; they do not exist without links with others.

Thus, it is a fact of nature – which we do know by simple observation – that human beings are different one from the other. But we also know that they cannot exist, they cannot survive without having social links, without being part of an "integrated society". However, the crucial problem to be solved in any society concerns the means by which it can be integrated.

It is obvious that individuals draw their wealth – not only materially, but also spiritually and culturally – from their differences. Whenever two individuals are different, trade between them is possible and profitable. By "different" one means either that their abilities (the supply side) or their tastes and preferences (the demand side) are different. The great merit of Western civilization comes from the fact it made possible for human beings to differentiate one from the other and to benefit from the specificities of others. Free markets and competition are the traditional economic aspects of this general principle: producers do not try to do the same as other producers – that is, to harmonize their productions – but to do better than them. The prosperity of the modern world comes from this ceaseless quest for differentiation. And such a differentiation is not opposite to integration, quite the contrary, since it is the very means by which a coherent development of human societies is made possible.

What is true for two individuals is true for groups of individuals. As there is no reason for two groups of individuals to be perfectly identical – we are not members of a beehive – trade is possible and profitable. Only under a totalitarian dream are individuals considered as perfectly substitutable one to the other, able to do all the same tasks, and to live exactly in the same way. But differentiation is *the* distinctive characteristic of human beings. Trying to diminish, to suppress differentiation – that is, *harmonizing* – means denying a man his very essence. Pushed to its extreme, harmonization would mean the disappearing not only of trade but also of civilization.

Now, we also have to admit that there are limits to the need for diversification. The clearest example is that of social rules. In order to facilitate our relations with others, we have to accept some specific schemes of behavior and it would not be efficient for anyone to try to invent a new rule for his own sake. Another obvious example is that of language. The relations between individuals, which are essential to their survival, would be impossible if they did not share common languages. Similarly, there are a lot of other fields in which human beings have an interest in avoiding differentiation, for instance in the case of telecommunications it would not be efficient for anyone to use a different standard from the one which is used by others.

On the other hand the innovator is always someone who breaks the generally accepted methods to behave, to produce, to act. He is the one who introduces more differentiation in a society. And competition, namely free entry on markets, is useful just because it induces people to differentiate through innovation. From this point of view, it is important to stress that the dominant theory of competition – the so-called theory of pure and perfect competition – is completely misleading since it does not correspond to the real world. Thus, it assumes that, in order for competition to prevail, there must be a great number of producers producing the same good with the same production techniques. However, when competition is correctly defined as free entry into markets, competitors do not try to be identical one to the other, but, on the contrary, they are inclined to offer a better product produced at a lower cost. One of the great virtues of competition thus comes from the fact it induces producers to differentiate one from the other. But, as we will see in the present book, the determination of the optimal degree of diversification and, therefore, the optimal degree of homogenization, is one of the great problems all societies have to solve.

Thus, the life of a society can be described as an endless process to determine the optimal mix of differentiation and homogenization between people. According to the evolution of techniques and knowledge, this mix is evolving. If they are free to act, people adjust to their human environment by choosing either to differentiate or to adopt common standards and common behaviors. Saying that individuals adapt themselves to their society through their search for differentiation and homogenization is saying that they integrate. Integration is thus the end result of numerous and endless processes of adaptation of some individuals to other ones. In a free society the degree of differentiation and homogenization is therefore steadily changing, according to the perceptions and the capacities to innovate of individuals.

We are now at a time when there is an explicit effort to open the economies of all countries and continents. Thus, in Europe the efforts towards integration are already old and play an important role in the design of day-to-day economic policies and politics. But this European story also bears witness to the ambiguities attached to the concept of integration. In fact there are two conflicting views of integration, one according to which it implies more competition, and one according to which it implies more centralized harmonization. In other words, recognizing that any society has to solve this problem of the optimal mix of differentiation and homogenization, the differences between several processes of economic and political integration concern the way by which this mix is discovered: Is it by a spontaneous process of trials and errors by individuals or is it through constructivist decisions of those who hold the state power and who have, according to the words of Friedrich Hayek, "the pretence of knowledge"?[1]

Due to the complex and ever-changing nature of individuals and, therefore, of societies, one ought to admit that it is impossible to decide in advance what has to be unified and what must not be. We do not know, for instance, to which extent Europeans, Africans or Latin Americans need a single currency and which currency. We do not know whether we can design a legal framework for firms that would be better than any other one. We do not know whether we need a unified tax system. As in any other field of human activity we have to experiment. And experimenting means competition.

As an example, it is widely admitted in Europe that there cannot be a single market – that is, an integrated market – without a single currency. In fact, most people believe that the diversity of currencies constitutes an obstacle to trade and, therefore, would not be compatible with the existence of the single market. However, if it were true that there cannot be economic integration without a common currency, it would be even more justified to say that there cannot be a single market without a single language. In fact, it is more difficult to imagine two traders who use different languages than two traders who use different currencies. Why then is not the slogan "no single market without a single language" fashionable? And, according to the traditional – but debatable – concept of integration, should we not consider language unification as a priority for European integration?

The very concept of a single market – considered as something different from, and more desirable than, a common market – is in fact ambiguous. It is quite often viewed as a space in which all individuals would meet a similar – unified – environment. All efforts in favor of harmonization – in taxation, in laws, in money production – stem from this general view of integration. People feel that in order for competition to be "fair", everyone has a right to benefit from identical conditions of production.

This centralized, constructivist view of economic integration between countries is opposed to another one, the only correct one for those who believe in an individualistic approach of economic and social problems. According to this view, economic integration just means competition and the spontaneous discovery of the optimal degree of diversification. It implies that anyone is free to enter into a market as a supplier or a demander, whichever is his nationality or his place of residence. But it certainly does not mean that all participants to this single market be in identical conditions.

Each individual is placed in a specific environment, as regards climate, the skills of people in his society, his history or the rules he has to accept. People benefit from their differences if they are free to exchange. And the great virtue of competition is to make possible an optimal differentiation between people, namely that differentiation which is desired by them. Thus, economic integration between European countries – or between Latin American countries, African countries or Asiatic countries – can enhance the welfare of inhabitants as far as it makes possible to suppress obstacles to trade and the free movement of persons, capital, rules and ideas, but certainly not if it means the unification of their environment.

As we already stressed, if they are free to act, individuals are able to limit the degree of differentiation. Let us take the example of language once more. We use a language to communicate with family members, neighbors or people who are very far from us, and we could dream of a single language in the world. But the variety of languages is a fact, and is the outcome of a long adaptation to the concrete needs of people. In a case such as that of Europe, in which national borders are falling and in which relations between people belonging to different linguistic areas become more intense, a common language might be useful. And, in fact, it may be that role which is increasingly played by English. Some people regret it, but it is the result of a spontaneous process of selection. English has not been imposed by force, but it has been spontaneously adopted as a common language. The use of this same common language is unavoidable for many activities, such as air transportation – in which there would be dangers if each pilot would speak his own language – or business relations.

However, it does not mean that the use of English as a common language implies that it could become the single language of Europe, just because the needs of people are very diversified. Many people just need to communicate with other people in their neighborhood and their needs can be perfectly well satisfied by a national language or even a local dialect. It is striking, from this point of view, to see that some minority communities have kept their own languages for centuries, such as Germans in Russia, Albanians in Italy, and so on. In fact, they use their native language to meet their need for cultural identity and the common language – the one of the country in which they reside – for business relations.

This ought to occur in Europe, as well as in other parts of the world. Even if the use of English is ever-increasing, it does not mean the disappearance of other languages: Integration means an optimal mix of those various languages. From this point of view, it is quite characteristic that constructivist efforts to introduce a new, common language – for instance, Esperanto – have failed: They did not correspond to a perceived need of people. And to make a comparison, the euro can be considered as the Esperanto of currencies. If there was really competition in the field of currencies, it might fail, as Esperanto failed. But it benefits from a special privilege, which did not benefit to Esperanto, namely that it has a monopoly position through the support of public authorities. But there is no more a priori reason to believe that Europeans need a single currency than to believe they need a single language. We would just need to experiment (that is, to accept competition).

NOTE

1. This is the title of the Nobel Prize lecture delivered by Friedrich Hayek on December 11, 1974.

PART I

Firms, markets and competition

1. The firm in a free society: following Frédéric Bastiat's insights[1]

Frédéric Bastiat did not devote much attention to the problem of the firm, so taking an interest in his thoughts on the topic could seem strange. Yet, the foundations for a realistic theory of the firm (and, more generally, of the distribution of human activities) are found in Chapter 14, "Wages," of Bastiat's classic book *Economic Harmonies* (1863).[2] Further, the way used by Bastiat to lay the foundations of his analysis are both original and profound. In the present chapter, I will review Bastiat's approach, develop it more fully, and draw some practical and theoretical conclusions about the nature of the firm.

1. FRÉDÉRIC BASTIAT AND THE FIRM

> "The wage system particularly has been the object of the socialists' attack. They have almost gone so far as to present it as something hardly less cruel than slavery or serfdom. In any case, they have viewed it as an oppressive and one-sided arrangement having only the semblance of liberty, as exploitation of the weak by the strong, as tyranny exercised by capital over labor."
>
> **Bastiat (1863), p. 366**

Here, Bastiat clearly explains the Marxist vision according to which wage earners are exploited by capitalist entrepreneurs, and working relations are basically asymmetrical. Bastiat's own approach, on the other hand, is a dynamic analysis of the emergence of wages in a world of uncertainty.[3]

Interestingly, Bastiat's chapter on wages does not address precisely the issue of wages. Instead, Bastiat makes a comparison between the specific role of wages and other human phenomena. By so doing, he demonstrates that the existence and role of wages cannot be understood except by referring to a more general theory of human action in society. The process by which there is a differentiation of roles inside the firm is exactly the same as the process that induces people to buy and sell insurance or to pay and receive interest payments. Thus, Bastiat analyzes some of the reasons why individuals cooperate not only through exchange but also by creating associations.

One important reason for cooperation is the fact that different people hold different subjective expectations about the possibility of losses. When risk is viewed as too high, individuals may find it profitable to create a mutual insurance organization. Each member, by contract, agrees to bear a given portion of the damages incurred by other members. In such an organization, each member plays exactly the same role (except that each share is different from the other if the values of the insured properties are different). Such an organization is created because each member of the mutual fund prefers a low risk with a high subjective probability over a high risk with a lower probability. As Bastiat puts it: "Fixity is very attractive for people. However, when considering the nature of men and of their activities, it seems that fixity is not compatible with it" (Author's translation). Thus, individuals create associations in order to gain more fixity.

There is an interesting point in Bastiat's explanation, which is a real contribution to understanding human activities in society. He stresses that everyone, even socialists, agree about the benefits of associations as a means to share risks. But, he adds, "Indeed, the socialists give the name *association* exclusively to arrangements of this kind. As soon as speculation is introduced, they say, association disappears. I say that it is improved" (Bastiat, 1863, p. 363; emphasis in original). Thus, according to socialists, as soon as a speculator – a profit-seeker – is introduced in an association, its very spirit and its very justification vanish.

On the contrary, according to Bastiat, the speculator's presence enhances the association's capacity to meet its goals. Taking a dynamic view of the development of human activities, Bastiat thus imagines that some entrepreneur (or some company) comes to the group of mutual insurance members and tells them the following (1863, p. 364; emphasis in original):

> By providing for mutual insurance, you have tried to purchase your peace of mind. The price this precious asset costs you is the indeterminate assessment you set aside annually to cover your losses. But you never know in advance what this price will be; and, on the other hand, your peace of mind is never complete. Well, I am here to propose a different procedure. In consideration of a *fixed annual premium* that you will pay me, I will assume the risk for all losses. I will insure all of you, and here is the capital to guarantee my promises.

From a practical point of view, it is likely that it is easier for one person (or the representatives of a company) to decide to meet the numerous members of the mutual fund rather than the reverse, and this is a logical implication of the theory of collective decision. However, from a theoretical point of view, it does not matter at all whether the negotiation between the entrepreneur and the mutual fund members has been initiated by one or the other. There is a fundamental symmetry in the arrangement, as in any contractual arrangement. The final arrangement ought to be the same whether an individual chooses to cooperate through contract with a group of individuals or whether several individuals decide in common to negotiate with him and to sign such an agreement.

In the real world, such as in starting a new business, neither the first nor the second situation prevails. Usually, the team of workers – analogous to the mutual organization – does not exist before the entrepreneur is present. Rather, a potential entrepreneur assembles the team of workers, according to his project, by hiring isolated workers who did not know each other. Likewise, the insurance entrepreneur establishes his project, and enrolls isolated insured persons who did not know each other. But, once more, this is not a substantial aspect of the problem. In any case, the relations between all of them are exactly the same.

The members of the association agree to pay a little more than their normal share in order to get perfect safety and peace of mind. According to socialists, says Bastiat, there is no more association since an intermediary has introduced himself between the associates. But, Bastiat argues, there is no fundamental change, except that the associates have found a way to remain in the association without having to care about its management.

As regards the entrepreneur, he provides two sorts of services. First, he takes away from the associates any remaining element of risk. Second, he takes care of the management of the association. Bastiat stresses the voluntary, and therefore beneficial, character of this contractual arrangement since, in any exchange, both parties to the exchange, given their differences in capacities and tastes, benefit from their specialization, which makes exchange possible. According to Bastiat (1863, p. 365): "The association thus transformed is in a position to improve in every way."

Bastiat uses his insurance example to show how purely contractual arrangements make it possible for individuals to better organize social cooperation and to better manage life's inherent risks. He then generalizes this approach, making it applicable to all sorts of human activities. For example, he is able to explicate the role of wages, profits and interests, and, by implication, the working of the firm.

It should be clear that while a firm is an association in the sense that Bastiat uses the term, it is not an association in the way that socialists use it. Thus, Bastiat writes (1863, pp. 366–7):

> Because of these same prejudices, this same ignorance, [socialists] rail constantly against *interest*, or else against *wages*, which are *fixed* forms, and therefore highly developed, for the payment of what is due to capital and labor. [. . .]

> Further, it is because of this fallacious approach of socialists that wage earners wanted to get rid of the wage system and to replace it by some sort of association, as if *association* and *wages* were mutually exclusive.

This mistrust in wages and in the wage system may seem overcome in our time, but, in fact, we just find it under other forms. It certainly inspires Marxists, since they describe the entrepreneur as someone who is in such a power position that he can extract part of the return that ought to be obtained by workers as a counterpart to their productive contribution to the firm output. The idea according to which only workers (wage earners) are productive, whereas the entrepreneur is a sort of parasite that extracts resources from the community of workers, has, explicitly or implicitly, inspired all experiments and proposals about worker management. Further, this idea is present whenever one disagrees with what his or her "fair share" is, an implication that wage earners ought to receive a part of the profits of a firm.

2. THE FIRM AS A SYSTEM OF COOPERATION

Following Bastiat's example – Bastiat, by the way, can be considered as a precursor of the modern theorists of contracts and agency problems – let us assume that a team of workers does exist. It can transform into a capitalist firm by two means:

1. An entrepreneur offers a new set of contracts by which he specializes in organizing the team and taking care of risk.
2. Workers decide to become wage earners so they hire the services of an entrepreneur who, according to the contract between them, only gets a residual income (that is, the part of value added which is not absorbed by wages and interests).

In any case, the firm newly created, through the transformation of the team of workers, is nothing other than a set of contracts. As such, its creation is necessarily beneficial to all, as is any contract that has been freely agreed upon by contractors. By substituting a more complex set of contracts (the firm) for a simpler set of contracts (the team of workers), those who voluntarily contract reveal that they consider the new set as beneficial for all of them.

It is true that, in some cases, they may have made the wrong choice and may regret it, but this is not the issue. At the time they accept the new set of contracts, they believe it to be beneficial. The fact that, throughout history, human beings have regularly selected the set of contracts known as a firm, rather than selecting other sets of contracts, is evidence that they have learned from experience that the firm is the most efficient set of contracts.

Bastiat identified two justifications for this differentiation in roles: a better organization of the productive process, and a better distribution of risk-taking. Let us consider them successively.

2.1 Organization by a Manager

In order to better analyze the improvements thus introduced by firms, let us first focus on the problem of personal capacities and specializations by considering a purely imaginary situation in which there is no uncertainty about the final production of a team of workers. Let us also assume that we are initially in a pure exchange economy without any economic organization. Each individual is endowed with primary resources and his own productive capacities (his mind). He transforms the resources he owns or the ones he got by exchange, and he sells any output that he does not invest or consume himself. His customer, in turn, transforms what he bought, and consumes, invests or sells the output. For instance, to build a car, one worker would build a chassis and sell it to some other worker. The second worker would add a body, and sell the product to a third worker who would add an engine – and so forth until the entire car is produced.

But to increase productivity and, therefore, the income of each member of this productive chain, a team organization is probably desirable. We will distinguish between two basic cases, one in which self-organization by the workers is possible, and another where such self-organization is not possible.

When self-organization is possible

If the productive process is simple and the team is small, self-organization is possible. The members of the team organize themselves, allocating a specific task to each according to their respective abilities.

However, a problem will appear as soon as the common product of the team has to be allocated. If the allocation is decided after the production has taken place, there is a great probability that producers will disagree about the share each is to receive. Let us assume that they somehow reach agreement about distribution (for instance, thanks to some voting process). In order to maintain peaceful relations within the team, all members accept it, although it may create a distribution of wealth considered as unfair by some of them. There also exists the possibility that the decisions about the distribution are brought about via coercion: the strong members coerce the weaker ones, as is the case under socialist production. The possibility of such an outcome under this type of decision process may lead people to be more reluctant to engage in team production, and therefore reduce the overall productive capacity of the society.

The best way to obtain a peaceful and agreed-upon distribution of the total return is for the team members to contractually agree on the rules before production takes place. Thus, economic calculation is possible and distributional risks are eliminated. This solution is beneficial for people because, as Bastiat wrote, people like fixity. While the cost of fixity may, in some cases, outweigh its benefits, in which case people will not buy it, in the present case, the cost is presumed to be smaller than the benefit, making it worthwhile to accept it. In fact, in this case, the costs are mainly negotiation costs. The members of the team have to discover supplies and demands for the various possible qualifications of members. The shares will finally depend on the contribution of each member of the team and on the relative scarcity of his precise ability; there is no reason to believe that such productive contributions will be equal, so there is no reason to expect all shares to be equal.

Thus, a system of cooperation based on a set of contracts has replaced a series of bilateral contracts and exchanges. Members of the team can sell their labor services, rather than their output, to a collective entity. In exchange, each member receives a previously agreed-upon share of the common output. The institutional change to a more complex and abstract set of contracts allows for an overall improvement in productivity.

An individual producer's share of the common production can be called a wage, but referring to this person as a wage earner instead of as a productive team member is only a specification of his more general status: He is a producer who acts and trades.

When self-organization is impossible

If producers are numerous and if the productive process is complex, self-organization may, in practice, be impossible. In such a case, the team members (the wage earners) will have an interest in looking for an organizer, as Bastiat suggested. We may call this organizer a manager, but it would be premature to call him an entrepreneur, since we have assumed for the time being that there is no uncertainty. According to their respective comparative advantages, the producers of the firm specialize either in this general management task or in another more specific productive task; thus, a differentiation of roles is introduced in the firm.

However, it would be wrong to interpret this differentiation as an asymmetry. The manager is not at the top of some hierarchical organization, giving orders to people with a lower status. The members of the organization engage in different tasks; there would, after all, be no sense in a contract between identical contractors. However, these differences do not and cannot imply any asymmetry; all members of the organization are equal in the sense that they have equal rights.

In the case of the firm, the manager and the other workers sign contracts with the abstract entity called "the firm" – which is the collectivity of members – and they are all linked by the same type of relations. From this point of view, we may as well say that the manager hires the other workers or say that the workers hire a manager. It is not substantial to the understanding of the working of the firm to decide who hires whom. In fact, it may be preferable not to use such a term as "to hire." Rather, we may be more satisfied with saying that the individuals are contractors, they are partners in exchange, and they get part of the output. We may imagine that, historically, in one case, the manager looks for workers and "hires" them and that, in another case, the workers look for a manager and "hire" him, but the result is exactly the same. There is an agreement between all of them for a given specialization of each one.

When the firm exists because all agreed to their respective contracts, workers sell their services to the organizer, who, in turn, sells the output on the market, pays the wages, and keeps his share of the output. The important point here is that such a set of contracts never constitutes a command system. Semantic confusion is introduced when one says that the manager or, later on, the entrepreneur, "hires" the workers, when, in fact, he buys their services. A similar confusion exists when one says that there is a hierarchy in the firm, with the manager giving orders to the workers. A hierarchy would imply a command system in which relations are unilateral.

Such a unilateral command system is the case with relations between the state and citizens. The former give orders to the latter, and use coercion to ensure that they are obeyed. Clearly, this can never be the case if relations are based on free contracts, as occurs in the firm. From this point of view, it is fallacious to describe a firm as an organization structured by a hierarchy. In a firm the managers are not at the top of some hierarchy; they just have a different and more complex role than other participants.

In any contract, there is a necessity for each contractor to make sure that others fulfill their specific obligations. Let us consider what happens when workers sell their services to a manager. The workers have the easy task of making certain that the manager pays the wages that have been agreed upon. The manager, on the other hand, has the far more difficult task of monitoring the workers – who may be numerous and who have varied skills – to ensure that they are performing according to their agreement. Thus, the manager spends far more time ensuring compliance of the workers than the workers spend ensuring compliance of the manager. This differentiation of roles and monitoring tasks gives the impression that there is a hierarchy. Again, let us be clear, the manager is not a commander-in-chief of an army of workers. A well-functioning capitalist firm incorporates monitoring procedures, but no hierarchical relations. *It could even be said that the capitalist firm has been invented because it is not a hierarchical system.*

Stressing this feature of the capitalist firm makes clear that such a firm is not essentially hierarchical, so it is inappropriate to define it as such. However, concrete appearances are not always as clear-cut as that. In reality, a contract can never stipulate all of the duties of a wage earner, so some broad language is likely to be included in the contract, such as saying that the wage earner will follow the instructions of the firm's owner or manager. This opens the door to possible misunderstandings or refusals to engage in particular actions under particular circumstances.

For example, contractual duties are more loosely defined in Latin countries than in Anglo-Saxon countries. This may allow Anglo-Saxon workers more leeway in disagreeing to take actions not explicitly covered in the contract, while leaving Latin wage earners feeling that they must follow orders and have less say over their contracts. Nonetheless, such contractual specifications (or lack thereof) do not transform the nature of the firm, namely the fact that it is a set of contracts between individuals who benefit from the same rights.

2.2 Uncertainty

Let us leave now the purely hypothetical case of a firm without uncertainty. Since people like fixity, they are ready to pay for the services consisting of suppressing uncertainty. As is well known, the entrepreneur is precisely the one who bears the cost of uncertainty. Since the value of the firm's future production is uncertain, the entrepreneur promises to the wage earners a fixed wage which is less than the expected value of their production. By the same token, the wage earners are paying the entrepreneur to take care of uncertainty. If the market value of the production is higher than the costs, the entrepreneur earns a profit; if it is lower than the costs, the entrepreneur suffers a loss. The wage earners earn the same wage in either case.

The wage earners could decide in advance, without knowing the total market value of their combined output, the share of the total output that is to be received by each worker. However, history has repeatedly shown that workers usually prefer to transfer the uncertainty to someone who specializes in the provision of certainty, in the same way as an insurer is paid for providing a safety service. As with any voluntary contractual arrangement, such a contract is beneficial for both parties. The workers buy more safety at the expense of a possible lower gain (but also, possibly, a lower loss) and the person who absorbs the uncertainty gets a more or less important return by selling safety services.

It is not necessary that the manager is the same person who absorbs the uncertainty, but there are two good reasons for them to be the same person. First, few would be willing to absorb the uncertainty without the ability to monitor the production process. Second, the manager has more incentive to efficiently control the production process and to innovate if the manager's returns depend on his own decisions.

Since the entrepreneur plays both roles, what we said previously about the relations between the wage earners and the manager still holds. The entrepreneur does not become a chief in a hierarchical structure merely because, in addition to his role as manager, he takes care of uncertainty. In no case is a firm built along the lines of a command system; it remains a set of contracts under any circumstance. The entrepreneur, who is both a manager and a sort of insurance company, is also a capital-owner, as has been well emphasized by Bastiat. After all, in order to be acceptable as insurer, an entrepreneur must own capital, making it possible to guarantee that he will honor his contracts, and attracting confidence from the other contractors.

Saying that the entrepreneur is the owner of the firm means that he owns part of the present means of production and rights on future profits. As an owner, he can sell the firm, that is, sell a complex set composed of capital goods, the specific organization he has implemented, the specific contracts he has signed, and so forth.

3. SOME IMPLICATIONS OF THE ANALYSIS OF THE FIRM

The traditional definition of the firm as a set of contracts is important and correct. Numerous consequences can be derived from this very definition. As already stressed, contracts exist because people are different. But differentiation does not mean asymmetry, which can only exist in a command system in which some people can coerce others. Relations are unilateral in a command system, bilateral in a contractual system. According to Mises (1996, p. 196): "There are two different kinds of social cooperation: cooperation by virtue of contract and coordination, and cooperation by virtue of command and subordination or hegemony."

As we know, individual goals are different and cannot be compared.

This has important implications to the free society and to the coercive society. Since there is no way to engage in interpersonal utility comparisons, it is impossible to claim that any voluntary relationship is asymmetrical, or that it benefits one party more than it benefits another. On the other hand, when individuals are parties to transactions via coercion rather than voluntary choice, it is quite clear that one side gains and the other side loses. In comparing these two situations, it is clear that there cannot be asymmetries in a capitalist firm.

A similar argument may be made concerning information asymmetries. Different individuals choose to get different information, and people enter into various forms of associations because they have different knowledge. For instance, a wage earner transfers to the entrepreneur the uncertainty about the demand for his own work, because the entrepreneur better knows how to meet this demand. Thus, merely to observe that different individuals possess different information does not imply asymmetries in their relationship.

3.1 The Goal of the Firm

Microeconomics textbooks often state that "profit is the goal of a firm." This same statement is also made by socialists who attack the firm under the pretext that a firm's very existence tends to create beneficial results only for a small set of individuals, namely the owners. However, the textbooks and socialists are in error.

As a firm is a set of contracts, it cannot have a goal, since only individuals have intentional activities. Further, the individuals who sign contracts have different and even divergent goals. The entrepreneur may look for profit, but also seek other goals, such as prestige, influence or satisfaction of curiosity. Wage earners probably look for high wages, but are also likely to be interested in a pleasant working environment, insurance benefits or an easy commute. Not only do we not know these various goals, we do not need to know them. Traditional microeconomic analysis uses a simplistic approach with a single, arbitrary variable (the maximization of profit) as the goal of a firm. An alternate approach, used by Bastiat and Mises, assumes that each individual participant's goal is personal utility maximization, which may or may not be consistent with profit maximization of the firm. Such an approach is logically superior to the mathematical approaches in modern textbooks.

There is a plurality of goals in a firm because there is a plurality of individuals whose goals are diverging or even antithetical to each other. One fundamental role of the entrepreneur, as an organizer of social cooperation, is to make these goals consistent with each other. In fact, it seems clear that a firm cannot work efficiently if this diversity of goals is not taken into consideration.

3.2 Decision-making in a Firm

While socialist societies create hierarchical organizations (wrongly called firms), and family-based societies are hierarchical, a capitalist organization is not hierarchical. In the capitalist firm, the owner and managers are not giving orders to wage earners; rather, they are fulfilling their own differentiated role as organizers, for the mutual benefit of all, wage earners as well as entrepreneurs. Some wage earners and some entrepreneurs are good at their respective roles, and others are bad. In such a mix, some outcomes may create the illusion of a command society, but this does not make it so.

Further, because no contract can specify every possible circumstance, someone has to decide how to face new situations. When facing some new challenge, the entrepreneur, being the organizer of the work in the firm, is the one who decides what the worker has to do. The worker can argue that the decision does not correspond to the terms of the contract and, at the limit, can quit.

Making the decision to leave the firm is more or less easy. It depends, for instance, on the expectation of finding a new job on the labor market, on one's compensation and a variety of other individual factors. It may also depend on the institutional characteristics of the firm. If, for instance, a firm benefits from a monopoly privilege and a wage earner's job is very specialized (train driver, professor of economics, and so on), he may have difficulties in finding a new job. Thus, a worker's expectations of finding other employment may have an impact on that worker's belief in the existence of a hierarchy in the firm.

However, the existence of orders coming from the top and going to the lower levels is not a *substantial* characteristic of a firm. The fact is that there are firms in which orders are never given. Even if a more or less great number of managers behave as if they were in a command system, a capitalist firm cannot be defined or described by the existence of orders and hierarchy. Analyzing the nature of the firm requires the analysis to look for a firm's substance, rather than to merely consider the incidental features of some firms.

3.3 The Act of Will and the Differentiation of Interests

While the preceding analysis of the firm constitutes an answer to many of the usual prejudices about the respective interests of wage earners and entrepreneurs, the leftists also offer a static and biased approach. Because they do not understand the wealth-creating process or the coordinating role of the entrepreneur, they consider that what the entrepreneur gets is at the expense of the wage earners.

Further, when they object to the idea of profit maximization as the only goal of a firm, they do so for incorrect reasons. Rather than recognizing the myriad of goals by participants in a firm, they are happy to attribute an act of will to a collective entity, such as a firm. Once they attribute this collective entity with a will, they argue that it should take into account the interests of both wage earners and profit earners.

From this wrong interpretation of the very nature of the firm come all sorts of fashionable ideas, such as those who argue that "social logic" should supersede "financial logic." Likewise, there are those who argue that firm governance should consist of decision processes that include stakeholders as well as shareholders. While they correctly recognize that people in different roles have different interests, they fail to recognize that the capitalist firm has its particular organization precisely *because* of these different interests. It is, after all, the voluntary capitalist structure that allows all these interests to be made compatible with each other. This harmonious coexistence of interests is completely ignored by all fashionable streams of thought, as well as by political decision-makers.

3.4 Differentiation and Symmetry of Rights

Let us return to the previously mentioned problem of differentiation and symmetry of rights. In a contractual arrangement, individuals may have different goals and bring different capacities, but they have the same rights so that there is no asymmetry. However, as regards the working of firms, language often creates confusion. When symmetry exists in a social reality – as is the case with voluntary contracts – then the same symmetry should exist in language. However, the language employed when discussing firms is more or less contaminated by Marxian-type concepts.

For instance, if one says that "an employer hires an employee," one ought also to say that "an employee hires an employer," since both parties are equal and voluntary participants, and each is in a position to accept or reject the other. Likewise, if one says that "an employer fires an employee" when the employer terminates a voluntary agreement, one ought also to say that "an employee fires an employer" when the employee terminates the voluntary agreement. However, these second sets are not used in conjunction with the first sets, so the usually employed language suggests that the employer can unilaterally determine whether an agreement exists (to hire) or whether an agreement is terminated (to fire).

Many labor laws are predicated on the idea that there is an inescapable asymmetry between the employer and the employee. To rectify this supposed imbalance, many such laws make it more difficult for employers to fire wage earners than it is for wage earners to fire their employer (to quit their jobs). While different people possess different capacities to act – it may be easy or hard for a worker to get another job, and it may be easy or hard for an employer to get another worker – this does not imply any asymmetry in rights. All parties *can* act to engage in a contract, to not engage in a contract, or to terminate a contract.

One may even argue that because the entrepreneur has to bear some specific constraints, those who believe in the existence of contractual asymmetries should really give the entrepreneur the additional protection. If a firm fails, the entrepreneur loses his past investment in time and savings, whereas wage earners take their accumulated human capital with them. If ever someone had to be protected – which, obviously, is not the case – why would it not be the entrepreneur since, after all, he bears the uncertainty? The wage earners have traded away uncertainty for fixity, so their main potential claim to needing protection is gone.

In reality, the specific protection of wage earners cannot meet any rational explanation. It is nothing but the result of the working of majoritarian democracy. Wage earners are more numerous than entrepreneurs, and they vote to create a legal system, which, at least they believe, works in favor of their interests. However, in many countries, excessive regulations and taxes have made it impossible for potential wage earners and entrepreneurs to sign labor contracts, which is a real cause of unemployment. Because these existing laws make it more difficult for a wage earner to find a new job after leaving a previous one, additional labor laws get passed to increase the protection of wage earners against firing. This, in turn, further reduces the incentives for entrepreneurs to engage in contractual relationships with wage earners, and unemployment is increased, not decreased.

3.5 Profit-sharing

A correct understanding of the nature of the firm leads to the rejection of proposals that mandate worker participation or profit-sharing. Since the distribution of roles in the capitalist firm is done according to comparative advantage, the participation by workers in strategic decisions is one that reduces overall efficiency unnecessarily.

Further, profit-sharing with wage earners is also a contradiction, since wage earners traded away the uncertainty of profit for the certainty of wages. It would be analogous to sharing profits with bondholders (lenders); bondholders chose to be bondholders, rather than stockholders, to ensure a lower risk. If wage earners (and bondholders) want to share in the profit, they need to share in the absorption of uncertainty by buying shares of stock on the market.

When governments mandate profit-sharing, they are changing the relationship of each individual to the firm, and changing the extent to which each individual absorbs the uncertainty associated with the firm. As such, it is foolish to legally mandate profit-sharing.

Still, voluntary contractors must be free to decide any sort of contract. Thus, for instance, some entrepreneurs and employees may decide that employees will receive both a fixed wage and some participation in profits. This is often done with stock options, which are used to create incentives for those who engage in strategic decisions to make good decisions. Indeed, stock options are sometimes considered by stockholders as a good way to monitor the managers.

At the same time, though, it is obvious that holding shares of stock would be unlikely to modify the behavior of an unskilled or low-quality worker in a big firm. After all, the decisions or actions by such an individual worker are unlikely to have any real impact on the stock price, so no incentive for better individual performance is created. This is the reason why stock options are generally only offered to a limited number of wage earners – generally only to those whose actions can have an effect on the stock price.

3.6 The Nature of the Firm

Explaining the limits between the firm and the outside market is a traditional problem (which could be called the "Coase problem"). If the market is "efficient" (as most economists believe), why does the firm exist? After all, it is well established that economic planning cannot work at the worldwide level, or at a national level, so why should it work at the firm level?

Alas, the very question is based on the assumption that the firm is a non-market organization that engages in planning. However, this approach to the nature of the firm is flawed; the firm is not a planning system – that is a system in which those who have power give orders to others and in which there are no prices. Rather, a firm is a system of contracts and, as such, it is a market system.

In understanding the workings of various human systems, reference to the market is inappropriate, since a market exists as long as any sort of exchange exists. Rather, one ought to focus on questions such as the following: Are there free and voluntary contracts, or is there coercion? How are property rights defined and enforced? Are property titles tradable?

A free society is not a market economy; rather, it is a society of legitimate rights and free contracts. As is well known, coordination between individuals is made through the price system, the use of traditions and general rules. In the pure exchange economy, individuals do not need anything else. In many other cases, though, some process of voluntary organization has to be added, and is considered an improvement. In such cases, coordination implies cooperation through some process of collective decision.[4] This process is collective in the limited sense that concerned individuals explicitly agree about some common rules or ways to behave and act. It does not mean that the organization by itself thinks and acts.

Such is the case with associations (condominiums, mutual funds, and so on). By entering freely into an association, a team or a firm, an individual agrees not only to pay his fee or to sell his services, but also to cooperate with others according to some specific rules which exist or which are to be developed.

In a firm, as in an association, individuals share something in common, which may give the impression that the organization has its own life, goals and existence. As an example, what is called a "firm culture" is not an objective reality, but the result of more or less common perceptions. In fact, it may even be more correct to say that there exists not only one single culture in a firm, but several cultures. Whenever this feeling of sharing something in common fades away, individuals may end their agreement and "leave" or, let us say, "fire" the firm.

4. CONCLUSION

As Bastiat stressed so well, socialists favor associations because they view associations as collective entities that possess the will to act. As such, socialists celebrate associations as being a superior alternative to capitalism. Further, they often use associations as unofficial parts of the state through which they can gain subsidies and privileges for themselves and their pet projects.

Libertarians are certainly in favor of voluntary associations, since libertarians understand human nature, and know that individuals are social beings. But they also know, as Bastiat made so clear, that firms are the most perfect forms of associations.

NOTES

1. Initially published as "The Firm in a Free Society: Following Frédéric Bastiat's Insights" (Salin, 2002). A previous version of this paper had been presented at the conference

"2001, Bastiat's Odyssey," Cercle Frédéric Bastiat, The International Society for Individual Liberty, Libertarian International, Dax, 3 July 2001. I thank members of the Séminaire de théorie économique Jean-Baptiste Say at University Paris-Dauphine (particularly Georges Lane, Jacques Raiman and Alain Wolfelsperger) for their comments on a previous version of this text.

2. Bastiat (1863). All quotations of Frédéric Bastiat in the present chapter are from the 1964 edition in English.
3. This uncertainty and its role in wage-earning is particularly stressed in Lane (2001).
4. Thus, cooperation is only one form of coordination, a form which implies the explicit organization of inter-individual relations, either under a hierarchical or non-hierarchical structure. The other form could be named "spontaneous order," as suggested by Friedrich Hayek.

2. Firm or market: where are the limits?[1]

The aim of the present chapter consists in evaluating to what extent the use of the main principles of economic theory can help in understanding the working of social organizations – more precisely enterprises – and the working of markets, namely these abstract places on which economic agents meet. In fact, one is too often tempted to use mechanistic approaches which are assumed to describe the working of entities which are artificially endowed with reason and will, although one can understand their working only by taking into consideration the behavior of individuals who are concerned by their working. From this point of view, one ought, for instance, to avoid doing statements such as "the firm is deciding" or "the firm is innovating," but also "the firm is paying taxes," and so on. It is true that one uses such statements for obvious language facilities, but in so doing, one runs the risk of using what Ayn Rand called "floating abstractions" – terms not clearly related to reality – and thus forgetting the human reality which is hidden behind this linguistic fiction. As a consequence, one uses the same term to mention the capitalist firm – which we will analyze later on – and a Soviet-type firm, which ought rather to be called a "productive organization."

In fact, many people consider a firm as a set of material and human means, which combined together make possible the production of goods and services that are to be bought by individuals or other firms. However, in order to fully understand the very nature of the firm, it is necessary to go back to its basic definition. As already recalled, a firm is nothing else than a set of contracts. In the case of a firm other than a one-person firm, there is first the initial contract by which the firm is created by shareholders, and later on the contracts signed between, on the one hand, the owners of the firm (or, possibly, their representatives, themselves appointed by contracts) and, on the other hand, wage earners, but also contracts with suppliers, lenders or customers. Each of these partners in exchange has a specific role to play according to the contract one has signed. Each firm gets its specific form according to the way by which these contracts are specified, changed and operated. But it is precisely because one has never seen a contract deciding, reasoning, acting or paying taxes that it is, strictly speaking, incorrect to say that "the firm" decides, reasons, acts or pays taxes. It is certainly by keeping in mind this definition – both simple and inescapable – of the firm that one can correctly analyze the working of an enterprise or a market, thus avoiding a mechanistic approach and the building of arbitrary concepts that may lead to management errors as well as harmful economic policies.

1. THE NATURE OF THE FIRM

Looking for the limits between the firm and the market – and, therefore justifying the very existence of firms – is a traditional problem (which could be called, as already mentioned, the "Coase problem," since Ronald Coase is the economist who has given the best systematic analysis of this problem [Coase, 1937]). In fact, many economists think that the market is the most efficient form of organization in order to meet the various human needs in the best way, so that one may wonder why other types of organization – such as so-called "non-market" organizations – may exist, which is assumed to be the case of the firm. The answer usually given to this question consists in saying that one would probably use only market processes if transaction costs did not exist. But contracting necessarily implies that the contractors must bear costs, at least because they must devote time to this contractual activity and time is the scarcest resource. In a completely imaginary world in which these costs would not exist, it could happen that the firm does not exist and that, at every minute, contracts be signed between the suppliers of work services and an entrepreneur who would decide the processes of production and would sell the resulting commodities on markets. But even in such extreme conditions, the production might not occur under optimal conditions. In fact, the entrepreneur has, among others, the fundamental role of taking care of production risks. But these risks would be increased if the contracts with the suppliers of labor services had to be renegotiated every minute, which, by the way, would also be a factor of risk for these labor suppliers. It is therefore obvious that labor contracts must be signed for a minimum span of time. But, to be sure, the optimal duration of a contract depends on circumstances and it may not be the same for the supplier and the purchaser of labor services. Therefore, it ought normally to be an important item for negotiation. Anyhow, the existence of transaction costs and uncertainty costs is an explanation of the fact that one gives some durability to a set of contracts. But when is it possible to say that such a set of contracts signed by an entrepreneur does constitute a firm?

By using extreme assumptions, one may have the possibility to bring some nuance to the radical opposition, which is usually done between market processes and "non-market" processes (which would be those of the firm). We first have to make the role of the market clearer. To evaluate and understand the working of an economic system, it is not sufficient to know to which extent markets do exist. In fact, a market can be defined as this abstract place on which exchange takes place. Now, exchange always exists, not only in so-called "market economies" but also in centrally planned economies. Therefore, what is characteristic of what is called a "market economy" is not the fact that people have recourse to markets, but the fact that trade takes place between persons who own individual property rights. This is the case with a capitalist system. The later one can be defined as a system of legitimate property rights, which means that these rights have not been obtained by the use of constraint, but by the personal creative efforts of individuals. Thus, capitalism has an ethical foundation and it is for this very reason that it is efficient. In fact, when the legitimate property rights of every person are correctly defined, the working of a society is based on a simple but powerful rule: respecting the rights of others. Then anyone knows what he is entitled to do and, therefore, he is responsible, which means that he bears by himself the consequences – good or bad – of his own act. Moreover, being responsible, he is induced to obtain the best possible use of his human and non-human resources, since he does know that he will be the person who will get the return or who will have to bear the possible losses. From this comes the efficiency of a capitalist system.

It is within this framework that one ought to look for the limits of the firm: Is there a fundamental opposition between the processes used on markets (more precisely, on capitalist markets) and those used inside the firm? First, it is inordinate to describe a firm as a "non-market" organization, since, as already recalled, a firm can be defined as a set of contracts. Therefore there is not a radical system gap when one shifts from the market to the firm. Thus, what is characteristic of the firm is not the fact that one should use non-market processes, but the fact that the constituent contracts have certain durability and that they are subject to coordination processes between them under the responsibility of the entrepreneur. This would be a reason for characterizing the firm not as an organization, but as a system of coordination of contracts. An army is an organization, namely a system in which a chief gives orders to subordinates. But, by its very nature, a firm is not an organization, even if the fact that the entrepreneur is the coordinator of contracts and can let people believe that he is the chief of an organization and even if, in real life, some entrepreneurs behave as "big chiefs."

In spite of this, it is important, in order to understand the firm and maybe also to manage it efficiently, to remember that a firm is a set of contracts. Now, in a contract there is not a dominating person and a dominated one, but two partners who are different and who, precisely, sign a contract *because* they are different, so that they can trade different commodities and services.[2]

2. THE WORKING OF THE FIRM

Thus, there is no fundamental opposition between the firm and the market, except for the fact that the firm is a set of coordinated contracts with a certain duration. However, is it possible to push forward the comparison between both? And, in particular, to wonder to which extent one may find inside the firm the characteristic features of a capitalist system? It is clear that the capitalist firm rests on the same principles: The owners of the firm have legitimate property rights and they legitimately receive the profit, namely what remains available from the value of the sold output, once all contracts have been honored; as regards wage earners, they are the legitimate owners of their labor services which they sell against a wage. Each one is deemed to be respectful of the others' rights. However, there are some practical difficulties, which may create some deviations with respect to the basic model. Most of these difficulties can be analyzed as particular aspects of the general and well-known problem of "the principal and the agent" (or agency dilemma): Partners in a contract are not necessarily and strictly respectful of others' rights, they can have an opportunist behavior which makes necessary the control of the "agent" by the "principal" as regards the way contracts are carried out. But this control is costly.

Let us take a first example of these opportunist behaviors. We have already recalled that, being responsible, the owner of a good was induced to use it in the most efficient way. However, in a firm, in most cases, the owner of material means of production is scarcely the one who uses them. The wage earner who is in charge of it, not being the owner, is less induced to do the best use of it. Therefore, it is necessary to control that available resources are not wasted, that maintenance is well done, and so on. Now, there exists a theoretical means to overcome this difficulty: organizing things so that the one who is using a resource be the legitimate owner of it, which means he is responsible. As an example, one could imagine a company specialized in transportation by buses or trucks in which each driver would be the owner of his own vehicle. Thus, one would get closer to the extreme model we had previously considered: each driver would constitute, in some sort, a small separate firm and he would sell his services to an entrepreneur who would be in charge of the coordination between the different drivers and customers and who, on another hand, would be the owner of the brand of this transportation firm which would be widely "dematerialized."[3]

Is not such a scheme very close in fact to the case in which there are several franchised firms linked by contracts? The coordination between activities, instead of being done in a centralized way (contracts between owners of firms and wage earners, for instance) is done in a *de*centralized way (contracts between the owners of a firm and franchised firms, then between these franchised firms and wage earners)? It is because it makes the discipline of responsibility more widely spread that franchising is an efficient system of production.

It is obvious that the control problem is particularly concerned with the implementation of a labor contract. In fact, this contract usually determines the level of the wage, the length of the labor period and, in very general terms, the tasks which are to be done. But a wage earner can always be tempted not to give the best he could give as far as he will not bear by himself the harmful consequences of his behavior. It could be possible to diminish such a temptation by two different means. First, by deciding in advance the work to be done by a wage earner second after second, and by controlling ex post the actual implementation of his tasks – but this would obviously imply considerable costs. Second, by having recourse to the assumption we have just suggested, the one in which, instead of being a wage earner, each supplier of labor services would be a small firm; instead of selling his labor services, he would sell the output obtained by his labor and, as the legitimate owner of this output, he would be induced to get it in the most efficient conditions. But, as we know, this solution would also imply high costs. One important task of the entrepreneur, as far as he cannot use one or the other solution, then consists in trying to minimize the costs of control.

To reach this target, one may try to make the wage earner more "responsible," which may imply, for instance, not asking him to deliver a given number of working hours, but asking him a given result which he is free to obtain by using the means which seem to him the most appropriate. Such a solution also has the advantage that the wage earner can experiment, which means that if he ever commits errors, he is induced to look for more efficient means to get the desired result, instead of just acting blindly in a way compatible with schemes which are imposed to him and even possibly of being so lazy as to resist any innovation.

It is also well known that the problem consisting of controlling the "agent" by the "principal" exists in relations between the owners of firms and their partners inside the firms. This is particularly true in firms the capital of which is owned by a very great number of very dispersed shareholders. This is the case, for instance, in the banking sector. By contrast, in the eighteenth and nineteenth centuries, there were a great number of small banks owned by a small number of shareholders. As owners, these later ones were responsible and they avoided taking too many risks in order to avoid bankruptcy. Nowadays, there are rather a small number of banks with very numerous shareholders. These later ones have not the possibility to exert a strict control over the decisions taken by the managers who are wage earners and not capitalists. As such they have no personal interest in protecting and developing the capital of the firm, so that they may be inclined to take too many risks, in particular if it makes it possible for them to get higher returns.[4]

From this point of view, it would also, therefore, be preferable to have production structures closer to those which we have mentioned, such as franchising, namely a system of coordination between capitalist entities. Thus, instead of having a single very large bank, with many dispersed offices over a very large territory, it would be more efficient to have a great number of small banks, owned by responsible capitalist owners, but linked together by a series of contracts and sharing the same single "brand." If such a structure is not frequent nowadays, it is for a large part because public policies encourage following the choice of the great dimension (the famous "too big to fail").

From a more general point of view, previous remarks imply serious doubts about the usual prejudice in favor of the great dimension. As one too often adopts a technical and material approach of economic problems, one generally considers that there are economies of scale in most activities, particularly because there are fixed costs, so that the larger the scale of production, the lower the unit cost of production. To be sure, such economies of scale exist, for instance, because the costs of information are the same for a trading activity on a financial market, whatever the number of operations made by a financial institution; the research cost for a new product or the cost of a marketing campaign are the same whatever the volume of production; and so on. But, by focusing on these technical aspects, one forgets that a firm is above all a system of contracts and of relations between human beings whose behaviors determine the working of the firm. But, as already stressed, there are "diseconomies of scale" which are of a human and institutional nature. The more numerous the wage earners, the more difficult it is to control the implementation of contracts by everyone and the more the discipline of responsibility is alleviated. From this point of view, big firms are fragile. As an example, it is characteristic that the greatest part of important innovations during recent decades has been the result of research made by teams of researchers, who were limited in size, but very flexible, in small or medium enterprises and not in the large laboratories of big firms.[5]

If this analysis is valid, one may ask why present structures of production are not closer to the decentralized capitalist model which we have suggested, namely a system in which small firms implement various processes of coordination between them. A main reason comes from the fact there is a legal definition of the firm and a wide range of legislation concerning the creation of a firm and its activities. The consequence is a considerable increase in operating costs and transaction costs (for instance, to modify the perimeter of a firm). This means that there are important fixed costs which induce looking for a sufficiently great dimension, and which decrease the institutional flexibility of firms.

However, it is also true that requiring firms in a country to adopt the rules defined by legislation brings an advantage: The information costs about the ways a firm is operated decrease. But there is also a very high cost by preventing firms from devising and experimenting different operating rules. In this field, as in any other field, competition is a factor of innovation and suppressing it is therefore harmful.

To put it briefly, determining the more or less extensive range of activities in a firm implies looking for the best way to make two opposite requirements compatible: minimizing transaction and uncertainty costs, but avoiding a lightening of the discipline of responsibility and minimizing control costs. From this point of view institutional flexibility would be desirable in order to adapt to specific concrete circumstances and technical evolutions (which modify operating conditions as well as transaction costs, information costs and control costs). But legal obligations decrease the institutional flexibility of firms and, by increasing information, operating and transaction costs, induce deciding a dimension of the firm greater than would be the case otherwise; so doing, they reduce the incentive to imagine and to implement coordination processes between productive structures. The opposition currently made between the firm and the market is thus reinforced, although one might consider as optimal a situation in which the frontier between "in-market" activities and "out-of-the market" activities would be blurred and more variable. It is all the more possible to imagine such a situation in our time since digital techniques make it possible to decrease transaction costs.

As we have already stressed, a capitalist economy is not mainly characterized by the fact it is a market economy, but by the fact it is a society of legitimate rights and free contracts. As is well known, the coordination between individuals is mainly made by the price system, the use of traditions and the respect for general rules of conduct. In a pure exchange economy, people do not need anything else. But in many other cases, one must add processes of voluntary organization that are quite often considered as an improvement. Coordination then implies cooperation via a process of collective decision.[6] This process is in fact collective from a limited point of view as far as concerned individuals explicitly agree to apply some common rules – such as the law of majority – or to adopt specific ways of behavior and action. But, obviously, this does not mean that the organization thinks and acts by itself.

Such is the case of associations (condominiums, mutualistic organizations, cultural or charitable associations, and so on), but also firms. By entering freely into an association, a team or a firm, an individual accepts not only to pay a member fee or to sell his working services, but also to cooperate with others, according to some specific rules which exist or which have to be imagined. In a firm, as in an association, individuals share something in common, which may give the feeling that the organization has its own life, its own aims and its own existence. As an example, what is called a "corporate culture" is not an objective reality, but it is the result of perceptions which are more or less common to the participating individuals. In fact, it would even be more correct to say that there is not a single culture in a firm, but several cultures. Anyhow, when this feeling of sharing something in common fades away, it may happen that individuals decide to end their agreement and leave the firm or, one may even say, that they "fire" the firm.

Finally, there is an important reason not to make a radical opposition between the firm and the market. In fact, it is well known that the market makes it possible to obtain the "harmony of interests." In other words, two persons or two groups of persons who have different capacities, knowledge and aims increase their welfare through exchange. When two persons freely decide to trade together, one is certain that no one is losing (if not, the exchange would not take place) and that both partners get a gain. It is precisely because they are different that exchange is possible and profitable. In fact, it is not the market that makes possible the harmony of interests, but free exchange and free contracts. Now, since a firm is a set of contracts, it makes possible the harmony of interests.

From this point of view, it is wrong to say – as is the case in all microeconomics textbooks – that the aim of the firm consists of maximizing profit. In fact, the owners of a firm may aim at maximizing their profit, but they may have other targets (enjoying entrepreneurship, liking risks, looking for recognition, and so on). The other partners of the firm have completely different targets. Thus, wage earners probably look for maximizing their wages, but also getting a job that they do like, having a pleasant working environment, and so on. Thanks to the coordination processes between individuals, these very different targets become compatible one with the other. It is in fact mainly the role of the entrepreneur to obtain this harmony of interests and it is when it is well implemented that the firm works in the best possible way.

3. CARTELS, A MODEL OF ORGANIZATION FOR THE FUTURE?[7]

Cartels are not well considered. They are generally viewed as organizations that are created by producers in order to plunder customers. More precisely, a cartel is usually defined as an agreement between several producers in order to get a monopoly power, namely in order to charge purchasers with a higher price than the competitive price.

In fact, if competition does take place between several producers of the same good, each of them is induced to decrease his prices in order to get a satisfactory market share. According to the traditional economic theory of competition, the competitive pressure gives an incentive to each producer to decrease his price to the point where his marginal profit becomes zero, which corresponds to an optimal situation for purchasers: A price lower than the competitive price would not be sustainable for producers, since they would get losses, so that production would disappear; a higher price would obviously be harmful for purchasers, but competition makes it impossible. Now this satisfactory order is disturbed whenever it is possible for producers to make an agreement in order to avoid competition. Thanks to their collusive behavior, they can diminish the quantity of goods supplied and thus increase the selling price of their products. Simultaneously, they must mutually promise not to differentiate their products in order to avoid reintroducing, via the characteristics of their products, a competition which they had suppressed in prices. In spite of the fact they are separate producers, they behave in exactly the same way as a monopolist would do. It is this traditional approach of cartels that is considered and condemned by most legislations that are supposed to defend competition.

But one may wonder whether such a view about cartels has a practical importance. First, a cartel built in such a way is basically unstable since it incorporates a fundamental contradiction. In fact, it is the interest of the whole set of producers that the total production be limited, in order to increase selling prices and to maximize joint profits. But, inside the cartel, each producer obviously has an interest in trying to increase his market share by decreasing his selling price beyond what would be necessary to maximize the returns of the cartel. Thus, the cartel may be destroyed. But it may also get a threat from outside as far as competition prevails, which means that any new producer may freely enter into the market in which there is a cartel. As private cartels are fundamentally unstable, the best answer public authorities could give to the possible existence of cartels does not consist in voting anti-cartel laws, but in making free entry into markets as easy as possible, which implies particularly the opening of competition to the whole world.

One of the great merits of competition stems from the fact it induces producers to differentiate in order to do better than others. But, in some cases – particularly in network activities – it is not optimal to have a very high degree of differentiation and there are gains from homogenization. In such a case, it may be efficient to have a single producer on a market. But it is also possible – and perhaps more efficient – to have several producers who coordinate at least a part of their activities. Thus, they obtain homogenization for some parts of their production processes, but they differentiate and compete for other parts. The plurality of producers makes it possible to maintain some degree of competition, either presently or potentially in the future. But their coordination makes it possible to save resources by homogenizing their production, which in fact benefits purchasers. In reality there may be an unlimited number of processes by which producers can coordinate a more or less important part of their activities. And one may accept the idea that there is no real difference between, for instance, a cartel and a system of franchising – already mentioned – or even the existence of a label that consists in homogenizing the characteristics of the production of different producers.

A dynamic economy implies a flexible productive architecture in which cartel agreements and competitive processes coexist and change over time. The free interaction between supply and demand gives incentive to look steadily for the best means to adapt production to the more or less diversified needs of clients. The coordination of producers through cartels is sometimes the best way to meet these needs. This is why legislation against cartels is not only useless, but harmful, as far as economic freedom prevails.

Thus, instead of opposing the firm and the market, one ought to recognize that individuals can coordinate their activities through a great number of different ways, from the individual firm to the market through the limited or unlimited liability corporation, the cartel, franchising or label. In a world in which transaction, information and risk costs would be smaller than they are presently, one could imagine continuous changes between all these possible processes of coordination, which, at the limit, would even make the concept of "firm" meaningless. Modern information techniques could help going in this direction. But the most important obstacle, which is preventing such an institutional flexibility, is certainly the existence of very rigid legislations and regulations. If they were to disappear, it could happen that the architecture of productive structures would be deeply modified and able to change rapidly. Thus, one could imagine that the durability of a brand becomes more important than that of a firm, since the production of a good to which a given brand would be given could be done by many different processes of coordination between a great number of productive units that could possibly change rapidly.

NOTES

1. Translation from Salin (2013a).
2. This idea has been developed in Chapter 1.
3. Thus, one would get closer to a project which had been considered some years ago and seemed unrealistic, the one in which there would be a great industrial firm without factories. In fact, such a project is not absurd at all.
4. Salin (2010) explains the consequences of this situation on the development of the recent financial crisis.
5. According to information given in *The Economist*, 24 April 2004.
6. As already mentioned in Chapter 1, cooperation is one possible form of a coordination process.
7. We develop more precisely the analysis of the role and the behavior of cartels in Chapter 3.

3. Cartels as efficient productive structures[1]

Cartels are considered as specific productive structures that allow producers to exert a monopoly power. But this traditional link between cartels and monopoly power is debatable. In fact, the evaluation of the working of cartels is closely linked to the theory of competition and monopolies which one adopts. Thus, Murray Rothbard[2] has made break-through contributions by persuasively showing that there is no monopoly power as far as there are only voluntary arrangements. We agree with such an approach and we consider that freedom of entry in production is the only relevant criterion to evaluate productive structures, so that one might dismiss as irrelevant all the traditional conditions of the pure and perfect competition theory. In the present chapter we will not address this general debate about competition and monopolies. Our precise aim is rather to look for the specific characteristics of cartels and to evaluate them under the light of our approach of competition. Cartels are generally considered negatively as formal arrangements to restrict production. After having discussed this approach we explain why cartels rather play a positive role in meeting some specific demands of the market. As a consequence they modify the frontier between the firm and the market.

1. THE CARTEL AS A RESTRICTIVE STRUCTURE OF PRODUCTION

The traditional theory of pure and perfect competition focuses on the number of participants and, as such, introduces a strong opposition between the competitive case in which demand is perfectly elastic (from the point of view of the individual producer), and the monopoly case in which demand is inelastic, which makes it possible for the monopolist to extract a "super-profit." In-between is the case of the oligopoly, namely the troublesome case in which there are a few producers on a market.[3]

What is wrong in the traditional theory is not the *formal* analysis of monopoly or oligopoly, but the confusion it has made between the end result and the process. The number of firms on a specific market at one given time is the provisional outcome of a specific process and it has no meaning by itself. On the contrary, the fact that the process is based on the use of public constraint or is purely spontaneous makes the difference. Thus, it is not true that the super-profit exists whenever there is freedom of entry on a market, since one cannot explain, in such a case, why there are no more producers trying to get such a super-profit. But the traditional analysis of the monopoly is clearly and directly appropriate when applied to the case of a public privilege, namely the existence of a public barrier to entry: In that latter case, the formal analysis of the monopoly is a correct description of reality. In this case only does a super-profit exist (but it would be more correct to call it a "super-privilege-rent").

Now, what about the case of a small number of producers, which is the scope of analysis both of the theory of oligopolies and the theory of cartels? Let us assume that for some technical or historical reasons, only a limited number of firms exist at one given time (the possible economies of scale not being large enough as to justify the existence of only one producer). Each producer has to elaborate a strategy of his own in an environment of imperfect information (since the decisions of each producer affect the state of the market, but no one knows about the intentions of others). Thus, authors such as Stackelberg have shown that the outcome of the process may be different according to the strategies followed by different producers. There are, for instance, cooperative and non-cooperative processes, equality between the producers or a distinction between a leader and followers, and so on. These assumptions may have interesting applications. But they are debatable as far as they tend to introduce the idea of a monopoly situation in the absence of any public privilege.

A distinction seems to be frequently made between an oligopoly and a cartel. A cartel could be defined as a specific oligopoly in which the different producers, instead of just interacting, enter into a process of explicit cooperation. Thus, a cartel is viewed as an agreement between different producers in order to follow common rules or behaviors; that is, a system of mutual and freely accepted obligations.

It is usually assumed that this agreement can be explained by a common *intention* of participants, namely creating a monopoly position. Therefore, participants who have not had to face a perfectly elastic demand are able to extract a "super-profit" from purchasers, which they would be unable to obtain without such an agreement. Thus, cartels are mainly viewed as having a negative aspect, as is expressed in the usual saying that cartels are colluding.

In the traditional theory the "super-profit" is shared between participants according to a priori rules, such as their market shares. It is well known that cartels are considered as unstable structures, since participants are tempted to become free-riders: Although they have an interest in others respecting the agreement, they can expect a larger share of the common "super-profit" by introducing some degree of competition with regard to their partners.

The cartel is sometimes considered as worse than the monopoly. In fact, it is often assumed that a monopoly exists for purely technical reasons, for instance because techniques are such that large economies of scale make it impossible for several firms to coexist in the most profitable way (natural monopoly).[4] In such cases no normative judgment is issued against the monopoly, but it is only argued that the state has to prevent the assumed "exploitation" of consumers by regulating the monopoly or by nationalizing it. The value judgment concerning cartels is more critical since it is assumed that there is no technical reason for any monopolist position, but that the cartel is created ex nihilo by an explicit agreement between producers in order to exploit purchasers. From this point of view any cartel arrangement ought to be prohibited. According to this view the cartel is created *in order to* create restrictive procedures.

In fact, as we see later on, this negative approach of the cartel is a direct consequence of the traditional theory of competition. According to it, there is pure and perfect competition whenever a great number of (identical) producers produce a homogeneous good. In fact this theory does not describe a real process of competition between real entrepreneurs, but the technical organization of managers in a non-innovative system, for instance the managers of plants in a Soviet-type centralized system of production: It is assumed that there is one single technique – an "optimal" technique from a purely technical point of view – to produce a given good and all (numerous) managers have to apply exactly the same technique to produce exactly the same good. In that sense, it can be said that the theory of pure and perfect competition is in fact a theory of central planning (see Salin, 1995 and 2014b).

The Austrian theory of competition leads to a quite opposite view. The end result of a competitive process is not the production of identical goods by numerous producers, but, on the contrary, the *differentiation* of goods produced by producers who are innovators and who are induced by competition – namely the free entry of potential competitors – to offer better goods at lower prices.

Therefore, as far as cartel agreements intend at the homogenization of goods (either of their specific characteristics and/or their price), one may wonder for which category of theories it could be a problem. From the point of view of a supporter of the traditional approach of competition, the problem may not be that of homogenizing goods, but one of creating monopoly power. From the point of view of the supporter of the Austrian theory of competition, there is no such thing as a monopoly power, as far as the process of cartellization-monopolization is spontaneous. But the reason for *homogenization* has to be clarified – which we will try to do later on – since the merit of competition relies on the fact that it induces *differentiation*.

The approach used by Murray Rothbard to study the specific case of cartels seems to be the following: He accepts the idea according to which cartels are a system of collusion aiming at introducing some restrictive actions in a productive system (rarefaction of production). However, he shows that on the one hand restrictive actions of producers are perfectly justified and that, on the other hand, cartels cannot create a monopoly power since such a power cannot exist as far as there is free entry on a market. Thus, in Rothbard's view, if producers organize themselves into a restrictive agreement (a cartel), it is to meet a demand by purchasers for a restrictive action. The argument goes as follows. A monopoly position can be reached by a single producer or a set of producers organized into a cartel only if demand is inelastic, which makes restriction of production possible and profitable. But, it is up to demanders not to have an inelastic demand: if ever they were unsatisfied with the cartel behavior, they could decide on having a perfectly elastic demand, that is not accepting an increase in prices through the restriction of production. As Rothbard wrote (1993, p. 565):

> If the consumers were really opposed to the cartel action, and if the resulting exchanges really hurt them, they would boycott the "monopolistic" firm or firms, they would lower their purchasing so that the demand curve became elastic, and the firm would be forced to increase its production and reduce its price again. If the "monopolistic price" action had been taken by a cartel of firms, and the cartel had no other advantages for rendering production more efficient, it would then have to disband, because of the now demonstrated elasticity of the demand schedule.

By saying that demanders could react against the cartel by lowering their purchases, Rothbard implicitly assumes that the good produced by the cartel has close substitutes, so that the demanders can decline the restrictive action of producers (and the corresponding increase in prices) by shifting to these substitutes, without any significant loss of utility.

Thus, if a cartel burns coffee in order to increase its price, the waste comes from the fact there has been an excessive production of coffee and not from the fact it is burned (since coffee has no other value than the one it gets from its relative scarcity in comparison with other goods). In some sense the restrictive action is not specific to a cartel, since on any free market one always restricts the production of a good in order to produce another one. According to Rothbard (1993, p. 569): "The cartel's action, in reducing the production of coffee and causing an increase in the production of rubber, jungle guiding, etc. led to an increase in the power of the productive resources to satisfy consumer desires." Rothbard also states that (1993, p. 584): "A cartel action, if it is a voluntary one, cannot injure freedom of competition and, if it proves profitable, benefits rather than injures the consumers." Thus, either the cartel results from the free working of the market and its possible restrictive actions are "wanted" by consumers, or it is the consequence of a barrier to entry and the restrictive action is a pure monopoly – that is, state created – exploitation of purchasers.

However, Rothbard seems to limit justifications for cartels to the case of voluntary and beneficial restrictions of production, although he does not exclude the possibility of other cartel actions when he writes (1993, p. 570):

> To regard a cartel as immoral or as hampering some sort of consumer's sovereignty is therefore completely unwarranted. And this is true even in the seemingly "worst" case of a cartel that we may assume is founded solely for "restrictive" purposes, and where, as a result of previous error and the perishability of product, actual destruction will occur.

However, the very notion of a "restrictive action" is by itself debatable, inasmuch as such an action can be labeled as restrictive only in comparison with a norm which could undoubtedly be named non-restrictive. Let us take the example of coffee producers burning coffee in order to increase its price and obtaining a maximum profit. A cooperative action is necessary in order to avoid free-riding. However, instead of burning coffee after it has been produced, producers could have decided a cooperative action before producing it in order to avoid over-production. They did not do it just because they lacked the necessary information on the future state of the market. Therefore, burning coffee is a restrictive action only in comparison with a specific state of affairs that had been freely chosen by producers in a situation of imperfect information.[5] Therefore, it would be preferable to avoid using the normative word of "restriction" and to just assume that the cartel aims at profit maximization.

Now, if ever there is free entry on the market, it is wrong to say that this profit maximization corresponds to a "super-profit." As is the notion of a "restrictive action," the notion of a super-profit is meaningless, since it implies a comparison with a completely non-existing norm, namely the rate of profit obtained in a situation of "pure and perfect competition."

The mere definition of a cartel does not imply anything about the more or less free entry on the market. The theory of monopoly has no scope as long as the reasons for the existence of one single producer are not made precise (barriers to entry, economies of scale or innovation). Similarly, the theory of cartel is meaningless without a clear understanding of the reasons for the existence of such a market structure. As we have seen, the possibility to introduce a restrictive action on a market is not an acceptable explanation and we have to consider other justifications for cartels.

If there is not a single producer but a couple of producers on a given market, it means, for instance, that there is no additional gain to be obtained from shifting from several producers to one single producer (the optimal size of firms has been obtained with several firms and there is no marginal economy of scale). To most theorists, cartels appear as unstable market structures, because they can find explanations for a situation with one monopolist or for a situation with a great number of producers, but not for any in-between situation. The cartel thus appears as a transitory solution to solve a specific problem. However, this intermediate market structure can be perfectly stable and optimal.

2. THE CARTEL AS A VALUE-PRODUCING ORGANIZATION

As just stressed, contrary to the traditional theory, competition has the merit of inducing producers to differentiate their production one from the other and not to try to produce exactly the same good with the same technique. Now, if we define a cartel as a structure that allows different producers to coordinate their production in order to suppress any differentiation in their products, does it mean that cartels can be viewed as anti-competitive organizations, or that some other reason might explain the emergence of such a productive structure?

There is a very general and simple answer to this question: If competition prevails in the sense that there is free entry on a market and if a cartel has existed for long, it necessarily means that this structure is the best one to meet some specific demand of the market. In other words, a cartel is not necessarily unstable – as is obvious from practical experiences – and if it remains alive in spite of potential competition, it means that it is a useful structure in this specific case. In other words, competition usually leads to differentiation of products (that is, imperfect substitution between them), whereas a cartel tends to induce homogenization (that is, substitutability). The benefits of differentiation are so obvious that there must be serious reasons for limiting it and introducing a higher degree of substitutability between products.

In fact, there are many specific activities in which there is a demand for homogeneity, especially in network activities, such as telecommunications, transportation or money production (which are frequently considered as public utilities and even natural monopolies). Generally speaking, such situations can be named situations of "sub-additivity," which includes externalities, economies of scale and economies of scope. In such cases one can obtain gains from coordinating several producers or from substituting one single producer to a number of them.

As an example, in the case of money production it can be considered that there are economies of scale and, therefore, decreasing marginal costs in the production of money, since, for instance, advertising costs on the characteristics of a currency may be more or less fixed and the centralization of reserves allows savings of resources. There are economies of scope, since information got by a financial intermediary can be efficiently used to create money against credit. And, finally, there may be externalities, since, for instance, a currency is more useful for one person the more widely it is used by others. Even if one disagrees on the precise reasons for "sub-additivity," anyone may accept the idea that it would not be "optimal" to have a very large number of different currencies.

Governments and all the "experts" who support them usually shift from such observations to the conclusion that there are natural monopolies, so that public monopolies or regulations are necessary in order to avoid the exploitation of buyers by producers. In fact, there is only one conclusion to be drawn from such observations, namely that there is a potential gain to be obtained from decreasing the degree of differentiation in the production of such goods. There are potential gains that can be obtained from substituting one or a limited number of goods to a great diversity. However, it does not mean that the optimal degree of diversification – or, conversely, the optimal degree of homogenization – can be decided a priori from a purely technical approach. Two remarks are important from this point of view:

1. If ever gains can be obtained by diminishing the degree of differentiation – for instance, because of economies of scale – it does not imply that it is also optimal to diminish the number of producers. As an example, if it could be proved that it would be technically optimal to have one single currency or one single computer standard in the world, it would not imply that there ought to be one single producer: Either a monopoly or a cartel can do the job. In fact, a cartel is a productive structure in which *different* producers produce the *same* good, so that they can be as efficient as a monopoly in meeting sub-additivity problems.
2. One cannot know in advance and forever whether there is sub-additivity in an activity. It has to be discovered. And competition – which we

> define as a situation of free entry into a market and which Friedrich called a "process of discovery"[6] – is the best way to discover to which extent sub-additivity does exist and to which extent it may change over time. More specifically, it cannot be generally said that sub-additivity exists in such or such activity, as it may exist at one given time at one point of the production process, but not all over it. For instance, in a telecommunication or transportation network, it may not be efficient to have more than one major "highway" in some parts of the network, whereas in other parts there would not be any economy of scale: the "highway" may be operated by one or "monopolist" producer or by several producers coordinated into a "cartel," whereas the other parts could be managed by different, not coordinated, producers as well as by a cartel (such as the one managing the "highway"). As new technologies can be discovered, the place of the cartel may change over time.

Therefore, cartels exist not only, or even not mainly, in order to make resources scarcer and to increase prices, but to increase the value of production and improve the productive processes. The cartel is not created to extract what the traditional theory calls a "super-profit", but to produce *coordination gains*.

Cartels, as well as monopolies, are the possible outcome of competition (that is, free entry on a market): competition makes it possible for real entrepreneurs to innovate, so that they are the only suppliers of the new product they have decided to offer to the market. As competition has the merit of inducing producers to be the first ones on a market – that is, to be what traditional theory calls "monopolists" – it is meaningless to compare a cartel situation and a situation with many producers. But it makes sense to compare cartels to monopolies. In fact, if ever there are gains to be obtained from homogenizing production, because of sub-additivity phenomena, it does not imply that it is more efficient to have one single producer than several ones in a cartel.

In fact, in a cartel there are possible coordination costs that may be opposite to the coordination gains obtained through the homogenization of production. However, the cartel may be organized along two different procedures, either spontaneous coordination or explicit cooperation. As an example of the first category, let us take the case of a free banking system and let us assume that, in a given area, several banks produce currencies that benefit from a convertibility guarantee in terms of gold. However, each bank discovers that, in order to make its own currency more attractive, it has to increase its liquidity and, therefore, it decides to accept the currencies issued by other banks of the system against its own without limits, at the fixed price given by their mutual gold prices. Such a system of spontaneous coordination makes all currencies perfectly substitutable, which means that the banks of the system have decided to eliminate any possible differentiation of their products. However, one may imagine that some degree of cooperation – that is, explicit coordination of decisions – may take place, for instance to decide a common name for the "common" currency, but it is not absolutely necessary, since each bank can decide separately to use the name of a currency already issued by one of them. Thus, one cannot define a cartel by the existence of cooperation – or what is sometimes called collusion – but rather by the fact that there is homogenization of goods produced by different producers, whether it results from explicit centralized decisions or from decentralized, individual, decisions.

Coordination costs are certainly higher the more cooperation exists in the system, since it is necessary to monitor the explicit cartel agreement. In such a case, as already recalled, each participant in the cartel has an interest in others honoring the agreement while trying to engage in free-riding in order to get a larger share of the common market. On the contrary, coordination costs are just about non-existent whenever the cartel is the result of the spontaneous decisions of its members.

On the other hand, a cartel may have some advantages in comparison with the case of a single producer ("monopolist"). The main gain stems from the fact that, although there is actual homogenization of production, the possibility of *future diversification* remains. As already stressed, the existence of coordination gains may change over time as new technologies are discovered. When a single good is produced by several producers in a cartel rather than by a single producer, there may be more incentives to discover new techniques. The traditional assertion according to which a cartel is necessarily unstable is not completely wrong, but it must not be considered as a negative aspect of the cartel, rather as a positive one. It means that the cartel survives as long as it is the most efficient productive organization. But that it may burst whenever other productive structures appear as more efficient. Moreover, the participants in the cartel are permanently induced to look for the possibility of inventing more efficient productive organizations, among which are those that imply the disappearing of the cartel and, maybe, the settlement of a new form of cartel.

Another possible gain brought by the cartel is a scale gain. Contrary to what is usually assumed, economies of scale do not generally exist. Moreover, whenever it can be assumed that there are economies of scale, they have to be viewed as *technical* and not as *institutional* economies of scale.[7] But there are also diseconomies of scale, which are mainly of an institutional nature. It is well known that the internal organization of a firm does not rely only on explicit exchange procedures, so that the production of information may be more difficult than in the case of market procedures. The larger the firm, the larger may be the organization cost. Thus, by coordinating their production – or cooperating – in a cartel, different firms are able to produce a good at the optimal scale, from the technical point of view, while minimizing institutional costs (diseconomies of scale).

The IATA (International Air Transport Association) has in the past given an interesting example of an efficient, rather stable, but changing cartel. Through an agreement that is not very costly to manage, different firms were able to give more value to their services, since the tickets issued by different airlines were (nearly perfectly) substitutable one to the other, at least as regards regular tickets. However, airlines were allowed some degree of differentiation – for instance, in the quality of service – and, on the other hand, they also produced services (special rates, charters) that did not enter the cartel agreement. Thus, the airline industry was characterized by an optimal degree of differentiation and homogenization from both the points of view of travelers and airlines. To some travelers, the substitutability between air tickets was very valuable; for other travelers the priority consisted of getting the lowest possible price. Thus, the airline industry had met the different needs of customers. But new techniques – especially due to the use of computers – as well as deregulation of the airline industry, decreased the gains obtained by such a cartel arrangement, since it made possible an extreme differentiation of prices not only between firms but within them.

The traditional theory of competition, as well as the traditional theory of the natural monopoly, has a global view of what they call a "good." It is considered, for example, that there is something such as "air transportation" or "telecommunications." Moreover, it is assumed that subadditivity exists in such network activities, so that there is the risk of a natural monopoly. In fact, as has been made clear by the "new" theory of consumption (Lancaster 1966, 1991), people do not demand "goods" but characteristics, and physically distinct goods are supplying bundles of characteristics in various proportions. The problem of production is to adjust to the immense variety of characteristics desired by different individuals. Now, homogeneity may be one valuable – and, therefore, demanded – characteristic, as is the case for money or air transportation. Thus, to be efficient a productive structure has to produce baskets of characteristics viewed as optimal by demanders, which implies that some baskets may include homogenized goods and others differentiated goods. The cartel – a mix of differentiation and homogenization – contributes to this adjustment. From this point of view it is an essential feature of productive structures. Contrary to the usual view according to which cartels are fundamentally unstable and, therefore, transitory, and contrary even to the view of Murray Rothbard who also considered cartels as some transitory organization, cartels have a durable, although changing, role to play.

3. THE CARTEL AS AN INTERMEDIATE PRODUCTIVE STRUCTURE

Thus, the cartel plays an important role in allowing an optimal combination of diversification and homogenization in production, according to the needs of demanders, and in providing an optimal combination of coordination and cooperation. From this latter point of view, it plays an interesting and intermediate role in productive structures.

Rothbard considered that a cartel aims at organizing a "co-operation to increase the incomes of the producers." He added (1993, p. 572):

> For what is the essence of a cartel action? Individual producers agree to pool their assets into a common lot, this single central organization to make the decisions on production and price policies for all the owners and then to allocate the monetary gains among them. But is this process not the same as any sort of joint partnership or the formation of a single corporation?

Comparing the creation of a cartel to that of a centralized firm, he concludes: "There is therefore no essential difference between a cartel and an ordinary corporation or partnership."

However, as already stressed, if ever a cartel and a big firm are exactly similar, why would cartels exist? Rothbard assumed that cartels are mainly transitory structures, contrary to what can be shown by reasoning or experience.[8] In fact, his conclusions are dependent on his definition of the cartel. Viewing the cartel as an explicit cooperation of firms in order to increase the joint profit – according to the traditional definition of a cartel – he assumed that the most efficient firms will be tempted to break the cartel in order to increase their market shares. In fact, as we have seen, a cartel cannot be defined by a strategy of market sharing, although it does exist, but by a coordinated – not necessarily cooperative – effort to homogenize production (which may imply identical prices). If this homogenization is desired by the market, the cartel is efficient and will last. If it does not meet any specific need of the demanders, but is only the end result of an effort by producers to maximize joint profits, it may fail rapidly.

As a consequence of his restrictive definition of a cartel, Rothbard thought that either the cartel is efficient and a merger will rapidly take place between its members, or it is not, and it will break down. As he wrote (1993, p. 579): "If joint action is the most efficient and profitable course for each member, a merger will soon take place." In reality, efficient cartels can and must last, possibly by transforming their structure and activities or the number of their participants. The best example may be that of money production. Under free banking the production of money by members of cartels was efficiently made without any destruction of the cartel or any merger into one single big producer.

Mergers do not occur precisely because in a cartel firms are independent profit centers, which make economic calculation more efficient. Instead of viewing a cartel as a set of firms which are about to merge, it may be both more realistic and efficient to consider a cartel as the ultimate stage of a process by which a big firm has been decentralized into various coordinated *decision centers* and, ultimately, split into independent *profit centers* with different owners.

As already recalled, by initiating the modern analysis of the firm, Ronald Coase gave an answer to the following question: If, as it is rightly assumed, the market is an efficient way for individuals to organize their mutual exchanges, why substitute other procedures, such as the cooperative and command procedures used inside a firm? The existence of transaction costs explains the coexistence of market procedures outside firms and non-market procedures inside firms. The market makes it possible to *coordinate* relations between individuals through voluntary exchange, whereas individual actions are made compatible inside a firm (or any other organization) through *cooperation*, but also coordination (that is, a complex mix of spontaneous and constrained actions). However, as we have seen, a firm is not a pure command organization, since it is basically a bundle of contracts.

It must be admitted that an optimal organization of production stems from the juxtaposition of two non-excluding schemes, cooperation and coordination. The market is a *coordination* process between voluntary actors and the firm – as well as any other organization – is partly a *cooperative* system in which the productive process is based not only on spontaneous interactions between individuals through contracts but through more vague processes of cooperation. In any firm there is a mix of command, voluntary decisions and initiatives, coordination through information processes, and so on. And it can be assumed that the larger a firm is, the more difficult the internal organization process is.

Instead of a "one or the other" approach, a cartel makes it possible to better combine various characteristics via a better use of both cooperative solutions (internal organization) and coordination processes (market). This is the reason why there is a great variety of cartels combining coordination and cooperation procedures in different ways. This is also the reason why cartels are not necessarily unstable. They are a part of firm strategies: If ever a firm considers any change in its production, it does not have to choose only between extending an internal process of cooperation or entering into voluntary exchange on the market. It may be preferable to combine cooperation and coordination under the form of a cartel.[9] The micro-computer industry gives an interesting example of such strategies. According to the evolution of markets, strategies, and technologies, producers decide their standards independently or enter into cooperative agreements, which can be considered as cartel agreements.

From this point of view it is preferable to abandon the definition of a cartel as an agreement between firms that *intend* to exert a restrictive action or any sort of specific action. The actual intention of participants is not relevant. Any action results from an intention, but the content of the intention does not matter from the market point of view. It may be that an entrepreneur enters into an agreement with some specific intention, but the outcome of the agreement is not the one intended, but another that appears just as beneficial, so that the agreement will be maintained. What is important in a cartel is that some mix of coordination and cooperation blurs efficiently the frontier between organizational processes and market processes.

NOTES

1. Initially published as Salin (1996b).
2. Particularly in Rothbard (1993). In the present chapter we rely mainly on this book.
3. The definition of a market is arbitrary, since it implies the possibility to differentiate perfectly specific goods. This would be possible without any ambiguity only if goods were not substitutable one to the other. As far as some substitutability exists – which is always the case – the definition of a good and of a market is arbitrary.
4. Anyhow, those who support such views do not usually consider the possibility of competition from producers located in other nations and are ready to support protectionist measures.
5. Moreover, in such a case, the cartel is only a transitory market structure to cope with the unexpected consequences of non-cooperative behaviors. However, in principle, the market is a coordination process that makes cooperation unnecessary.
6. The justification for such an approach of competition is given more precisely in the following chapter.
7. As Murray Rothbard rightly wrote: "The critical problem is not the size of the plant, but the size of the firm" (1993, p. 577) and "Economics can make few valid statements about the optimal size of a firm except that the free market will come as close as possible to rendering maximum service to consumers, whether we are considering the size of a firm or any other aspect of production" (1993, p. 578).

8 "In many cases, a cartel can be considered as simply a tentative step in the direction of permanent merger" (Rothbard, 1993, p. 573).

9. Franchising in retail trade is a well-known example of such strategies, as already mentioned in Chapter 2.

4. Property rights, competition and the European Union[1]

Linking together concepts such as property rights, competition and the European Union may seem strange. However, it makes sense because, in fact, these concepts are at the very roots of European problems. By focusing on property rights and competition, we are induced to direct our attention towards the real actors of the integration, namely individuals. Property rights cannot be separated from individuals and if we really want to understand and to evaluate the process of European economic and social integration, we have to go back to the foundation of this problem, which means caring about property rights.

1. THE LEGITIMACY OF PROPERTY RIGHTS

Let us first clarify the reasons why property rights and competition are two inseparable expressions of liberty. There are many ways to care about property rights. There is first a quite obvious utilitarian reason: if someone is the owner of something, he has a greater interest to take good care of his property. And as a consequence, the society and the economy become more efficient if property rights are clearly defined. But there is also another dimension, which is even more important: the ethical dimension of private property. We all live in a world of scarcity and all people have to face scarcity. It means that not all people can dispose of all economic resources. Any human society must define exclusions, by deciding who is going to have a right to use some resource and who is going to be excluded from the use of this same resource. In this sense, we can say that property rights exist in all societies.

To really differentiate these societies we have to wonder to which extent is the definition of property rights legitimate or not. And here, the ethical dimension steps in. Are the property rights legitimate, or not? On what is this legitimacy based? In order to answer these questions we have to take account of the characteristics of human beings. A human being is characterized by his creativity. He lives and survives thanks to the use of his reason. He thinks before he starts acting. It means that all the wealth called economic wealth is always a result of a process of creation. A human being is a creative being and he is such because he uses his reason. As a consequence, the creator is a legitimate owner of his creation. From this point of view, it is impossible to claim that a human being is free – which means that he is the owner of his own body and his own reason – without admitting at the same time that he is the legitimate owner of the fruits of his activity, that is of his creation. Such is the legitimacy of individual property rights.

Unfortunately, it is clear that we are very far from a satisfactory recognition of property rights in most of our societies. We hear, for instance, about the redistribution of national income, as if the national income was somehow obtained by miracle and created above people's heads so that some further redistribution was necessary! But, the only legitimate redistribution is the one done by the creators of the wealth themselves, because they are the legitimate owners and they can, as a consequence, distribute it, give it, sell it, rent it, and so on.

The ownership thus seems to be an absolute principle, a criterion to be used in the evaluation of all societies. As soon as property rights are defined, duties are defined as well. In a free society based on ownership it is a duty of all to be respectful of the rights of other people. And from this point of view, we may mention an important distinction, the one which exists between what we may call "universal ethical principles" on the one hand, and personal ethics on the other hand. Now, there is only one single universal ethical principle – or, at least, one principle that can become universal – which is the principle of ownership and duties attached to it. In effect, as soon as we have defined the property rights of every man and also the duties attached to these rights, we have defined a coherent system, a social order. This being done, anyone of us can add to these rights and duties some more duties, which he personally favors and which are based on one's personal ethics, such as some general rules of behavior that should be obeyed, like generosity or similar feelings.

But these duties are purely personal and these specific personal rules of behavior of innumerable persons may certainly conflict one with the others. The duty according to which one has to be respectful of the rights of others can be considered as the only universal ethical principle.

We have already mentioned that the legitimacy of rights comes from the creation of resources. But how can these rights be determined? We may give some attention to this problem because it is important to evaluate the working of the process of European integration. In fact, to state it briefly, one may remind that there are two great traditions. One tradition is based on jurisprudence, on judges who, whenever there is a conflict about the legitimacy of property rights, define the property rights of the parties. This is specifically an Anglo-Saxon tradition, but we can find it in a great number of civilizations. The second tradition uses legal definition of rights, as it is done in the Napoleonic Code and it seems that most European continental countries share this tradition.

According to this second tradition, the rights should be defined by some political authority. This tradition seems dangerous, because, quite obviously, if you define rights in such a way, there is a risk of an arbitrary approach. Today, both traditions do exist or coexist in Europe.[2] This is certainly one of the greatest difficulties in the process of European integration. It is a difficulty that is discussed quite rarely, even though it is very important since it concerns the fundamental basis of our societies.

The previous statements about property rights were very brief, but they are sufficient for a correct understanding of the strong relation that exists between the problem of the definition of property rights and the problem of competition (which itself is closely linked to the problem of economic integration, as we see later on).

2. THE DEFINITION OF COMPETITION

The traditional theory of competition, known as the theory of pure and perfect competition, is the dominant theory both in academic circles and in the legislations of most countries in the world and, more specifically, in Europe.

Thus, the European competition law is implicitly based on this traditional theory of competition, which implies that this theory has extremely important practical consequences. The traditional theory is characterized by several assumptions which can be found in any textbook in economics. To make it short, competition is defined as a situation in which a large number of producers produce the same kind of goods, under the same conditions of production, in a world of perfect information. Some other conditions are sometimes added, but this one is the most important. Moreover, this theory shows that all these identical producers end up in a situation of zero profit. This situation of zero profit and similarity of producers is often considered as a competitive optimum.

This traditional approach can be criticized in many respects. First the assumption of perfect information is absurd, because information is never perfect. We could even say that any human action always consists in looking for and creating information. As already stressed, a human being is a rational being, someone who uses his reason. There is no activity, however practical it is, that is not at the same time an intellectual activity and an activity consisting of creating information. The assumption that we can have perfect information is therefore absurd. And a theory based on an absurd assumption deserves to be forgotten. It definitely does not deserve to become an inspiration for legislation, or for decisions of the European Union. The traditional approach is in fact a purely technical vision of competition. It assumes that some production methods do exist (independently from any human intention and decision) and that the only role of entrepreneurs consists in applying these production methods. But this is a wrong view of the real nature and the real behavior of entrepreneurs. An entrepreneur is somebody who tries to anticipate the future, and the needs of the market, who tries to innovate and create something new with the help of new methods of production. In other words, he is someone who creates information. Therefore, the focus on material techniques of the traditional theory does not reflect the real world. The real world is a world of innovation and a world of profit, because profit is precisely the return obtained from innovation. And this is the reason why one may even say that the traditional theory of competition is in fact a theory of planned economy, deprived of real entrepreneurs and where a central authority is ordering producing units to use the technology defined by this authority.

The traditional theory of competition is obsessed with what is sometimes called "market power." It is believed that it is optimal to have a great number of identical producers on the market, so that none of them can have a particularly large "market power," for instance by imposing any high price to purchasers. And this is where the implicit normative aspect of the traditional theory springs.

However, this idea comes from a semantic confusion, namely an inappropriate meaning of the term "power." In fact, speaking of a "market power" is meaningless: Power means constraint. But no constraint prevails on the market; there is only freedom. Consequently, the idea according to which a producer could have any power whenever the market works freely is a contradictory idea, which does not make any sense. It is quite the opposite concerning the activities of the state, in which case the term "power" is used correctly, because the state is an institution that holds a monopoly on the use of legal constraint. Needless to say, this traditional theory of competition is strongly linked to the traditional theory of monopoly. A monopoly is thus defined as a situation in which there is a single producer of a good on the market, which implies that he can reduce the quantity of goods supplied in order to increase prices and to make a so-called super-profit.

So in reality, this traditional theory leads to a paradox. As a matter of fact, it seems to be very rigorous. It is developed with the help of all sorts of mathematical models. But its application is fully dependent on personal judgments: A judge or a member of the European Commission, who is supposed to determine whether competition exists or not, is going to decide according to his own arbitrary considerations that competition does not exist if the threshold of such or such market share is overpassed. He will decide, for instance, that the merger of two enterprises cannot be authorized because it would result in too large a firm. Or he will decide, completely arbitrarily, that such a merger is acceptable.

Hence, it is strange to have a theory that is supposed to set rigorous criteria for the definition of competition, but in reality leads to something absolutely vague that gives perfectly arbitrary power to those who are entrusted with defending competition. In reality, competition cannot be understood without taking into account what could be considered as an ethical criterion, namely the criterion of freedom. Thus, we are proposing the following definition of competition: Competition exists on a market if ever producers are free to enter into this market and consumers are free to choose the producer whose goods they desire.

This simple definition based on the freedom to enter into the market has several merits. First, it corresponds to common language. Thus, as is widely accepted, saying that, for example, two sportsmen compete with each other does not mean they are trying to be identical, but on the contrary that each of them tries to be better than the other one. On the contrary, the traditional theory of competition assumes that it is good that all of them be similar. The second merit of this definition of competition is that it is coherent with the correct definition of rights that we briefly mentioned, and as we will explain later on. But let us first mention a third possible justification of this definition of competition, based on the freedom to enter into a market. It is a utilitarian justification. Our approach of competition implies that, if there is free entry into a market, then all producers have to face the risk that someone offering better goods or cheaper goods will appear. If there is free entry into a market, producers are induced to work better than others, which means that they better meet the needs of the customers. Such is the reason why Friedrich Hayek defined competition as a "process of discovery." This brings us to an essential and important point: If competition is defined by the free entry into a market, it leads to *differentiation*. If competition really prevails, producers will try to differentiate themselves from one another, whereas the traditional theory of competition assumes that they try to be identical. And this is because it is a purely technical vision. It presupposes that there is only one satisfactory technique of production for any good and everybody has to adopt it. This approach is in fact considering the special case of a static world in which profits do not exist. But the real world is different. It is a dynamic world, a world of innovation, a world of stimulation. And competition plays an essential motivating role within this world, because it induces producers to differentiate one from the other. Let us accept it, the problem of differentiation or similarity seems to be one of the main problems we have to consider whenever we are concerned with human societies.

Now, the reasons why we have mentioned all these problems may become obvious. We do believe that it is the only way to clarify one of the main concerns of European integration, which is usually viewed as a process of harmonization. But while the most widespread vision of integration is a vision of homogenization, competition leads to a totally different world, a world of differentiation. One may even say something which may seem paradoxical, namely that it is a great merit of competition that it induces producers to obtain a "monopoly position" (according to the traditional meaning of the word), since each of them makes an effort to be the sole supplier of a particular product on the market at a given time. But, of course, in such a case a producer wants to be the supplier of a product that is better than others.

To say it otherwise, there are two sorts of monopolies and language is too vague and too poor since it does not help in stressing the differences between both. There is first a "monopoly," which is the result of an ability to innovate. The one who innovates and supplies a new product gets 100 percent of the market for this product, as can be expected. If one is using the traditional point of view, he is inclined to say: "Uh, this producer has 100 percent of the market, he is a monopolist, there is a risk he will abuse his dominant position and will plunder the customers. We have to prevent the monopoly and forbid to do this and that." However, from a dynamic point of view, we must say that this superior position – the existence of a 100 percent market share – is the result of an innovation which is necessarily benefiting buyers (since they freely decide to buy this new product instead of anything else).

Now, there is the second sort of monopoly, a monopoly which is the result of a restriction, or a ban, to enter into a market. It is created whenever the state – and no other entity can do this – provides a privilege to some public or private company to produce something. This means that the state forbids others to enter into the market. In such a case the monopoly deserves to be considered as a harmful producer, because it can plunder its customers. There is a great number of monopolies of this sort – some of them work satisfactorily, but many of them do not. As an example, we should not forget that the twentieth century was a century of inflation, along with all the negative consequences it brought. But we should not forget also that it was a century in which money in each country was produced by state monopolies, contrary to what had happened earlier in history. To illustrate the dangers of a real monopoly, this example could be sufficient. Anyhow, it is utterly paradoxical that we have legislations trying to condemn alleged private monopolies in most countries and in the European Union, while these legislations do not apply to the only real monopolies, monopolies of state origin. There is in fact no monopoly other than the monopoly of the state.

Another justification of competition is a justification of ethical nature, which is closely linked to what we have said about property rights. According to our definition, competition prevails when the entry into a market is free. But it also means that there is freedom of contract and that people can freely enter into any relation. This is why competition, so defined, seems to be inseparable from the definition of property rights. If we forbid legitimate owners to handle their resources, their property, as they desire, that is, if we forbid the use of contractual freedom, we in fact take away their property rights. It is not possible to really be respectful of individual property rights without contractual freedom, that is, without the existence of competition. To put it differently, the term competition is synonymous to contractual freedom and to respect for property rights. All these notions are absolutely inseparable. And that is why we can say without any restriction that free exchange and free international exchange is a moral principle.

If we prevent, via tariffs or other barriers, two individuals from exchanging, only because they live in two different countries, it means that we interfere with their rights, with their contractual freedom. As a consequence, it creates a situation in which their freedom is limited. Therefore, we cannot imagine that there could be a protection of property rights without the existence of competition (that is, the freedom to enter into a market and to do contractual arrangements). It is also not possible to imagine real competition without the existence of property rights.

3. ECONOMIC INTEGRATION

These statements bring us to the heart of the problem of economic integration in the European Union. We have stressed that there are two approaches of competition. One is based on the idea that competition exists only if all producers are similar, if all converge towards a single model. On the contrary, the second view – which we consider as the correct one – is based on the idea that everyone tries to do better than others, that everyone tries to differentiate himself or herself from others. These two theories are absolutely opposed. In the first case, it is believed that it is necessary to homogenize, but the second case is in favor of differentiation. By the way, this seems to be quite natural, because every human being is somehow different from others and even wants to be different.[3] There is one single human nature and we all belong to one single human race. We are all rational beings, but this fundamental unity does not suppress individual differences of each of us. That is the foundation of the wealth of mankind. And therefore this differentiation should be considered as something fully desirable.

Thus, there is a perfect parallel between, on the one hand, the mentioned opposition of two approaches of competition (implying two views of property rights), and, on the other hand, two diverging views about the integration of several countries, as is the case of the European Union. According to the dominant view, to complete economic integration it is necessary to create a supernation, and for that reason we need to harmonize, to have the same regulations everywhere (the same taxes and so on). According to the second view, integration does not require harmonization, but in fact the opposite. Integration should be founded on the recognition of differences among human beings and their activities. Of course we are inclined to prefer this second approach, which is probably and unfortunately a minority view (but, happily we do know that truth is not determined by a majority of votes so that one may feel quite comfortable even when being in a minority position).

To put it differently, there is, on the one hand, a political, centralist and constructivist vision, and on the other hand, an economic vision that is human, decentralized and favorable to personal differences and innovations. When people speak about integration, they use this term in a very vague way. According to the usual interpretation, this term means, as already stressed, an effort to homogenize behaviors, activities, institutions, and so on. But, it should be defined completely differently. A system is integrated if all its different parts can work in a coherent manner. And what can make any human system coherent? Nothing else than the rules we have met previously: recognition of property rights, contractual freedom – which means competition – the rule of law. If all these conditions were met, we would find ourselves in a peaceful society, because they exclude any conflict, so that we would have an integrated society. Of course, we can achieve this under the condition that the general rules are coherent rules. And the rules that we have specified above (when speaking of property rights and competition) are precisely such coherent rules. From this, we can deduce that the real meaning of the word "integration" simply corresponds to competition. This is the reason why we thought it necessary to talk so extensively about something that might have seemed too specific, such as competition. But it was simply because the problem of competition is at the heart of the problem of integration. Getting the integration of a human society means allowing contractual freedom, even if we do not know what will be the outcome of this freedom.

Europe is now facing a more or less hidden conflict between these two visions. At the beginning of the process of European integration, there was a correct view of the whole process. What was the aim at that time? A "common market." And what was the meaning of this common market? It simply implied suppressing barriers to exchange. It was said that producers from the European countries could offer their products anywhere in Europe. And that European consumers could choose any producer without having to care about his nationality. The tariffs and other obstacles to exchange were removed. The first steps of the process were correct, even if they were limited to the exchange of goods (and, unfortunately, to European countries and not to the rest of the world). Later on, another well-chosen step consisted in implementing a common market for factors of production, such as the free movement of people and capital. It would have been sufficient to go on in such a way, and to create common markets – that is, competitive markets – in regulations, norms, tax systems, and so on, to give producers and customers the freedom to choose and an ability to select what suits them best.

Unfortunately, the European Union has chosen a different path and it is diverging still more and more from its initial path. People more and more accept the wrong idea according to which competition can be fair and viable only if producers operate under the same conditions. A confusion is thus made between competition on the one hand, and harmonization of the conditions of competition on the other. But one reason for competition to be desirable is precisely that it allows people to work under different conditions, in different environments, to compete with each other and to be present on markets. As already stressed, it induces them to *differentiate* from other people. Competition means diversification. And the harmonization of the conditions of production is absolutely the opposite. Let us take an example. European producers of tomatoes work under different conditions. They can use free sunrays in Italy, Spain or southern France. On the contrary, in the north, for example in the Netherlands, they grow tomatoes in greenhouses heated with natural gas. Both of these groups then meet on the market and compete, in spite of the different production environments. If we wanted to strictly apply the dominant ideology of harmonization, we would have to oblige the southern producers to cover their fields with canvases so that they would not be in more favorable conditions than the other producers, because they have more light and heat. This would be the only solution to get identical conditions of competition. Doing such seems absurd and *it is absurd*. But, is there any difference between the harmonization of the conditions of sunlight and the harmonization of tax, regulatory or education conditions? To be sure, the conditions of education are different in different countries, as are all sorts of conditions in the environment of firms. Competition is possible, and one may even say it is desirable, precisely when people are different and live in different conditions. Unfortunately, the idea according to which competition is a stimulus to diversification is generally not understood and not accepted. This results in a great number of harmful consequences.

We will not give a comprehensive list of these consequences for the time being (some of them will be analyzed in subsequent chapters). But let us mention a very specific one. The official importance given to the harmonization of many conditions of production has precisely been the reason why the countries of Central and Eastern Europe that freed themselves from communism had to wait many years to enter the European Union. In some sense, it had been easier to tear down the Berlin Wall than to enter the European Union! But why was it so? These countries could have joined the countries of the European Union immediately, if the European Union had only been an area where competition and contractual freedom prevailed. But European authorities and most European governments do not aim for "common markets," they aim for the creation of "organized markets" (which mainly implies "harmonized markets"). As a result, the countries that are candidates to become members of the European Union are obliged to adopt what is called "*acquis communautaires*". It represents an obligation to adopt a considerable number of regulations, European directives, practices, and so on. No differences are accepted, all countries have to fit into the same format. This dominant view is particularly dangerous and is worth criticizing.

Thus, it seems correct to say that the problem of competition is at the very heart of the problem of integration. The previous statements make it possible to analyze all the problems raised by the process of integration, such as those concerned with tax systems, monetary systems, trade, rules, laws and regulations, and so on. In the coming chapters we will mainly have the opportunity to debate monetary systems and tax systems. We will see that the politicization of decisions does not make European integration easier and more efficient, quite the contrary.

All these questions are very important. Unfortunately, there is a general agreement according to which only one approach to integration is possible, the one that stresses harmonization, centralization and politicization. And we can see it by looking at the terms used. Those who support a centralizing and constructivist vision of Europe are called "Europeans" (or "pro-Europeans").

And those who support a different vision are labeled "anti-Europeans" or "Euroskeptics." Personally we believe that being confident in the spontaneous process which is the outcome of the behaviors of free individuals is more coherent with what has been the main characteristic of Europe over history, namely a world of diversity and individualism, a world respectful of individual property rights and individual responsibility.

NOTES

1. Adapted from a lecture given on the occasion of the presentation of the Liberalni Institut Annual Award for the Contribution to the Proliferation of Liberal Thinking and Making Ideas of Liberty, Private Property, Competition and the Rule of Law Come True (Prague, 9 October 2003). A slightly different version has been published in Salin (2007a).
2. Lady Thatcher once said – in a private audience – that these two European traditions are totally incompatible. And she added that, if she had reservations regarding the process of European integration, it was precisely because she believed that the Anglo-Saxon tradition is incompatible with the continental tradition.
3. Once a French biologist was asked on TV whether all humans are equal. He answered: "Yes, all human beings are equal and identical in their capacity to differentiate themselves." This is a crucial and realistic message.

PART II

Globalization and international economic problems

5. Arguing in favor of globalization[1]

What does globalization mean? It is in fact more or less synonymous with the traditional term, free trade, but it is more fashionable. In reality, one may consider that there is a slight nuance between both expressions: When speaking of free trade, people have in mind trade in commodities and services, whereas globalization may have a broader meaning, including free exchange not only of commodities and services, but also of factors of production, knowledge, culture, laws and rules, and so on.[2]

Globalization has been a matter of growing concern during recent years. Its growing importance can be explained by institutional factors (multilateral liberalization of exchange, economic integration) and by technological factors (the development of internet and telecommunication techniques). However, if one takes a much longer historical perspective, globalization has existed – at least over some parts of the world – for centuries. It mainly shrank during the twentieth century under the influence of nationalist policies. From this point of view the present globalization is significant in comparison with the world structures of the twentieth century, but it cannot be considered as a specific characteristic of our time.

It is also an obvious fact that many people fear globalization.[3] They fear it because it evokes unknown threats, those which can be manipulated by some far away and anonymous producers who could endanger their jobs and their ways of living. They would feel safer if ever they could be locked into their national, regional or even local world, the one they know, the possible changes of which they can more or less appraise.

However, beyond passion there is reason. And reason clearly tells us that the fears linked to globalization are unjustified. In order to be convinced, one has only to accept a little effort towards abstraction, which is the only way by which we may understand reality. In fact, it is enough to understand the main statement from the theory of exchange – what we later call the exchange principle – and its extension to the field of international trade. What we have to learn from the general theory of exchange is absolutely clear and it can be considered as an eternal and universal truth. We are told that, as all individuals are different and endowed with various talents and capacities, each of them finds his own interest in specializing in the activity (or the activities) in which he is relatively more efficient (in comparison with other potential producers). We may also add a consideration not linked to the logics of action, but to the mere observation of facts, namely that whenever people specialize in one given activity they learn and discover more efficient ways to produce, so that exchange thus brings a possible additional gain.

What is true for one individual remains true for several individuals, for instance those who constitute a country.[4] Without having to ask them, one can be certain that exchange is profitable for those who do it, at least if they freely decide it: if two persons decide to trade together, although they are not obliged to do so, it is necessarily because each of them finds that exchange is profitable. But there is no reason for the gains of trade to disappear whenever trade takes place between two individuals (or two groups of individuals, such as two firms) located in different national areas. This is why one can say without any doubt that *globalization is necessarily profitable*. Now, if the case seems so clear, one may wonder why globalization is opposed so forcefully, as well by the supporters of the anti-globalization movements as by many producers, politicians or journalists.

In the present chapter we will first try to trace out what seems to us the fundamental roots of the opposition to free exchange, which will allow us to criticize some of the most usual arguments against free exchange. We then stress that disagreements about free exchange and globalization are not mainly based on technical aspects of the problem, but on (often implicit) ethical arguments. As a consequence we will address the possible strategy to counter opposition to free exchange.

1. THE ROOTS OF THE INTELLECTUAL ERROR CONCERNING INTERNATIONAL EXCHANGE

As just mentioned, the field of international trade and trade policy offers a unique paradox: Although the merits of free trade – and more generally of free movements of activities, goods and factors of production – have been forcefully demonstrated for at least two centuries, and although they correspond to an undebatable principle, an innumerable number of people and governments are still supporting limits to free exchange and believe, or seem to believe, that restrictions to trade are justified.

Moreover, it is surprising that millions of people have learned the principle of comparative advantage in schools and universities, but they seem not to be able to use it whenever they have to evaluate a concrete problem related with international trade. For instance, they usually believe that all producers in a country would suffer from a loss of so-called "competitiveness" if ever the value-added tax (VAT) was higher in their country and exports were not tax-free. They do not understand that "competitiveness" is a relative concept and not an absolute concept, so that an activity in a country seems to be competitive only to the extent that some other activities are not. Therefore, if ever the VAT were not reimbursed on exported products, the relative competitiveness of different products and services would not be affected by a higher or lower tax rate (which, by the way, means that no tax harmonization is justified, for instance among the EU countries).[5] Similarly, those who claim that developed countries suffer from the "unfair competition" of low-wage countries just fail to understand that low wages only give the corresponding countries a relative advantage in labor-intensive activities (or, rather, in activities intensive in poorly educated labor) whereas they have a relative disadvantage in other activities.

Thus, we have to face a fascinating intellectual phenomenon: Nearly everyone, I believe, is able to understand the famous Ricardian "two countries, two goods" example of the theory of international specialization. But many people find it difficult to imagine the "n countries, m goods" case, which corresponds to the real world. However, the problem is not a problem of mathematical techniques, quite the contrary: focusing on the purely formal aspect of the Ricardian principle may prevent people from getting a deep understanding of the principle of exchange. It seems that very few people – even among professional economists – have reached this state of mind through which the understanding of the real meaning of the comparative advantage principle has been translated into an intellectual reflex which makes it possible to grasp spontaneously a concrete situation by referring instinctively to the general theory of exchange.

This problem may also be made more obscure by the fact economic education too often presents the comparative advantage principle as a principle to be applied in the field of international trade and not as the general principle of exchange. As such it is given a collectivist meaning and it belongs to the realm of macroeconomics and no more to that of microeconomics. From this point of view it is characteristic that the development of the international comparative advantage principle in the history of economic thought and that of the general principle of exchange have been more or less independent one from the other. In reality, the genuine understanding of the general principle of exchange could only emerge once the theory of subjective value had been clarified by "Austrian economists," which made it possible to claim that exchange between two individuals (or two groups of individuals) was creating (subjective) value. To really understand the theory of exchange one must have previously understood the theory of value. Unhappily, although many students in economics have learnt the comparative advantage principle in international trade theory, they may not have a sufficient education in the theory of subjective value.

Now, reducing the exchange principle to the field of international exchange has two unfortunate consequences:

1. It provides the principle of exchange with an abstract and purely formal character. International trade is implicitly assumed to take place not between individuals located on different territories, but between abstract entities named "countries." As soon as one accepts an economic theory founded on a fiction, that of the nation, nothing can put a brake on the accumulation of fictitious abstract concepts. Thus, one will speak of national interest, national income, national rate of growth, and so on. And the designers of economic policy will be able to find all sorts of legitimizations for a mechanicist approach in which the maximization of subjective value by each individual will have been completely removed from the attention of economists.
2. It induces people to give a relative meaning to the general principle of exchange by stressing that the comparative advantage principle has been developed by Ricardo for a given period and place. But it is often said that a principle that could be acceptable then may not be any more valid since the conditions of production and exchange have changed. Such claims can be made only if one is making a confusion between the general principle of exchange and some specific assumptions of a specific model of international trade.

As an example, Ricardo had assumed that production factors were immobile internationally and that techniques of production were different in different countries, which implies that knowledge is not internationally mobile. Such an assumption is quite acceptable since knowledge is not something that could exist independently of those who think and act: As information is costly and individuals are rationally ignorant, there is no reason for knowledge to be the same all over the world. And as exchange is not a technical phenomenon but the result of human action, it is the outcome of the processes by which individuals obtain and create information.[6] But, to be sure, quite different assumptions can be made in that respect – as the diversity of assumptions in international trade theory bears witness – without hurting in any way the validity of the general exchange principle. It is therefore important not to miss any opportunity to restate the principle of exchange with its most general meaning, as it must be. The relative character which is too often attributed to the principle of exchange (at least in the field of international trade) easily leads to the use of a number of various criteria to estimate the costs and benefits of international exchange (as we see in the next section).

The intellectual error would have been more frequently avoided if one had been cautious enough in always adopting an individualistic and not a collectivist approach: Instead of speaking of trade between nations, one ought to refer to the situation of an individual exchanging with other individuals, which finds an interest in specializing. By adding that the problem is not modified at all if ever the two partners in exchange are located on different national territories, one makes it perfectly understandable for anyone.

However, it is also true that, quite often, people have difficulty extending a piece of reasoning from the individual scale to a social one. They consider, more or less implicitly, that there are collective realities that are different from individual ones, and that there are, for instance, national interests that have nothing in common with the individual interests of citizens. In fact, these so-called national or collective interests are nothing but the interests of the members of specific categories and they cannot logically exist independently from individual interests. Unhappily, the same people who do understand, at least from their own experience, the meaning of individual interest and the behavior of individuals are unable to accept the logical link which would allow them to understand the working of a global society. To illustrate the difficulties met by so many people in understanding the exchange principle and/or its specific application to the field of international exchange, let me just quote the following example. Paul Samuelson once said that he had been challenged a long time ago by the mathematician Stanislaw Ulam who asked him to name "one proposition in all of the social sciences which is both true and non-trivial." It was several years later that Samuelson (1969) thought of the correct response, namely the comparative advantage principle in international trade: "That it is logically true need not be argued before a mathematician; that is not trivial is attested by the thousands of important and intelligent men who have never been able to grasp the doctrine for themselves or to believe it after it was explained to them."

Paul Samuelson was certainly not wrong in saying that the comparative advantage principle was absolutely true. But, as a good economist, he could have given the answer within a couple of seconds and not several years later, and he ought to quote the general principle of exchange and not its specific application to international trade.

In the present chapter we try to look for the reasons of this strange paradox, namely the existence of a gap between the formal understanding of the principle of exchange and the deficient understanding of both its generality and its applications.

Now, if ever people do not believe in an idea that can be demonstrated as absolutely true, it is either because they are ignorant or because their reason is dominated by their passion and interests. This may explain the gap we are analyzing in the field of international trade. As already mentioned, globalization just means competition extended to the whole world. Now, competition – which can be defined as the possibility for anyone to enter into any market as seller or buyer, that is as a partner in an exchange – is a demanding discipline, as is the discipline of liberty. Competition constitutes an instrument for change and changing implies effort. It is quite understandable that people may be reluctant to accept the necessary effort to adapt to the changes in the external world, even if they could understand the argument in favor of liberalization. It is even understandable that they prefer not to obtain the future (and uncertain) benefits of international competition, because the cost of the present change is viewed as too high (in other words, they have a strong preference for the present).

However, saying that it is understandable does not mean that it is legitimate. Similarly, it is quite understandable that people demand a subsidy from the state, but it does not mean that this subsidy is legitimate. It is important to make this distinction between what is understandable and what is legitimate, because the confusion between both is often made implicitly. It is the case whenever it is said that liberalization, although it may bring about a gain to some people in the future, may impose a present burden on others and that it is fair to take into account the loss of welfare of those who suffer from liberalization. By introducing an argument of fairness, one makes possible both to accept the general principle of exchange and to legitimate limits to its application to the real world. In other words, there would be a trade-off between an "efficiency argument" – the one based on the principle of exchange – and a "fairness argument" – the one based on the changing welfare of different people and categories of people.

We will discuss this so-called ethical argument later. But, for the time being, we just want to stress that this "ethical" argument makes it possible for people to reconcile in their minds two things which are in fact absolutely not compatible, namely the understanding of the principle of exchange and the support of state-imposed limits to the freedom of exchange.

2. THE BELIEF IN EXCEPTIONS TO THE EXCHANGE PRINCIPLE

There are a lot of arguments against liberalization either in academic publications or in media and political debates and we do not intend to consider all of them here. How do the supporters of such critical views make their arguments compatible with the general exchange principle? To this end two main ways are used. First, it is claimed that the exchange principle is not as general as usually stated and that it is based on some specific assumptions. By modifying them, different conclusions can be found. Second, it is stressed that one ought to consider the existence of a trade-off between the gains from free exchange and other social targets such as employment or development.

In reality both ways are used simultaneously in order to make a plea for some protection. Such is the case with the famous infant industry argument. This argument – which is widely accepted – comes from the conjunction of two intellectual errors: the belief in the relative character of the comparative advantage principle and the belief in a specific ethical norm (which, as we see in the next section, is not acceptable). As regards the latter, it is commonly stated that competition cannot be fair if potential competitors are not placed in the same starting position. Thus, the infant industry argument is held even by people who sincerely believe in free markets, but who think that a free society implies equality of chance. Let us not consider this normative aspect of the discussion for the time being and let us rather focus on the positive argument.

According to the infant industry argument, when the development of a new activity is envisaged in a less developed country, it has to bear higher costs than foreign producers from more developed countries, because the latter don't have to bear the specific costs linked to the launching of a new activity. Therefore, there is a risk that the new activity in the less developed country could not overcome these specific obstacles and bear the losses of the first period, in spite of the fact it would be profitable in the long run. Thus, the normative argument about fair competition reinforces the positive argument according to which the theory of comparative advantage would be a specific theory, which would be valid only as far as one takes a static view of international trade, ignoring possible long-term changes in relative competitiveness. The apparently logical conclusion of this reasoning is that liberalization could be particularly harmful for less developed countries.

The crucial point in the argument thus consists in stressing that an activity could be beneficial in the long run, even if it is not in the short run. But what can be the meaning of such a statement? Let us imagine a potential entrepreneur considering the launching of a new activity. He does know that there will be a first period – a couple of years – during which he will be losing money because one needs time in order to build the production process, to get in touch with the market, to educate the employees, and so on. But he will decide on making the investment if ever the discounted value of future expected gains is higher than the discounted value of short-run expected losses (and if this net discounted return is higher than in any other activity he could imagine). If not, he would lose money, which would mean that he is destroying existing wealth rather than creating new wealth (or, at least, he would earn less money than he could get in another activity). This is true for any activity, at any time, in any place, with no exception.

Thus, saying that an activity can legitimately be protected in the short run because it would be profitable in the long run is perfect nonsense. Protection means that one is hiding part of the costs (the short-run costs) in order to allow an activity to seem profitable, although it is not. But there is necessarily a cost of protection, which is borne by other producers and consumers (and, as is well known in theory, the cost imposed to others through protection is higher than the gain obtained by the one who is protected). In fact, the infant industry argument must not be viewed as an exception to the general exchange principle, but as inconsistent with it and, therefore, as unacceptable. As the exchange principle is universally true, the infant industry argument is definitely and radically wrong.

The exchange principle is true because it takes into account the necessary interdependence of all human activities: Someone chooses an activity not because it is profitable in some absolute way, but because it is relatively more profitable than other possible activities. Someone chooses to specialize and to trade because he is relatively more efficient in the products he is producing than in the products he can get through trade. The infant industry argument adopts a partial view of human activities and just ignores the fact that human action consists in choosing the activities that seem to be relatively more profitable. The infant industry argument consists in falsifying the terms of human choices, creating the illusion that an activity is more profitable than it really is and, consequently, making other activities less profitable. Moreover, it substitutes the choice of activities by incompetent and irresponsible persons to the choice by competent and responsible persons: the process of protection does not consist in protecting all the activities of a country – since it is impossible, protection being always relative – but in protecting some activities at the expense of others. But this process of selection, instead of being the result of numerous decisions by a large number of businessmen who are relatively better informed and who are interested in taking the best decisions, because they are responsible, is made by politicians and bureaucrats who cannot be better informed and who are not responsible. Thus the infant industry argument has to be definitely abandoned, precisely because, far from being an exception to the exchange principle, it is in contradiction with it and depends on incoherent statements.

The infant industry argument is particularly harmful because it may lead to a situation in which wealth-destroying activities are chosen in a country at the expense of wealth-creating activities. Thus, less developed countries adopting protectionist policies under the pretext of protecting new activities may be trapped in a process of decline. Moreover, it is harmful because it assumes that one has to restore similar conditions in countries that have followed different paths historically. But, in order to create some equality of chances and similar production conditions, one has to rebuild history and to establish a state of affairs that is completely imaginary and does not correspond to the concrete history of the inhabitants of a country.[7]

Similar remarks can be made about another line of reasoning that also pretends that there are exceptions to the general exchange principle. According to this, the exchange principle would have a limited scope because it assumes perfect competition and the absence of externalities or economies of scale, which is contrary to what exists in reality. As far as externalities exist and competition is not "perfect," the comparative advantage principle would no more be generally valid, which could justify limitations to free exchange.

This view is reinforced by the fact already stressed, namely that people frequently use the comparative advantage principle from a collective point of view and are ignorant of the individualistic foundations of it. In fact, if one considers purely inter-individual exchange, it is impossible to demonstrate that the existence of externalities or imperfect competition could limit the validity of the exchange principle: If two individuals enter voluntarily into an exchange agreement, it is because it is profitable to both or, at least, because they believe it. By deciding this agreement, they may create (positive or negative) externalities on others, but it remains true that both benefit from the exchange. On another hand, it is certain that the traders cannot be perfectly informed and it may happen that one or the other regrets the agreement in the future, because it appears to be less profitable than it seemed to be when it was decided. But the exchange principle just states that people trade because they believe that trade is profitable for them. And as information is always "imperfect," it may happen that the real benefit is different from the expected one. But this does not imply any limit to the scope of the principle. The only human reality is necessarily a subjective one and the exchange principle rightly deals with subjective valuations, choices and gains. There is no justification for any external observer to decide about the importance of the gain obtained through trade, since he is necessarily less well informed than the concerned traders about their subjective desires.

Now, those who adopt a collective approach of the comparative advantage principle and forget about individual preferences and choices believe that it is possible to define some social welfare, which cannot be determined only by referring to individual welfare. Thus, if externalities exist, all individuals in a society may be satisfied with the exchange they are performing, but they may impose a cost to the collectivity, so that some exchange activities have to be limited, forbidden or taxed in order to maximize "social welfare."

Thus, we meet in the field of international exchange exactly the same problems as the ones we can meet in any other field of economic theory. Therefore, it does not seem necessary to devote too much time to such a well-known debate about externalities and competition. We will, however, give some more thought to the problem of externalities in the following section from a specific point of view. For the time being, let us just recall that externalities seem to exist whenever property rights are not well defined, basically because the cost of definition seems too high in comparison with the gains that could be obtained (or because the state makes the definition of property rights impossible). In that sense, there is no real discrepancy between individual welfare and social welfare. Moreover, the idea of neo-classical economists according to which the maximization of social welfare can be obtained by voluntary exchange only to the extent that pure and perfect competition prevails, is based on a fallacious concept of competition. If competition is defined – as it ought to be – as free entry on a market, the supposed problem just disappears. Free exchange makes it possible for all individuals to maximize their welfare (so that "social welfare" is maximized), although information is not perfect, the producers of a given product are not numerous, there is a very high level of differentiation of goods, and so on.

To be valid, the exchange principle does not need a situation of perfect information, with a great number of producers creating the same products (once more the myth of equal conditions in different countries . . .), it just needs free entry on the markets. Whenever free entry and free trade are limited (for instance, under the pretext of coping with externalities and imperfections in competition), individuals can no longer maximize their own welfare and get all the potential benefits of trade.

However, such debatable ideas constitute the foundation of a modern – and, maybe, dominant – approach of international trade, known under the heading of "the new theories of international trade"[8], which may suggest that the "old theory" based on the comparative advantage principle is no more adapted to the modern world. The "new international economics" pretend to bring new justifications for protectionism, derived from the fact pure and perfect competition does not exist in the real world. It assumes, for instance, that there are economies of scale and that these gains can only be revealed over time. Therefore, a dynamical theory of specialization has to be substituted to the traditional, supposedly static, approach.

Thus, let us assume that an activity can be developed either in country A or country B. But the one who first develops this activity can reach the "optimum size" before the other and, thus, prevents the latter from developing. It may be justified for the state – according to the new theory – to subsidize or to protect a national activity if the future gain obtained from a monopoly position can be higher that the initial cost of the subsidy or the protection. There is a "national gain" that can be redistributed, in particular to those who had borne the initial cost.

However, this new international economics is not very different from the traditional theories of protection, such as the infant industry argument or the theory of the optimal tariff. Traditionally, the theory of protection demonstrates that the gain obtained by the protected producer (and the state) is achieved at the expense of other nationals and foreigners. But the theory of the optimal tariff pretends that it is possible to extract a global gain from foreigners by manipulating the terms of trade, so that if ever it is possible to design an efficient redistribution policy in the country, all nationals can benefit from this protectionist policy. The new international economics is, in reality, very similar to these old theories of protectionism. It pretends that there are specific circumstances in which one can obtain a global gain for a country thanks to a specific protectionist policy – strategical trade policy – which manipulates the terms of trade and gives a monopoly position to a national producer.

But it remains true that this "national" gain is obtained at the expense of foreign producers, because, for instance, by giving an artificial competitive advantage to the national producer, one prevents the development of the similar activity outside. In the long run, it is assumed, the state is able to redistribute the gain obtained from this monopoly position to those who had to finance the policy initially, either as customers of the protected activity or as taxpayers who paid for the subsidy.

The supporters of such a policy pretend that it is justified because, due to the existence of economies of scale, there is a situation of potential natural monopoly. The monopoly is defined as a situation in which only one producer can exist in the market (in contra-distinction to a situation of pure and perfect competition in which there are a great number of producers). Therefore, it is a "national interest" to make it possible for a national producer to be the first one on the market and to reach this potential monopoly position. Now, if one defines a monopoly – as it ought to be – as a situation in which there is no freedom of entry into a market, except for one single producer, it is impossible to define the case just considered – that of an activity with economies of scale – as a monopolistic one. As far as there is freedom of entry initially, there is competition. If one producer chooses to enter first and another potential producer prefers to wait – in spite of the fact he would be free to enter into the market – the latter cannot claim later on that he is prevented from entering because of the existence of a monopoly on the market: He has more difficulty entering, but he is not prevented from doing so, which is quite different. He freely decided to take the risk not to be the first to enter and no one is responsible but himself if ever he finally regrets his initial decision. Thus, paradoxically, the supporters of the new international economics justify a protectionist policy under the pretext that there is a potential monopolistic situation, and it is in fact this very protection that creates a real monopoly, namely a situation in which the use of state constraint makes it possible for a producer to be the only one on a market.

But the most important objection that can be raised against this protectionist argument is the following: It implicitly assumes that the state does know in advance that, by using subsidies or protectionist measures in order to support the entry of a national producer, this producer will obtain a monopoly gain in the future, because of economies of scale, and that it will be possible to redistribute this gain in order to compensate those who had borne the initial burden. But, if such a situation of perfect information could exist, this same information would be available for any potential producer. And if it was certain that it was possible to obtain such a monopoly gain by entering first on the market, there is no reason for any private producer to decide not to enter and to launch such a profitable activity; and there is no reason for the state to protect him or to subsidize him. Obviously, in reality, such a situation of perfect information does not exist and the potential producer accepts a risk by entering first into a market. But he expects to get a reward in the future, which is not the "super-profit" of the monopoly described in traditional textbooks, but a normal profit on a risky investment. We thus find the same sort of flaw in both the old protectionist theories (infant industry argument and optimal tariff theory) and the modern versions (new international economics).

In fact, one can find a lot of different specific assumptions in the new international economics which all aim at demonstrating that the long-run comparative advantage may be opposite to the short-run comparative advantage. According to these theories, it may happen, for instance, that less developed countries suffer from trade liberalization because it induces a path of specialization different from the one which would have been followed in autarchy, and implies a lower rate of growth (if not a negative one). Consequently, free trade does not allow the concerned country to obtain an optimal rate of growth and protectionism, contrary to what is suggested by the exchange principle, is justified. It is clear that these theories give an apparent justification to protectionist policies as far as it is easily considered as a norm for less developed countries instead of being what it is really, namely a special theoretical case. But one danger of these theories stems from the fact that they are based on a counterfactual argument: they state that it may happen that liberalization causes a lower rate of growth, but one cannot know in advance which specializations would be chosen in the country either under free trade and under different possible protectionist policies. As a theory of economic policy, they are based on the pretence of knowledge.

However, such practical arguments against the new international economics are not sufficient. In fact, one could say that, as far as it is a theoretical possibility, no matter if it is actual or not, the theory has demonstrated that there are exceptions to the exchange principle. This is why it is important to evaluate whether these theories are valid. However, examining them and their possible founding assumptions in detail would certainly go far beyond the necessary scope of the present chapter. From a very general point of view, in order to obtain the desired discrepancy between short-term and long-term comparative advantage, these theories introduce into a model of international trade specific assumptions according to which, due to liberalization, producers in a country are induced to adopt specializations that are less growth-enhancing than would have been the case under autarchy. These special assumptions are usually constituted by externalities and economies of scale – already considered – but also by phenomena such as agglomeration effects or dynamic education effects.[9] In fact all these assumptions are very similar to those used in the theory of endogenous growth. It is assumed that there are cumulative processes so that when there is free exchange between two countries, they may diverge one from the other.

Let us take the example of agglomeration effects. It is quite true that there are cumulative effects due to agglomeration: By concentrating in the same area, people get information at a lower cost, they are closer to their markets, they benefit from a diversified labor force, and so on. Similarly, capital flows are attracted by financial centers where it is possible to find better opportunities and better financial techniques.

Thus, if free exchange prevails, not only for commodities, but also for factors of production (free migrations and free capital movements), activities will concentrate into the richest countries and the less developed countries may lose their most beneficial factors of production. In any case, there will be a cumulative process of growth in the more developed countries, because of the agglomeration effects, and a cumulative process of lower growth (or negative growth) in the poorer countries, because of declining agglomeration effects. Therefore, the rate of growth will be lower in the poor country and some protection (which one?) would be justified in order for the country to reach a higher level of income and to be able to better benefit from agglomeration effects.

The crucial point in this theory (or this set of theories) stems from the fact that it is based on a collective approach and not on an individualistic one. It may be true that the rate of growth is lower with liberalization. But what does it mean? What is the relation between the rate of growth and the welfare of the country's inhabitants? The rate of growth of a country is the rate of growth of its national income (or gross national product [GNP]). But the very notion of a "national income"[10] or a "national product" is meaningless since the income or the product do not belong to the nation – a purely abstract concept that cannot think, act, produce and receive an income – but to individuals. Now, from an individualistic point of view, liberalization opens up new opportunities. Let us assume, for instance, that, due to openness an individual in the poor country can transfer his capital to another country and benefit from a higher return. His welfare is increased by liberalization. But from a purely quantitative – and disputable – point of view, there is less capital in the country and the rate of growth is lower. But, in spite of that and thanks to liberalization, inhabitants benefit from opportunities to increase their welfare.

Moreover, as far as liberalization opens up new opportunities, one cannot know in advance to what extent people will take these opportunities and adapt to them. In some sense, the theories that aim at proving that openness may decrease the rate of growth in a country implicitly assume that entrepreneurs are unable to invent new specializations, in particular in less developed countries, so that they stay in low-growth activities. A similar remark could be addressed to the theory of "immiserizing growth" initiated by Bhagwati (1958). It assumes that the growth in the production of an important exported commodity in a country deteriorates the terms of trade to such an extent that the country loses, instead of gains, from growth. But one may wonder why producers do not react to such a price signal by shifting to other productions. In fact, the problem is not a problem of openness; it is a problem of flexibility and adaptation. And once more, one cannot know in advance to what extent entrepreneurs can adjust to new situations.

3. THE ETHICAL ARGUMENT IN FAVOR OF FREE EXCHANGE

As in any other field of thought, in order to support or to reject liberalization, one may use arguments based on measurable criteria, or more ethical arguments. A great number of economists would explicitly prefer the first because they favor a value-free approach of economics. However, in order to propose policy solutions, they have to choose some criterion to evaluate different situations and this choice is necessarily arbitrary. We already presented an example of an approach based on measurable criteria when we discussed the meaning of the maximization of national income. Thus, the supporters of free exchange would point out that the rate of growth of a country is maximized when exchange is not impaired and those who support state interference with international exchange would point out the possibility of protectionist positive sum games or immiserizing growth in open economies. One reason for such divergent views among economists – who may have had the same education in economics and who may accept the same foundations of economic theory – comes from the fact that any policy measure has distribution effects. These effects are differently evaluated by economists who, quite often, surreptitiously reintroduce their own preferences and prejudices in what they pretend to be a value-free analysis.

A symptomatic example of such a drift is given by the traditional theory known as the theory of "optimal tariff" (which seems to provide one more exception to the general exchange principle, as is suggested by the term "optimal"): Protection could be profitable for a country as far as it makes possible a higher income. Why could a country be better off with a tariff than without it? The basic reason is that a tariff is a tax and, as is the case for any tax, there is a redistribution of the tax burden between both partners in exchange, whoever is formally paying it to the tax administration. Under a specific conjunction of demand and supply elasticities, the authorities of one country may manage to determine the tariff rate so that the greatest part of the tax burden has to be borne by foreign producers. It may thus happen that the tax received by the protectionist state more than compensates the "social loss" incurred by the inhabitants because of protection, so that the latter could be compensated for their losses. Now, it is clear that this tariff – although it is supposed to be "optimal" for this abstract entity, the protectionist country – is certainly not optimal for other countries: Their inhabitants have to bear the tax burden without receiving any "public good" in exchange. This is not a situation of optimality, but a situation of exploitation of foreigners by the national state. From an apparently scientific point of view, this tariff is labeled as "optimal." From an ethical point of view, it cannot be labeled as anything other than robbery.

Let us consider another example concerning the internal distribution effects of protection. Let us imagine that there are two individuals in a country, A and B, and a state. B is able to obtain protection from the state, in which case he would gain 80 and A would lose 100. To prevent such an event, A may propose to pay 90 to B in order for him to abandon his project. The utilitarian would say that, in such a case, free trade will be preserved and the national wealth would be maximized. However, it remains true that B received an additional wealth at the expense of A by using the threat of a public constraint, making possible a despoilment of what A owns legitimately.

Thus, lacking a clear standard of what is valid and what is not, those who pretend that they are developing a value-free analysis are necessarily led to invent some decision criteria, such as the maximization of the national income or the welfare of poor countries. They, in fact, quite often adopt an implicit ethics, especially when their proposals imply distribution effects and they decide arbitrarily to give a specifically higher weight to the welfare of such or such category (for instance, the welfare of one given "country," that of farmers, wage earners, and so on).

Now, they have to be blamed not only because they are using implicit ethical arguments, but also, and mainly, because their ethical arguments are not consistent. As already stressed, one must carefully make a distinction between two sorts of ethics: universal ethics and personal, subjective ethics. By universal ethics we mean a system of ethical principles that could potentially be accepted by all individuals all over the world, without any possible inconsistency (even if this ethics is not actually accepted by a more or less important part of the world population). The only ethics that can correspond to this definition is the ethics of property rights: Whenever individual rights are defined and respected, there cannot be conflicts between individuals, and any human situation can be clearly evaluated. The same is not true with personal ethics. As respectable as they may be, they are not necessarily shared by other people and there cannot be a universal agreement about some ethical criterion. Thus, according to their own personal ethics, someone may consider that the welfare of nationals is more important than everything else, and another may give priority to the poor, another to farmers or to bureaucrats, and so on. All these subjective value judgments are inconsistent with one another. The implicit value judgments present in so many theories of international trade belong to this category.[11] They cannot provide a basis for any general explanation of the world. As such they are not scientific, contrary to what they pretend to be.

Conversely, the universal ethics of property rights provides a sound basis for a theory of exchange and, consequently, for any statement in the field of international exchange. In fact, any limit or prohibition imposed against free exchange constitutes an attack against one's rights. Those who freely agree to make an exchange do not violate the rights of anyone, but their own rights are harmed whenever their desired exchange is prohibited. It is also true that their agreement may have consequences for other people (called "externalities" in traditional economics), but it does not mean that it is injuring the rights of these other people. Thus, let us imagine that a grocery store has been present in a street for a long time and sells to customers located in the same area. If a new store settles in the same street and attracts customers by selling better products at a lower price, the first one is not entitled to ask for any protection since it is not the owner of the customers and it has no rights over the newcomer. Certainly, the first store suffers from a "negative externality," but this externality is legitimately created.

Similarly, in the field of international exchange, if ever an activity has been protected for long in a given country, it means that the owner of this activity benefited from an illegitimate privilege, obtained through public constraint, and implying a violation of others' rights. If liberalization occurs, the rights of those who suffered from the protection are re-established. Simultaneously, the one who was protected has the feeling that a cost is imposed upon him (a negative externality). But suppressing an undue privilege must not be interpreted as a cost imposed upon the former beneficiary. Those who pretend to prove scientifically that protection may be justified for reasons we have previously mentioned (externalities, economies of scale, endogenous growth, infant industry, and so on) are necessarily inconsistent with the logics and the ethics of property rights. If two approaches are incompatible, then we have to choose just one of them. As the ethics of property rights is the only possible consistent approach, it has to be preferred. The best answer to be given to all theories arguing in favor of limits to free exchange is the one provided by the ethics of property rights.

4. CONCLUDING REMARKS: STRATEGIES TO SUPPORT GLOBALIZATION

The present chapter began by underlining the existence of a gap between the universally true character of the exchange principle and the numerous statements – by academics or the general public – that are not compatible with this principle. We now have to answer the following question: How to fill the gap?

The answer is not that easy. In fact, in the previous section we stressed that there is no valid theoretical argument against free trade, but also that the defense of free exchange may ultimately be made through an ethical approach. Free exchange has to be defended without any exception just because it means freedom to act for individuals. Having this conviction, we believe that pragmatic arguments in favor of free exchange – for instance, pointing out some link between growth and free trade – ought not to be used just because they miss the fundamental point and/or because they cannot be universally convincing. However, the difficulty in communicating in favor of globalization comes from the fact that most people are used to these sorts of arguments and consider ethical arguments – based on the ethics of property rights – as unscientific or unacceptable, given their own ethical prejudices.

Thus, let us take the statement that the countries that are the most open on the outside world are the most prosperous (or have the highest rate of growth). Such a statement can be developed with the use of the analytical tools of economics and it can be tested econometrically (with a good chance of being validated). Those who are in favor of liberalization are satisfied by such econometric results.[12] However, should we use such empirical arguments? In fact, we do not need such a proof of the benefits of free exchange, as long as we believe – as we should – that the exchange principle is universally true and empirical tests of it do not add anything to our knowledge.

But a real difficulty comes from the fact that what is satisfying for a significant number of academics – namely the fact that a universal theory cannot be proved to be wrong by facts – is not convincing for most people. Therefore, we are left with the following choice: adopting a radical attitude by reminding people endlessly of the exchange principle or accepting some compromising attitude by trying to demonstrate the benefits of free exchange. The first approach may be preferable, since academics must not abandon what constitutes the specificity of their contribution to the social debate, namely the search for a general theory that makes it possible to understand the working of the real world.

However, one may say, there is also a practical problem to be solved: The problem of globalization is not only an academic one and it is not sufficient to try to convince just the academics. Globalization is a practical and urgent problem, especially if one considers the influence of antiglobalization movements all over the world. This is certainly true, but it does not introduce any weakening in the belief just expressed, for the two reasons that follow.

First, academics have a "natural" specialization in communicating with other academics and even if they have the opportunity to address other audiences, they have a comparative advantage in academic communication. And other people, who have been educated by academics and have learned the good principles, will be able to address these other audiences.

Second, one may also consider that the ethics of property rights, as far as it corresponds to a correct view of human relations, can be understood well beyond the limits of the academic world, possibly expressed in simple words and clear statements. These intellectual efforts are certainly not sufficient since, as already stressed, opponents to globalization are successful because ignorance and individual interests are at work – but they must still be considered.

Finally, there is also a striking fact that deserves some thought, namely the contrast between the principle of exchange – which is universal and straightforward – and the new international economics – which is sophisticated and often taxonomic. This may induce us to ask the following question: Do we really need economists to create new theories of international trade? In fact, existing principles have been known for a long time and are sufficient both for an understanding of globalization and for the determination of economic policies (or, rather, to prevent any economic policy . . .). But the caste of professional economists has vested interests in developing these new theories. Thus, they obtain consideration, positions and money, mainly by bringing to governments apparently scientific arguments in favor of policies to "regulate" globalization. In comparison, those who just remind others of the "old" principles may be viewed as old-fashioned, but they may be the *real* economists. In fact, they have mainly a negative role: trying to convince that new theories are biased, inconsistent or arbitrary. They have to fix the breaches steadily made in the foundations of knowledge, but their role seems less glorious than inventing a new theory of international trade. In reality, in a world in which principles would be known and respected, we would need very few economists. But everyone would have to know economic reasoning.

NOTES

1. A previous version of the present chapter was presented at the Mont Pèlerin General Meeting, "Classical Liberalism in a Global Context," Salt Lake City, 14–19 August 2004. I thank members of the Jean-Baptiste Say seminar at University Paris-Dauphine (and, more specifically, Antoine Gentier, Guido Hülsmann, Georges Lane and Alain Wolfelsperger), as well as Alberto Mingardi, for very useful comments.
2. However, given the fact that, strictly speaking, globalization and free trade (or free exchange) can be considered as synonymous, we may use one or the other in the present text. We apologize for any inconvenience it may bring to readers.
3. All supporters of anti-globalization ideas do not share exactly the same opinions. For instance, most of them may be in favor of the mobility of persons, but more or less opposed to the mobility of capital.
4. A country can be defined not as a specific area but as a specific set of individuals who are using the same system of laws, rules and rights.
5. We analyze more precisely this problem in Chapter 7.
6. If a country is defined – according to the Ricardian assumptions – as an area of relative immobility of information, there is no reason for this area to coincide with the current definition of a nation as a juridical and political area.

7. One may also see in the infant industry argument an example of an apparently positive theory based, in fact, on a normative assumption, surreptitiously introduced: "Fair competition" would imply that different producers be in the same initial conditions.
8. There has been much important literature published in this field, particularly Helpman and Krugman (1985, 1989). This literature focuses on the consequences of all supposed discrepancies from the traditional model of pure and perfect competition (externalities, scale economies, oligopolies, and so on).
9. See, for instance, Romer (1987); Grossman and Helpman (1991); Rivera-Batiz and Romer (1991).
10. We even believe that the concept of income is largely arbitrary, contrary to that of utility or welfare (see Chapter 17). It may even be that most people would not know the level of their income – which means that it would be meaningless for them – if the income tax did not exist.
11. Thus, it can be argued that the new international economics have been clearly designed in order to make statements about economic policy, or more precisely to define "optimal" economic policies which are intended to increase the welfare of citizens. This, in turn, implies the (implicit) determination of value criteria, particularly when there are distribution effects (which necessarily exist).
12. Thus, it is comforting to read in the *Index of Economic Freedom* (published every year by the Heritage Foundation and *The Wall Street Journal*) that there is a strong link between economic liberty – which includes freedom of international exchange – and prosperity.

6. World regulations and harmonization[1]

It is often considered that the globalization of economic activities should go with a so-called "globalization of policies" or, more precisely, that globalization should need a counter-balancing power in increased worldwide regulations and harmonization of policies. In fact, many people have now accepted trade liberalization on the one hand and deregulation on a national basis on the other hand (in countries where it has occurred). They have noticed that trade liberalization is beneficial, as far as consumers can get a larger choice and lower prices. Meanwhile, the development of internet and of e-business contributes to the acceptance of a worldwide perspective and to the awareness that markets are international.

However, many object to the assumed perverse effect globalization has on employment, low income workers being supposed to suffer from the competition of workers from less developed countries. Also, the disappearance of regulations limiting competition inside a country where globalization has occurred has obviously contributed to more competition between national producers, and people are often opposed to more competition from the outside. Therefore, although the "globalization" of activities is increasingly felt as a fact of life against which it would be unrealistic to fight, the nostalgia of protectionism and state regulations exists everywhere. Many people feel that one has to minimize or to suppress the assumed perverse effects of deregulation and world competition. The instruments for this new view are world harmonization of policies, and world regulations.

According to mainstream thought, in order to avoid anarchy one has to substitute the previous scattering of regulations with global rules, as the previous scattering is considered as unsustainable. Since economic problems have become worldwide problems, they have to be solved directly at the global level. Moreover, the claim for global policies also stems from the idea that there are desirable policies that cannot have their full effect as they are decided at the national level. In fact, it is assumed that two main obstacles prevent these nationally based policies from being fully efficient.

First, there would be spillover effects, so that the result of one given policy in one given country would not depend only on its own implementation, but would also depend on the design of policies made by other countries. In other words, there would be externalities and in order to reach an "optimum situation" governments ought to coordinate their policies to minimize negative externalities and to maximize positive externalities. Second, there would be "public goods" or "public bads", which, by their very nature, are produced at the world level. One obvious example of this would be atmospheric pollution.

Therefore, our task seems to be the following: to look for any apparently acceptable argument from this dominant economic approach of globalization (although we doubt that there may be one); and to look for the best arguments we might use in order to explain its main errors.

1. DIFFERENTIATION AND HOMOGENIZATION

> One fears diversity, one stigmatizes it under the name of anarchy; but it is necessarily the outcome of the very diversity of intelligent minds and convictions, a diversity which furthermore tends to be erased by discussion, study and experience (Bastiat, 1848).

One ought to meditate on this beautiful argument by Frédéric Bastiat in favor of diversity and his trust in the ability of free human beings to converge progressively towards the common discovery of true knowledge, particularly in a period such as ours during which there are constant efforts to standardize human situations by compulsory methods. In fact, "unity in diversity" could be considered as a major characteristic of humankind: unity implies that individuals are rational, which means that any human action is directed by the use of reason. Diversity exists because one human being is concretely different from any other and even aims at differentiating himself from others. And, as is well known, it is this concrete diversity that makes exchange possible and profitable, so that a human society can be defined as an exchange society. These very facts of human nature imply that there is necessarily a tension between a need for unity and a need for diversity. In some sense, one might say that one of the main problems human beings have to solve is finding an optimal limit between homogenizing – because they share the same human nature – and diversifying – because they are different, they have various aims and knowledge. Some of the problems to be solved are: the extent to which rules or activities have to be harmonized; who has to choose the optimal degree of differentiation (and, therefore, of homogenization); and which are the best processes to find the best mix of differentiation and homogenization. From what has been said, it seems obvious that one cannot accept as valid a statement of "homogenization is always profitable" (it seems to be a motto in Europe).

To be sure, there are few general rules that can indeed be considered as universal and which, in that sense, are common to all human beings, such as the principle according to which one has to be respectful of others' life and property or the principle according to which "the contract is the law of the contracting parties." As far as these principles are considered universal, they are identical for all individuals and there is no room for any diversification of principles. It is certainly true that some people do not believe in these principles or even do not believe that universal principles may exist. However, as far as one considers that they are inherent to human nature, it would be inconsistent to admit that they are not valid for all individuals. But the fact they are universal does not imply they have to be "harmonized:" It is their very nature to be universal and they are recognized as such, so that no explicit act of will is necessary to make them universal. It also necessarily means that no worldwide regulations have to be adopted in order to enforce them: They are recognized or they are not recognized.

Now, one may consider that, apart from these universal principles, which, by definition, are common to the whole of mankind, all human activities are specific, which reflects the concrete diversity of human beings. Therefore, we can assume from the start that diversification is normal and even desirable. From this point of view the present and fashionable push towards harmonization seems to rest on a misunderstanding of the real behavior of individuals. If we accept the view that differentiation is a basic reality, we then have to wonder to which extent, and according to which criteria, any homogenization or harmonization is justified.

To be succinct, there are two diverging views of social processes that may underlie any precise social or economic theory: Collectivists view individuals as parts of a broader society and they do not care about the individual specificities of human beings, whereas individualists insist on these specificities. These are the real differences between the diverging theoretical approaches. Let us take as an example the problem of competition (and, therefore, the problem of monopolies and cartels).

Mainstream theory – the theory of pure and perfect competition – suits the prejudices of those economists who belong to the first stream of thought, the collectivists. As we already mentioned, it is generally assumed that competition prevails whenever there is a great number of producers producing exactly the same good under the same conditions. In fact this approach is technological and not economic, since it focuses on purely technical characteristics. It is assumed that, for any commodity, there exists one optimal technique, which is available to all producers. And competition, thus defined, is supposed to determine an "optimal" situation (in the sense that it is impossible to improve the satisfaction of anyone without decreasing that of someone else). Economists from the individualistic stream – mainly "Austrian economists" – consider that competition prevails whenever there is free entry and producers are free to discover the best techniques and the best institutional organizations. From this point of view, the great merit of competition stems from the fact it induces producers to *differentiate* one from the other. In other words, the collectivists believe in the "harmonization" of economic activities, whereas the individualists believe in differentiation.

Being convinced that the traditional theory of pure and perfect competition is fundamentally wrong, we are left with the idea that it is optimal to have the highest possible degree of differentiation in all activities, so that our main question can be formulated as: Are there exceptions to the general case, implying that in some situations a process of harmonization can be profitable?

In fact, there are many specific activities in which there are gains obtained from decreasing differentiation. The reasons can be found either on the supply side or on the demand side. On the supply side such situations occur, especially in network activities such as telecommunications, transportation or money production (which are frequently considered as public utilities *per se*, or even natural monopolies). In particular, whenever externalities, economies of scale or economies of scope are supposed to exist, one can obtain gains by coordinating several producers or by substituting one single producer with a number of them. On the demand side, there are costs of diversification because demanders have to bear costs of information in order to know the specific characteristics of each good and the extent to which these characteristics meet their particular needs. Information costs are thus decreased by the introduction of standards and labels.

One may consider – as governments frequently do – that the best way to meet the alleged need for homogenization is to replace a number of producers by a single one – a legal monopolist – who can both extract gains from producing at the optimal technological level (that is, exploiting economies of scale) and decrease information costs for consumers. The total gain is then supposedly shared by both producers and demanders. But another solution consists of maintaining a diversity of producers who invent some means to obtain coordination gains. This solution could be called a "cartel solution." A cartel can be defined as a productive structure in which different producers make their products perfectly substitutable one to the other. They produce homogeneous goods, which means that they "harmonize" their productions. In that sense, cartels do not deserve the usual negative reactions they arouse. As we have already stressed they are an efficient method of meeting a specific need for homogeneity.[2] Whenever there is free entry on a market and where cartels do exist, it does not mean that producers organized themselves in order to exploit demanders (since free entry would necessarily induce an outsider to compete with them), but it is a rational answer to meet a specific need for "harmonization."

As stressed when analyzing cartels in Chapter 3, we can certainly accept the idea that a maximum differentiation of goods and activities is not necessarily the best scheme, which means that for one given activity at one given time, there are gains obtained from homogenization, or in other words, from a perfect substitutability between goods (which, even when made by different producers, share the same characteristics). Thus, it is obvious that it would not be optimal for each individual to use his own unit of measurement or that there exists a very great number of telephone networks. In such cases, a higher degree of homogeneity would be profitable both for producers and consumers. But it does not necessarily mean that marginal gains are always positive, so that the optimum dimension for such activities would be reached in the case in which the same goods would be produced all over the world (by a single producer or a world cartel producing perfectly substitutable goods). This would imply, for instance, that it would be optimal to have a single world currency, a single world language, a single world telephone network, and so on.

Those who believe in the necessity of such harmonization share a technological view of production instead of a human (or praxeological) view. They believe that it is possible to define optimality (an optimal dimension, an optimal organization) without any reference to individual minds. But economists know (or ought to know) that it is meaningless to define optimality independently from individual wants and perceptions. Each individual, as a consumer or as a producer, has his own perception of what he considers as the optimal degree of differentiation (and, therefore, of homogenization) for the various services he may desire. For instance, some consumers may desire to buy a car offering them basic transportation services, whereas others would prefer to have a very broad spectrum of choice. Some producers choose a strategy of differentiation (for instance, Apple in the computer industry) and others choose a strategy of homogenization. Therefore, it is meaningless to claim, from purely technical considerations, that it would be optimal to have a certain number of car models in the world or one common standard for computers. It is not only a matter of technique; it is a matter of individual choice. Given the fact that the optimal degree of differentiation is not the same for all consumers and for all producers, they cannot obtain exactly the degree of differentiation they would prefer and therefore a maximum degree of satisfaction. It is the role of the market to adjust to the diverging wants of market participants as regards differentiation.

Thus, we know that for any activity there is an optimal limit between differentiation and homogenization, but we do not know where this limit is and how it alters over time because of changes in the wants and perceptions of consumers, in production techniques and in the strategies of producers. We have to discover this (changing) limit, and the best way to discover it is obviously competition, that is the free entry of producers on markets.

On the contrary, those who share a technical approach to the problem assume that they do have enough knowledge to know the optimal degree of homogenization. If ever they believe that what they consider as the optimal degree of homogenization is not reached by the spontaneous working of the market, they consider it justified to "harmonize" the characteristics of produced goods in order to increase the efficiency of production and to bring a higher degree of satisfaction to consumers. This is the reason why so many people favor world (or at least regional) harmonization through some constructivist process. They pretend that it would be more "efficient" to have a single world currency, a single world language or a single world system of laws.

It may happen that, in some cases, worldwide homogenization is the end result of the market process, but we cannot know this in advance. And if it does not occur, it just means that such a worldwide homogenization is not optimal. Let us take the often-used example of language, a typically network activity. It is quite clear that if ever each of us used a different language, each of these languages would be perfectly useless. Thus, we gain by diminishing the degree of language differentiation. If one assumes that the marginal gain is always positive, one may consider that a world single language would be optimal. But this has not happened over the whole history of mankind. To be sure, languages have not always been free from state interference and authorities have frequently forced their citizens to use a so-called "national" language. However, language is certainly a domain in which competition has prevailed. In spite of this fact a constructivist would consider it more efficient to have a single world language. More precisely, it is more and more true that there is a common world common language – English – and many local or regional languages (which possibly incorporate Anglicisms). It means that languages play different roles and, according to specific needs, the same person may use one or the other. World language harmonization would mean imposing a single language for all uses, either an existing one (English) or a fiat language (such as Esperanto). A similar process occurs in the field of opinion: Mainstream opinions exist because people find it rewarding to use the opinions of others instead of bearing the costs of developing personal opinions. From this point of view there is a spontaneous homogenization of thought. But meanwhile, a great diversity of opinion survives to some extent because people like to differentiate one from the other.

2. THE DIMENSION OF NATIONS AND THEIR DISTORTING ROLE

The present world is a world of nation states. Each nation state can be defined as a territory on which the state benefits from a position of monopolist of legal constraint. The state – or, more precisely the men of the state – decides that it is the only producer for some activities (national defense, money, transportation, public utilities, and so on) and it has the power to regulate other activities. Ad hoc theories (public good theory, natural monopoly theory, and so on) support such a claim by giving it an apparent scientific justification. By definition, the activities carried out by the state monopoly are "harmonized," since no one else is entitled to compete with it for these activities and to introduce differentiation. Moreover, regulations also tend to impose common standards to private activities. In that sense, the state can be considered as an instrument of harmonization, which, therefore, makes diversification impossible.

Now, we have previously stressed that, in many activities, there are coordination gains, implying that there is an optimal degree of homogenization or an optimal productive area. But the existence of nation states makes it difficult to reach the optimal dimension in each activity for three main reasons:

1. The optimal dimension of the productive area is not the same for all activities so that there is no chance that the existing dimension of a nation coincides with the optimal dimension of any activity. It may be too large or too small. For instance, the theory of natural monopoly rests on the idea that there are activities in which marginal costs are steadily decreasing (for instance, because of network effects). It is therefore assumed that only one producer can survive and that competition (in the traditional meaning of the word as "the existence of several producers") would be wasteful. In order to avoid a social loss due to suboptimal production, it is therefore considered that the state has to exercise such an activity. Among many criticisms which can be addressed to this theory, one is relevant for the present discussion: How could it be possible that the optimal production area (for instance, for telephone or electricity distribution) would be the US on the one hand and a country such as Zimbabwe on the other? The

dimension of a nation is a legacy from the past and it has no theoretical, and therefore no practical, justification.

2. When speaking of the optimal dimension or the optimal scale of production in any activity, we do not refer necessarily to any territorial dimension, but only to the set of producers and consumers and the number of units produced all over the world. For instance, an optimal monetary area, contrary to the traditional theory, may not have any territorial dimension. It is just composed of a set of transactions that are using a given currency.[3] This is one more reason for the optimal area in many activities not to coincide with the borders of any nation.
3. As stressed previously, the optimal dimension for any activity needs to be discovered and the best way to discover it is to allow competition to play its role. Meanwhile, competition induces people to invent new technologies and new institutional arrangements so that the optimal dimension changes over time. Whenever there is a territorial and legal monopoly, innovation is hampered and there is no possibility of finding the optimal degree of differentiation and homogenization.

All this implies that it is meaningless to try to define an optimal dimension of nations as far as they can be considered as territories in which some harmonization is obtained for a number of different activities. If one embraces the now traditional definition of the nation as a nation state exerting a lot of different activities in a given territory, the dimension of such a nation cannot be optimal. Looking for an optimal dimension of nations would more easily appear as meaningless if one would give – as it ought to be – a purely subjective meaning to the concept of nation, namely that a nation is a set of individuals who share a common feeling of belonging to the same culture, set of traditions and/or language, so that each one determines by himself to which nation he belongs (for instance, the Provençal nation, the French nation, the French-speaking nation or the European nation).

This suggests that there is no justification for the current process of political integration (that is the enlargement and consolidation of state monopolies). This is in perfect contrast with economic integration if it is properly understood not as the merging of nation states that have nationalized many activities and developed a regulatory power over citizens, but as the removal of obstacles to exchange (that is, the establishing of more competition). In fact, the argument in favor of world economic integration under the form of free entry of producers and consumers on markets – world free trade – cannot be disputed: It stems from a purely logical argument, one that is derived from the universal principle according to which trade is beneficial for both the parties who exchange. One cannot find any argument against worldwide free competition since it is pure logic, whereas there is no theoretical justification for political integration that is only the outcome of political power games. This also means that world competition is preferable to regional political integration, such as world free trade to the European Union (EU).

From this point of view there is a dramatic and not wholly involuntary confusion in concepts. So-called economic integration is usually interpreted as consisting of the merging of several nations to create a super nation state as if one could take for granted that it would be optimal to increase the present dimension of nation states. In fact, any system can be considered as integrated whenever the working of any part is consistent with the working of others. In some sense, speaking of an integrated system is nothing else than speaking of an ordered system. And we know, particularly from Hayek, that social order does not imply a rationalist harmonization from the center, but a cybernetic system of interrelations. Truly speaking, the integration of Europe, for instance, in no way implies the development of a central state to harmonize activities, but free competition in all activities.

Thus a nation or super nation can be defined as a space of harmonization, but it cannot be an optimal space for all activities. The best solution would certainly consist of suppressing nation states. But it is more frequently believed that one comes closer to the optimum by harmonizing the policies of several different states.

Let us assume for the time being that there are justifications for regulations and the public provision of some goods ("public goods"). In the present organization of the world, these regulations and public goods are produced by states. Moreover, the present world offers a contrasted picture: The constructivist approach of politicians pushes towards the enlargement of nations and the creation of super nations (as is the case for the EU) to which the power to regulate and to produce public goods can be transferred. Meanwhile, there is a pressure from populations for a more divided world and the dissolution of nations (for instance the claim for independence by many people in Scotland, Catalonia or Venetia). Truly, this pressure may come from politicians who have no hope to succeed on a larger political scale and who are developing the nationalist feelings of a more restricted population in order to come to power. But it may also be the consequence of a general recognition that there are no specific costs from belonging to a small nation and that, on the contrary, it allows citizens to be closer to the central power.[4]

The political approach is parallel to the one that may be dominant in industrial economics, the idea that there are economies of scale in nearly all activities. But such a belief stems from a purely technological approach. An institutional approach (such as those developed by Coase, Kirzner,

Hayek and Demsetz) does stress that there may be institutional diseconomies of scale: The larger the scale of production, the more difficult economic calculation becomes.

In the private ("industrial") sphere, there is a present tendency to shift from big production units to a networked production. The same could happen in the public sphere. The transformation in productive structures cannot give any support to the idea according to which existing nations are too small and have to be replaced by larger ones, but, on the contrary, it implies that a transformation in the working of nations has to parallel the evolution in productive structures: Functional federalism and competition ought to substitute for political integration.

3. WORLD OR REGIONAL HARMONIZATION

Harmonization is often considered as desirable since it evokes the idea that anarchy is avoidable. However, as stressed above, harmonization (that is, the suppression of differentiation) cannot be considered as a valuable target: in a free market economy people do not systematically aim at harmonizing, but rather look for an optimal differentiation (or optimal homogenization). When speaking of harmonization, one usually refers to explicit policy measures aimed at decreasing differentiation between nation states. In fact, harmonization thus defined means international cartellization of policy measures. But, contrary to a private cartel, emerging in a world of free entry, a public cartel cannot be beneficial, for two main reasons:

1. It is built from national areas which are arbitrary and do not correspond to the optimal dimension of all the activities which are regulated or fulfilled by states. Therefore, the cartellization (homogenization) of these public activities and regulations have no reason to bring net gains. There is no possible criterion to decide whether a regional or world harmonization of regulations could be an improvement.
2. Such a public cartellization prevents competition and makes diversification impossible.

Now, one may say, a world of private property rights with absolute freedom of action and exchange and without interference by any state could be considered as a first-best solution. But the world is not shaped that way and states do exist. Regulations and taxes decided in one given state have effects on citizens in other nations (the externalities argument). Therefore, other states have to make decisions in this second-best world.

Can it be the case that, in a world of regulating states, harmonization of regulations is preferable to differentiation?

Let us take the example of protectionism. There is an international organization – that is, a cartel of states – named the World Trade Organization (WTO). Why does it exist (this question could be raised about any international organization aiming at international cooperation and promoting the harmonization of policies)? Certainly not for reasons of principle: Economic theory cannot offer any justification for the harmonization of trade policies instead of independent decision-making processes. In fact, the WTO exists for purely practical reasons linked to the actual working of politics.

In fact, let us consider a free trade world with perfectly determined individual property rights and no public constraint (no state). Let us assume that a group of people creates something called a state in a given area inhabited by a certain number of persons (called country A). This state decides to introduce a tax or a regulation on some or all of the citizens. It certainly impinges on individual property rights. We have shifted to a second-best situation (except if one could imagine a hypothetical situation in which all citizens, without any exception, desired to be taxed or regulated that way, in order to get some "public good," the production of which they view as the best possible use of their resources).

Now, let us assume that, instead of levying a tax or imposing a regulation to its citizens, the state decides to create discrimination between "internal" exchange and "external" exchange. For instance, it decides a tariff on imports of wine to protect its own producers. As is well known, the burden of this tariff is shared at least by both traders, as is the case for any tax levied on the occasion of an exchange. In other words, the state impinges not only on the property of the inhabitants of country A (who, it is assumed, benefit in return from the production of a "public good"), but also on that of individuals in the rest of the world (ROW). It is true that some of the individuals who live in the ROW suffer from a deterioration of their situation (a negative externality), but this is not sufficient to justify any further intervention in the ROW or any world harmonization.

So let us first assume that, given this situation, a state is created in the ROW (country B). The state in country B has no means nor, overall, any justification for preventing the state in country A from imposing the tariff: As long as the inhabitants of A accept the idea that their state can extract taxes from them, it is perfectly legitimate for the state to impinge on the citizens' property by imposing a tariff. The buyers of imported wine in A (who are also sellers, for instance, of corn and other commodities) react to the corresponding change in the relative price of wine against corn. And it is because of this reaction that part of the burden of the tariff is in fact shifted to the inhabitants of the ROW. What is often called an externality is nothing else than the normal outcome of any change in an exchange economy. As human beings are trading with others, anything that happens to any one of them has consequences on others. There is a generalized interdependence of human beings in an exchange society and one does not add any additional knowledge to the understanding of this fundamental characteristic of human societies by assuming that some human activities create externalities, which have to be centrally managed and possibly harmonized: We all naturally depend on everyone else. There is in fact no difference between the assumption we have made, namely the creation of a tariff in A, and the appearing of a hurricane in A which would destroy corn crops and raise the relative price of corn against wine. There is no more or no less externality in one case than in the other (which, by the way, means, that there is no more justification for harmonizing tariffs than for harmonizing hurricanes . . .). This means that externalities do not exist as far as property rights have been defined: People in country B cannot complain because citizens of A have "accepted" a despoilment of their property or, even, suffer from an unwanted despoilment by the state. They have not a property right on a "just" price of wine (against corn or any other good) or any right to export a given quantity of wine; they have a property right on the wine they are producing with their own land, minds and bodies. They are free to offer the output of their work, but citizens from country A are not obliged to buy it and are free to put obstacles to the purchase of it.

This case is completely different from the one in which, for instance, a producer in country A would produce smoke that would darken the house of a neighbor located in country B. This is clearly an attack against the neighbor's property and *he* is entitled (not his state) to ask for compensation or for the discontinuance of the damage. The fact that both individuals are located on different sides of a border is not substantial: one is responsible for the damage he is causing to others, whether they are in the same country or another country. There is a problem not because there is a so-called "externality," but because one's property is harmed.[5]

Now, let us come back to the previous case in which the state in A had imposed a tariff on imports of wine from the ROW. If a state exists in the ROW (which means that the ROW becomes country B), it may want to struggle against the "externality" imposed on some of its citizens by the tariff. Using constraint (for instance, a war against A) would not be legitimate since no one in A – not even the state – has infringed on the legitimate rights of the citizens of B (they suffer from the consequences of what is going on in A, but it is a quite different matter). The state in B may try to negotiate by arguing that its citizens suffer from protection in A. It may even retaliate – for example, by imposing tariffs on some imports from A – in order to be in a better position to negotiate. By so doing, it certainly imposes not only a burden but also an injustice on its own citizens. Whether it knows it or not, the state in B believes it will make easier the dismantling of protectionism from A. Once more, the only theoretical criterion we possess to evaluate this decision is that it impinges on the property rights of citizens in B. We cannot find any general justification for the policy decided in B (the state may be right or not in forecasting that it may succeed better in its negotiation with A by retaliating, but we cannot develop a general theory implying that its protectionism is justified).

Now, we are in a situation in which both countries are protectionist (and the inhabitants of these countries may not even understand that they are mainly harmed by their own government policies). Although, in principle, anyone would gain from deciding a unilateral liberalization, let us assume they do not want it because no one wants to be the first to suppress protectionism. If ever they believe in the merits of free trade, they will initiate a process of cooperation to negotiate "balanced" liberalization, possibly leading to free trade. They may, for instance, create something like the WTO, the official aim of which would be to make possible international cooperation in trade policies.

The important point is the following: as economists, we cannot find any general theoretical justification for such an organization as the WTO. It may be wise to create it from a strategic point of view, given some specific political and institutional facts. But any such organization is not founded on a universal principle. There is an unquestionable theoretical – and therefore practical – argument in favor of free trade, but there is no theoretical argument in favor of any world regulation of trade liberalization. And we find exactly the same result as regards any activity or problem. We may have personal evaluations of any process of negotiation or state cooperation, some people being in favor of such systems, others believing in different processes, and there is a high probability that there will be disagreement between observers. But there cannot be any universally accepted justification for international cooperation between states, whereas the principle according to which (internal or external) trade is beneficial for both parties is a universal principle.

What has just been stressed about tariffs can be identically stressed about all sorts of regulations. Since any regulation in any country changes the conditions of production and exchange, it has consequences on international trade, which are reflected in relative prices. If, for instance, the state in A imposes some sanitary regulations on food production, the relative cost of food against other commodities is increased, which modifies the conditions of international specialization and exchange. The producers in A claim that they suffer from an "unfair" competition from the outside so that there is a need for a world harmonization of sanitary regulations in order to avoid unfair competition. As already explained, competition does not imply that all producers are in exactly the same environment. It is quite the contrary: Competition induces producers to compete in spite of different productive situations by imagining different production processes or specializing in different productions. Therefore, there is no justification, for instance, for tax harmonization (at the regional or world levels)[6] or for the introduction of a "social clause" in trade agreements under the pretext that foreign producers have an unfair advantage over national ones whenever they are not obliged to apply the same costly social laws.[7]

4. RULES, NORMS AND STANDARDS

As markets become more and more global, it seems increasingly necessary that regulations become worldwide. This can be done by two different ways: either one national state tries to regulate an activity for the whole world, or specific world organizations are in charge of such regulations.

The first case is met with regulations about competition. For instance, when the US Department of Justice sues Microsoft because of an alleged monopolist behavior, it does not consider only the American market, but the whole world market. Similarly, the EU Commission more and more frequently considers that it has the right to investigate whenever, for instance, a merger between two big American firms could give them too large a "market power" outside the US.

As regards the second case, international organizations increasingly aim at obtaining a world regulatory power. It is the case, for instance, with the World Health Organization (WHO), which has launched a global campaign against tobacco and is designing regulations (which have to be adopted by national governments and parliaments in order to be actually implemented). This evolution is particularly dangerous, since it can be interpreted as the emergence of a world system of surveillance of individual behaviors. Whatever are the real dangers of smoking, it is a purely individual problem. The usual arguments to justify a world regulation (externalities, economies of scale) cannot apply in such a case. But to play the game it seems sufficient to claim that the WHO is in charge of world "public health" and that smoking enters that category.

As we do not see any justification for such regulations and more generally for any regulation, we obviously have trouble in imagining how the internationalization of regulations could be anymore justified. In other words, the problem is not, for instance, that regulations in favor of competition and against monopolies are national in a world of globalization. The problem is that such regulations exist.

But let us consider the specific problem of norms and standards. By definition, a norm or a standard is more useful the more it is adopted by a great number of people, and from this point of view there is certainly a need for homogenization. But, once more, the market can do this.

However, and as already stressed, public national norms do exist and, apart from the solution consisting of suppressing all public norms, one may wonder whether a second-best solution would consist of replacing national norms with international ones. This is in fact the preferred approach in the EU. It may seem that this approach is justified as far as a decrease in the number of norms is beneficial both for producers (who can sell to broader markets and/or exploit economies of scale) and consumers (who have less information costs to incur and get compatible goods). But our previous reasoning can be transferred to this specific problem. Instead of making norms uniform, one may prefer competition in norms, including public ones.

From this point of view, institutional arrangements are important. Thus, a famous decision of the European Court of Justice (judgment "Cassis de Dijon") specified that a European country cannot prevent the import of a commodity produced in another country in which different norms are imposed to producers (for instance, for health or safety reasons). This does mean some degree of competition in public norms: Consumers – who must be considered as responsible persons as regards their own health or safety – have the right to choose between different norms. It can be expected that, little by little, the market selects the most desired norms. But full competition in norms would imply not only that imports of goods produced according to different norms be accepted, but, moreover, that in any country the producers be allowed to use the norms which are used in any other country (for instance, at least, other European countries as regards the EU). Similarly, it is often claimed that it would be preferable to have a single business law in Europe (for instance, to define the working and the organization of firms). A more competitive approach would consist in allowing any firm in any country (of the EU) to be constituted according to the law of any member country. One may guess that, little by little, the market would choose the type of organization that is preferred (by shareholders, creditors, wage earners and suppliers).

The usual justification for a public intervention in the definition of private norms is the following: Either there is a multiplicity of norms – which is not efficient – or one norm becomes dominant and there is the risk of a monopoly position. In such a case, in spite of the fact there is free entry into a market in principle, in reality new producers cannot enter because there is a "dominant" producer. The first producer on a market benefits from a sort of snowball effect. In particular, in network activities there is a cumulative process: People buy a good (computer, program, telephone, and so on) according to a certain standard because they know that many people are using the same. Thus, they reinforce the market share of the producer. States care about this problem for two reasons:

1. It may happen, it is argued, that consumers are "obliged" to use a given norm because it is dominant, in spite of the fact it is technically not the best one. There are many examples of such situations, such as typewriter keyboards, the VHS standard (which, at least in France, was said to be inferior to the French standard), and so on. Thus, a system of world cooperation to define common standards would benefit consumers by making it possible for them to get the best technical norms.
2. The existence of a dominant norm, used by one given producer, would create barriers to entry protecting the "dominant" producer from any competition, so that free entry would be only virtual.

These arguments have been prevalent in the Microsoft case.[8] And they are used to push ahead the public definition of standards, possibly for the whole world. In reality they are not acceptable: The choice of a standard has to be considered as one, possibly fundamental, element in the choices of firms concerning their strategies and production processes, as is well illustrated by the history of the computer industry. More fundamentally, it has even to be considered as necessarily implied by freedom of contract. Obviously, there is not a single set of norms for the entire world and we know, for instance, the difficulties one has had in the past when wanting to communicate between the PC world and the Apple world. However, the competition between the two different operating systems has spurred innovation. It seems that Apple has been ahead in developing new techniques, but did not obtain the dominant market share, which seemed to be warranted by its technological advance, just because it did not choose the best marketing strategies.[9]

One might dream of a world in which there would be a single standard for all computers and some might be tempted to ask for a regulation imposing the "best" standard. However, as far as the choice of norms cannot be separated from the choice of overall industrial strategies, it is an illusion to believe that anyone can decide which standard is the best for the present time and the future. And we may easily imagine that the dominant norm – that of Microsoft – becomes obsolete with the appearing of new standards, especially as technological developments are very rapid in the world of computers and the internet.

The diversity of norms has a cost, but it brings profits to consumers as far as it is a vehicle for innovation. From this point of view, the differentiation of norms can be viewed as equivalent to any investment: Investing means bearing a cost to get a future return. Those who adopt a technological approach of economic problems consider that the optimal number of standards in any domain is one, so that the fastest way to obtain this result is for some world authority to impose it (assuming that those who decide know which is the best norm). But it is likely that, from an economic and realistic point of view, the optimal number of standards is higher than one. As already stressed, the optimal degree of differentiation or homogenization cannot be decided from the "outside." It has to be experimented; it has to evolve over time. As Friedrich Hayek stressed, we ought not to care about results, but about processes. If there is free entry, the market will determine the optimal number of standards and there is no room for any determination either by a world authority or by some process of cooperation between national authorities.

If ever, at one given time, there is a "dominant" firm and standard, it does not mean that the process of competition is not working and that the state must intervene to impose competition (which is a contradiction in terms), as the American Department of Justice has done in the Microsoft case. The often-used argument of "barriers to entry" implies that, for some specific technical considerations, whenever a firm owns a standard it makes it impossible for other firms to enter into the market, so that competition cannot be said to prevail. This argument is completely fallacious. In fact, when the firm that is dominant today first entered the market, anyone was free to enter and to propose its own standard. If other firms have not done it or if they have failed, it just means that they have made bad choices or that they dared not take the risk of developing this new activity and/or this new standard. One cannot and must not rebuild history. If public authorities are entitled to cancel a process whenever those who have not invested in it are not satisfied with the result, innovation would be more risky and many activities would not develop. There are no possible barriers to entry, except for those decided by the states. If some harmonization is necessary, it is only the one that would consist in suppressing all obstacles and regulations built by the states.

5. INTERNATIONAL PUBLIC GOODS

The strongest case in favor of world regulations and harmonization seems to be that of so-called international public goods. In some sense, among the problems we have already considered, international norms and standards can be viewed as international public goods (which, obviously, is not the case for health recommendations, concerning, for instance, smoking). But we have also seen that the nature of norms and standards does not justify a public production. However, the belief in the existence of international public goods is widespread and it is the basis for many international agreements and international organizations (such as agreements to protect endangered species, tropical forests, sea resources or the atmosphere, all considered as a "wealth of the humanity").

However, saying that these resources are wealth of the humanity is also saying that they have no owners, so it is impossible to define individual responsibilities for their preservation. In fact, the best way to make certain that a specific animal species may disappear is to declare it as a wealth of humanity and to have states sign international agreements to protect it. As is well known, the only way to protect elephants, rhinos or tortoises is to privatize them. In reality, it is quite obvious that protecting these animals does not correspond in any way to the traditional definition of a public good, since exclusion is possible and rivalry in the use of these resources does exist. Therefore, even those who strongly believe in the traditional definition of public goods ought to recognize that applying it to these animal species is meaningless. And it ought also to be obvious as regards, for instance, forests: the problem of the Amazon rainforest, for instance, comes from the fact the Brazilian state is the legal owner of the forest and it allows woodcutters to cut trees. The latter have no incentives to grow new trees, as they are not owners of the land and would not benefit from such an action. The best way to save this wealth of mankind, the rainforest, is to privatize it (without forgetting to leave part of it to the first settlers).

Now, it seems that the problem is quite different as regards, for instance, the seas or the atmosphere, since it is impossible to privatize moving pieces of water or air, so that only a global public management (with possible concessions) can be imagined. As exclusion seems to be impossible, they would be perfect candidates to what is defined as public goods: No one, for instance, has any incentive not to pollute the atmosphere, but if all human beings are polluting they all suffer from the global pollution. It would be in their interest to accept regulations or taxes in order to decrease the level of air pollution. Such was the initial inspiration of the Kyoto Principle and it seems that there is a very large consensus about a public management of seas and the atmosphere.

To evaluate these arguments we would be tempted to enter into the discussion of public goods. But it would certainly go beyond the limits of the present chapter. Let us only stress that no good, no service might be considered as a public good by nature and forever, which, in some sense, means that public goods do not exist. Obviously, there are innumerable cases in which people prefer not to define property rights, because the cost of defining them with the existing techniques would be too high in comparison with the benefits thus obtained. Instead of labeling these goods and services as "public goods" it would be preferable to label them as "non-owned goods." Among them, some are not produced, some are produced by individuals who do not care about the fact other people benefit from their production without paying (for instance, private streets) and some are produced according to collective decision-making processes. Among the latter, an important distinction has to be made between two categories of goods:

1. Those produced by people who freely enter into voluntary agreements. It is the case, for instance, whenever one buys a flat in a condominium and accepts in advance a collective rule of decision – such as majority rule – for the provision of common services.
2. Those produced by constraint, namely the use of the tax power and the regulating power of states. The underlying idea is that no citizen would voluntarily pay for the provision of the so-called public good in spite of the fact he would benefit from its production, so coercion is necessary: Each one is obliged to pay as far as others are also obliged to pay.

Now, the only case in which it can be said that there is consent to constraint is the one in which there is unanimity: All citizens accept to pay the tax in order to obtain some provision of the public good. But this case is obviously purely fictional (except in very small communities). Most often, there is disagreement between individuals and the majority rule, for instance in the way by which a group of persons compels another group to pay, under the pretext that the produced good is a public good. The probability of disagreements is greater the larger the number of people involved in the decision-making process. Meanwhile, the larger the nation, the more difficult it is for people to vote with their feet. This is an important reason to oppose political integration and, on the contrary, to favor the splitting of existing nations into smaller and smaller entities. A world of millions of small condominiums ("states") is better than a world articulated around a limited number of super-nations (Europe, North America, and so on). The absolute nightmare is a world government, since individuals have no way to opt out. Therefore, one might have very great difficulties in trying to find convincing reasons for world political integration to be acceptable in some fields.

Let us repeat, it is not as easy to determine property rights on seas or on atmosphere than on animals and trees. However, we know that accepting the production of a good by constraint (public good) is the extreme and worst solution, so that we have to explore other options. More precisely, we can make the assumption according to which there may be technical or institutional solutions to overcome the apparent difficulties in the definition of property rights and, therefore, in the definition of individual responsibilities. We do not claim that we know the solutions, precisely because the solutions have to be discovered over the years, centuries and millennia to come. But, as is well known, in this field as in any other, whenever there is a public monopoly technical and institutional innovations are impossible, since no one has any incentive to develop them and this ought to be a sufficient justification for declining any public provision of goods, even those which seem to be international public goods.

The existence of national zones in seas and oceans makes it impossible to invent ways to define property rights in the use of water and its resources (fish, mineral resources under the sea, and so on). The existence of international norms for pollution or the development of ecological taxes by international cooperation makes it impossible to improve the precise definition of the respective rights of the polluters and the polluted. However, other solutions could exist and below we give brief sketches of the possibilities.

Let us take the case of fisheries and imagine that nations have no rights on seas (there is no distinction between international and national seas and all seas are open to private appropriation). The fundamental principle is the right of the first settler. One does not own all the seas because one has used a part of them, in the same way the conquistadors could not pretend to be the owners of the entirety of Latin America just because they had put their feet on the continent first. As regards fishermen, there is no need to define private property rights, so long as there is no scarcity of fish. But the users of a specific area have an interest in fish resources not becoming exhausted. Therefore, if the entry of new fishermen puts a threat on the renewal of the fish, the first users have an interest in defining and protecting their specific use of the sea in specific areas (but not everywhere and for any use). Then, they can decide not to allow the entry of an additional fisherman or to sell him fishing rights. As owners of property rights, fishermen have an interest in avoiding an over-exploitation of the sea. One might say that it is difficult to define and to protect such property rights. Certainly it is. But, it is no less difficult for a state or a set of states to define over-exploitation and to prevent it. And incentives are different.

But the most difficult problem to be solved may be the one of atmospheric pollution. As an example, let us take the famous case of the hole in the ozone layer. It is assumed that there is a causal relation from the production and use of CFCs to the progressive enlargement of the hole, this, in turn, having undesirable effects on health. The usual approach of the problem consists in imposing regulations and ecological taxes to reduce the ozone hole. Now, it should be obvious that we may care about the ozone hole only as far as it may have precise unwanted consequences on the health of concrete individuals. But the important point is the following: Either we have good information on the causal relationship and we know who is producing the harm and who is suffering and to which extent, or we don't. If our information is imperfect – as it seems to be, since scientists strongly disagree about this problem – the mere fact of taxing or regulating the supposed cause does not create any new information about the process. The level of regulation or taxation cannot be "optimal:" The changes in the allocation of resources brought about by these policies may be too important or too small, in comparison with the usefulness of alternative uses of resources. Moreover, there is some paradox in the use of ecological taxes to reduce global atmospheric problems. In fact, if these problems have an importance it is only as far as they are creating potential victims. Why should the state rather than the victims receive the tax revenues? The important point here is not to decide upon taxes or regulations to solve a global problem, but to better know the problem and to find the best institutional ways to come closer to the optimum level of pollution. And such a level cannot be defined independently of individual desires and choices.

A judicial solution, stemming from the principle of responsibility, would imply that an individual who believes that he suffers from some disease because of the ozone hole, with visible and specific damages, will look for those who may be responsible for his health situation, such as the producers of CFC, in order to get compensation. Putting the problem that way is underlining that it is not a global problem – a public good problem – but a problem which has very different consequences on different individuals: As far as there are no concrete victims or the alleged link between the damage and someone's actions cannot be proved, the damage problem is purely fictional.

It will certainly be objected that a system of individualized responsibility cannot be efficient, since an isolated individual has no real possibility to sue a great number of wealthy producers, even if a great number of individuals are in the same situation. Thus, no one would have a personal interest in fighting those who are destroying the ozone layer, before concrete damages are observed. Under such conditions it could be considered that it would be simpler that a small number of governments, helped by experts, determine ideal health conditions and act accordingly. This is exactly the traditional foundation of the public good theory.

In fact, there is no reason to believe that an individual has no means to defend his own health whenever it may be deteriorated by pollution, which would imply that a purely judicial solution can be envisaged. Individuals have a necessary interest to act since their own health is concerned. In fact, if it is easy to evaluate the causal relationship of "issue of CFCs – ozone hole – health damages" (as is implicitly assumed by states who decide ecological regulations and taxation), the cost of the judicial act is low. And if it is not easy to demonstrate this causality, why should governments impose taxes and regulations to prevent a phenomenon, the existence of which or the consequences of which are not at all certain?

Anyhow, how could a victim sue a great number of polluters? We cannot imagine all possible solutions, but we know that in such a universe founded on the recognition of individual rights, new solutions would be invented. Therefore, the examples we are giving must be considered only as illustrations of possible solutions. First, associations of victims can be created and sue the offenders. The advantage of this solution over a statist solution comes from the fact the association is composed of concrete victims who suffer from concrete damages. And the very threat of a judicial action from future victims would certainly modify the behavior of polluters, if ever they think that the causal relationship does exist and that they could be convicted in the future. Evaluating actual risks and looking for solutions would thus be gradual, according to real needs and without brutally troubling the whole equilibrium of human choices. In some sense, scientific expertise would be produced at an optimal rhythm, accordingly to the needs of those who are concerned.

But the most likely outcome of a purely individual approach to pollution problems would be that insurance firms would play a role of intermediary between the victims and the polluters. A potential victim would be insured against "global pollution" and polluters would be sued not by individual victims, but by insurance companies, thus reintroducing a better balance between both parties. Moreover, modern techniques of insurance would certainly make it possible to replace a great number of insurance companies by one or several big re-insurance companies.

Equally, a potential polluter could be insured against the risk of causing indirect damages to some individuals, so that there would be incentives for insurance companies to play a role as regulators of pollution, since they would have an interest in controlling polluters and demanding insurance premiums, which would be higher according to the size of the potential risk. Little by little a complex system of risk transfers and risk controls would certainly emerge and, without being perfect, would make possible the convergence towards an optimal degree of risk.

Such a solution would be superior to the usual government solution. When the environment is nationalized, possibly by a world organization, any environmental evil is considered as a fatality: No one is responsible. The future victims of the environment would therefore not get any compensation, whereas huge ecological taxes would enter the coffers of national states and world organizations.

In short, there are no worldwide problems, no such thing as sustainable worldwide growth, no international externalities or international public goods. There is only a world network of individuals who have rights and who are interdependent. They have to invent solutions to their own problems, and the price system and the juridical system are the powerful instruments they can use in ever-changing systems of adjustment.

NOTES

1. The present text was presented at the Mont Pèlerin Society General Meeting, Santiago de Chile, 12–17 November 2000. It was originally published as Salin (2001) and reprinted here with permission of The Independent Institute. I thank François Guillaumat for his comments on a previous version of this text and for his useful suggestions.
2. For a more detailed analysis of the role of cartels, see Chapter 3.
3. The optimum monetary area in the theory developed by Robert Mundell has a territorial basis, since it is based on the assumed "optimal" adjustment obtained from the use of various policy instruments. We propose another, non-territorial definition of the optimum monetary area in Chapters 10 and 11.
4. It is characteristic that tax havens are generally small nations, which may mean that it is more difficult to despoil citizens in this case. Moreover, the smaller the nation, the easier it is to vote by feet.
5. The difference between both cases – the tariff and the smoke – might seem slight, since in both cases citizens in B suffer from what has been decided in A. However, in the case of tariffs, if ever it is considered that it is legitimate for the state to levy taxes, it may decide to levy taxes on those who import from the outside. Certainly, the exporters from B will suffer from this tariff, but there is no attack on their property. In the case of trans-border pollution there is a direct attack on property. In other words, imposing tariffs is certainly an obstacle to freedom of contract, as is any tax on transactions – and this is a fundamental reason to oppose them – but the state in A does not directly oppose the freedom of citizens in B to export, it opposes the freedom of its own citizens to import (which, obviously, has consequences on exporters in B). However, it is also true that tariffs have sometimes been considered as ways to extract resources from the citizens of other countries through constraint. Such is the case with the so-called theory of the "optimum tariff:" As for any tax, the real burden of a tariff is not paid only by the one who actually pays, but part of the burden is shifted to the other contracting partner. If ever one could really know all supply and demand curves, it would be possible to define a tariff structure such that a government could extract a maximum amount of resources from foreigners. However, this transfer is purely and simply a despoilment of foreigners who, in exchange, do not receive any "public good," contrary to what is generally assumed to legitimate taxation. Calling such an act of despoilment an optimum tariff is equivalent to saying that it is optimal for an individual to obtain goods not by his own productive efforts, but by robbing others of their property. In fact, it is meaningless to speak of optimality without referring to individual property rights. There is no "optimal

allocation of resources," except the one that is made by individuals for the resources they legitimately own.

6. For instance, by the EU or by the OECD (The Organisation for Economic Co-operation and Development), which have for a long time been pushing towards an alarming system of harmonized minimum taxation of capital returns.
7. These examples deserve a more developed analysis, which is provided in Chapter 7.
8. On this problem one may read a very interesting book: Liebowitz and Margolis (1999).
9. As is well known, Microsoft chose to make its software available to all computer producers, whereas Apple chose to link the production of software and hardware, before deciding finally to become compatible with Microsoft. Moreover, the marketing strategy of Apple has often been relatively deficient in comparison to PC producers and Microsoft.

7. International tax problems: between coordination and competition[1]

As stressed in different chapters of the present book, the argument in favor of harmonization usually rests on a wrong definition of a common market and on confusion between competition – which allows market integration – and the harmonization of the conditions of production. A common market implies competition, it does not imply the harmonization of the conditions of production: When there is freedom of entry into a market, different producers can compete, although they are in different environments and produce under different conditions of production. In the present chapter, we apply these general ideas to the case of international tax problems.

Why are there international tax problems? Simply because nations exist! A nation can be defined as a specific area in which a government benefits from a position of monopoly to use legal coercion, which allows it to raise taxes. Now, individuals want to move or to trade from one nation to the other. These individual wants may be impaired by the existence of national tax systems. Conversely, the national tax monopolies of governments may be cut down by the existence of international flows of men and goods. Thus, international tax problems stem, on the one hand, from the shock between the free wants of individuals and the coercion exerted by states and, on the other hand, from possible diverging targets of national governments.

In the present chapter we first adopt a positive approach of international tax problems, in order to develop some general statements about the influence of national tax systems on international flows of commodities and factors of production. These general statements will help in evaluating normative approaches of international tax problems, in particular the two polar cases of tax competition and tax coordination.

1. A POSITIVE ECONOMIC APPROACH TO INTERNATIONAL TAX PROBLEMS

In order to develop a correct analysis of international tax problems, one must keep in mind a few very general statements about taxation, among which the following ones seem particularly important.

1.1 General Statements about Taxation

Before considering international problems specifically, we first stress two general statements about taxation, which are relevant not only for international tax problems but for *any* tax problem:

Tax neutrality is a myth

Any tax, even the lump-sum tax of textbooks, has effects on consumption and production. If we assume that there are two activities in one given closed economy, and that some proportional tax with a single rate is levied on both activities, there is no discrimination between them and people might be tempted to say that this tax is "neutral." However, there are changes in productive and consumption patterns, except in the extreme case of unitary income elasticities for both activities and "equal" distribution of the corresponding public benefits. It could be said that this extreme case – in which the percentage of each activity remains the same in production and consumption – is one of tax neutrality.[2] However, there is no justification for neutrality, thus defined, to constitute a criterion for tax policy.

A tax could be considered as perfectly neutral if public revenues were redistributed to citizens according to what they have actually paid (assuming that the public activity is costless). Now, *taxes exist because they are not neutral* and tax neutrality is nothing but a myth. Taxes cannot be neutral in the sense that a situation with taxes cannot be the same as a situation without taxes. And if ever it were to be the same, there would be no justification for taxes. Taxes exist precisely because they are not neutral. They have effects, some of which are intended by the taxing authority, some others being unintended.

Whatever the consequences of a tax on production and consumption are, it remains true that there is no discrimination between both activities if ever there is a single proportional rate.[3] However, a tax is never comprehensive for practical reasons: The tax administration is unable to register and tax all human activities. We may consider, for instance, that usually only *marketable* activities are taxed, which means that the tax system introduces discrimination between marketable and non-marketable activities. However, in the following pages, and in order to avoid lengthy arguments, we consider as non-discriminatory a tax that is the same on all marketable activities (which does not mean that it is neutral).

As just stressed, any tax has effects on the structure of production and consumption. Let us call these effects *structural effects*. Because of the changes they induce in production and consumption patterns, relative prices of commodities are certainly influenced by taxation. However, we may distinguish this cause for relative price changes from another: Whenever taxes are discriminatory, they induce – and are even intended to induce – further relative price changes. Let us call these *relative price effects*. Thus, there are two reasons for relative prices to change because of taxation: structural effects and (pure) relative price effects. In the following pages we shall assume away structural effects and concentrate on relative price effects.

Taxes are always paid by individuals

Tax laws and tax textbooks classify taxes into different categories, such as direct taxes and indirect taxes, taxes paid by firms and taxes paid by individuals, and so on. In fact, taxes are always paid by individuals, although individuals sometimes pay taxes because they have undertaken a specific activity.

As an example, it is pure illusion to claim that a firm pays a tax, since a firm is nothing but a set of contracts. A contract cannot think, act and pay taxes. But the individuals who have signed the contracts certainly think, act and pay taxes. It means that taxes (or compulsory health insurance contributions), which are assumed to be paid by firms, are in fact paid by some of these individuals (owners, wage earners, suppliers). But, those who actually bear the burden of such taxes do not usually know it.

It can be said that there is a single tax base: human activity. All taxes are levied from this same base, although the rates may be differentiated according to some specific events. As an example, let us consider a simplified case. Let us assume that taxes (and the state) do not exist initially in a closed country. Now, for one reason or the other, the financing of a "public good" is decided[4] and a tax at a rate of 10 percent has to be levied on all market values. Let us consider two possible cases:

1. The government decides to introduce a proportional income tax. If, for instance, distributed incomes (wages, profits, interests) are equal to 100 in a firm, after-tax returns of individuals will be equal to 90. After the tax has been introduced, the firm is distributing the same amount of income, but people get fewer private goods (90) and more public goods (10).
2. The government decides to introduce a value-added tax (VAT), with the same 10 percent rate. Now, the firm distributes only 90 to income earners, but people are exactly in the same situation as in the case of the income tax: They get a value of 90 in private goods and 10 in public goods.[5]

The effect of the tax on standards of living depends on the use of tax proceeds by the state. If the taxpayers value the public good financed by the tax more than any good or service they may have been able to obtain on the market by spending the sums confiscated by the state, their standard of living increases. If the state is less efficient than private producers to provide the goods it is supplying, there is a loss for citizens.

Anyhow, the income tax and the VAT are two ways – administratively different but actually equivalent – of levying a tax on the productive activities of individuals. From this point of view, it can be stressed that the VAT is not a tax on consumption, but a tax on factors of production, contrary to what is usually assumed.[6] More generally, it could be shown that any tax is a tax on the productive activity of individuals. However, tax bases are more or less comprehensive, more or less narrowly and arbitrarily defined. Therefore, in present tax systems, in which a great number of taxes do exist, a given activity may be taxed once, twice, three times or not at all.

1.2 Effects of Taxation on International Trade

Let us begin with the traditional Ricardian model of international trade in which commodities and services are internationally mobile, but factors of production are completely immobile between nations. For the time being we do not take monetary prices into account and rather focus on relative prices between commodities (as is generally the case in the theory of international trade). Moreover, we assume for the time being that taxes are non-discriminatory, which means that all activities are taxed at the same rate in one given country. Therefore, we shift to a later stage the analysis of custom duties, which by definition are discriminatory: The taxes are not the same for activities originating in the country or abroad. The standard question to be raised within this framework is the following: To which extent is taxation affecting international trade? The answer is straightforward, given our two abovementioned statements about taxation.

Let us first consider structural effects. As we have already stressed, an after-tax situation cannot be identical to the pre-tax situation. In other words, whenever a tax is introduced or modified (change in the definition of the tax base or the tax rate), the whole structure of production and consumption is potentially modified all over the world. More deeply, this consequence is a mere illustration of the fact that all human beings are interdependent and a decision by any of them has consequences on all the others (even if most of these effects are infinitesimal).

As already stated, we do not want to focus on these (obvious) structural effects. However, it may be important at this point to stress a usual and dangerous confusion, the one made between interdependence and externalities. From the fact that any act of ours has consequences on others, we must not infer that others suffer from negative externalities or benefit from positive externalities, so that we would have to compensate for these effects. As already recalled, externalities do not exist if the legitimate rights of individuals are not affected.

Let us now concentrate on the relative price effect. We shall mainly consider the effects of VAT, since it is quite often said that differences between national tax rates affect international trade. We assume that in our Ricardian model there is free trade (a "common market") between two countries (A and B) and that the state does not initially exist. There are only two commodities, wine and corn, and no money, so that one of the commodities has to be chosen as a unit of account (for instance, corn). For whatever reason, country A is relatively specialized in wine and country B in corn: A produces wine and corn, but exports only wine, B produces wine and corn, but exports only corn. The international relative price between wine and corn is assumed to be 1/2 (one pint of wine is exchanged against two pounds of corn). According to the "law of one price" this relative price prevails both internationally and internally. It depends on the various factors – personal preferences, available techniques, factor endowments – which influence all demands and supplies in both countries.

Suddenly, a state – an organization that does not sell its production, but which covers its costs of production by using constraint (compulsory tax payments) – appears in country A. Let us assume, for instance, that road building – which was a private activity until the appearance of the state – becomes a public activity, the cost of which amounts to 10 percent of total production. The government decides to finance it with a non-discriminatory VAT with a 10 percent rate.

Relative prices are unaffected by the creation of the tax (except, possibly, in the short run, due to various adjustment lags): A 10 percent tax on value added, both in the wine production and in the corn production, does not change the relative price of wine and corn, which remains equal to 1/2. It is true that VAT is a tax on the income of factors of production – which are the counterpart of the value added in a firm – and not a tax on consumption. In fact, the weight of a newly created VAT cannot be shifted towards consumers (which would happen only if there was a simultaneous increase in the quantity of money, making it possible to increase all nominal prices, but this is not implied by the creation of the VAT). It can therefore be shifted only towards income. This fact has very important implications, in particular:

1. *International trade between A and B is unaffected* by the creation of the tax in A (which could be interpreted as a differentiation of tax rates between countries, the rate being 10 percent in A and 0 percent in B), except for the structural effects, which we have decided not to consider. From this point of view, the usual opinion according to which tax rate differentials cause differences in "competitiveness" is erroneous. Since trade is explained by *relative* conditions of production and these are unaffected by (changes in) taxes – as far as tax rates are the same for all production costs in one given country – the creation of a tax such as the VAT or the change in its rate have no influence on specialization and trade. From this it follows that there is no reason to harmonize tax rates (for instance, to impose a 10 percent rate in B or a zero rate in A), contrary to the usual opinion prevailing in Europe, according to which a single market implies harmonization of the VAT rates between countries. A similar (wrong) assertion is also frequently held as regards, for instance, the free trade arrangement between the US, Canada and Mexico. And there are even people who would favor a world VAT harmonization! By pushing towards harmonization the EU Commission and many European governments are orienting tax reform towards a completely meaningless target, although radical and meaningful tax reforms may be needed, as is certainly the case in European countries nowadays.
2. *Trade is not affected by the inclusion or the exclusion of the VAT in prices of exports.* Let us assume again that there is only one VAT rate in each country, this "normal" rate being, however, different from country to country. Presently, when a commodity is exported to another country, the VAT charged on previous stages of production is reimbursed to the exporter and the VAT is paid by the importer on the full value of the import at the rate of the importing country (destination principle). The other possible system would be a "tax-included export system" (origin principle), in which an export would bear the full amount of the VAT, as any other commodity sold and used in the exporting country. In such a case, an imported commodity would have borne the tax in the exporting country, and the VAT would be charged in the importing country only on the new added value, as is implied by the very name of the tax.

Both systems are perfectly equivalent, for the simple reason already met: A tax with a uniform rate does not change relative prices and, therefore, the conditions of international specialization. Consequently, there is no fundamental reason for adopting one or the other system.

The shift from the destination principle to the origin principle – which has been recommended by the EU Commission for a long time – is usually called a "suppression of tax barriers" and is considered as a necessity in order for the European market to look like present national markets, in which consumers pay the same price – tax included – all over the national territory. Thus, it is felt that, in order to have a "single market," tax techniques have to be the same all over the European territory. In fact, as both systems are equivalent, one may say that the *single market had already existed* even before 1993 – which was assumed to be the beginning of the single market and which, in fact, did not add anything significant – since competition prevailed in trade relations.

All over the world, the destination principle has been adopted when VAT has been introduced, since it is usually believed that this is necessary to avoid "distortions in competition" or "artificial differences in competitiveness." It is generally considered that without this technique, the producers in countries where the VAT is higher would be "disadvantaged" in comparison with those in other countries – which is wrong. And it is also wrongly assumed that for this same reason, the country with the higher VAT rates would risk suffering from a "balance of payments deficit."

In reality, a "zero-tax export system" (destination principle) is similar to a system in which all exports are subsidized and all imports are taxed at an identical rate. It is well known from the theory of international trade that a subsidy on exports is identical to a subsidy on imports. A tax on imports is identical to a tax on exports. Such statements can be easily understood: Whenever an export is subsidized, the corresponding import is also subsidized since one cannot separate the purchase side from the sale side in a transaction. What is, in fact, subsidized is not only the sale, but the transaction: In our previous example, in which country A sells wine and buys corn, subsidizing the sale of wine is equivalent to subsidizing the purchase of corn. Similarly, when a purchase (import) is taxed, the other part of the transaction (the sale) is also taxed. Thus, relative prices are not modified if, on the one hand, a transaction is subsidized (under the pretext of subsidizing sales) and, on the other hand, it is taxed at the same rate (under the pretext of taxing the purchase).

Thus, there is no strong reason to adopt one or the other system and it is completely misleading to label the present system as a system in which there are "tax barriers". Tax barriers exist when there is a protectionist effect – that is, when there is a change in relative prices – which is not the case with either the destination principle or the origin principle.

However, we would like to stress one important aspect of this problem: It is regrettable that the destination principle be chosen when a VAT is created. Although the adoption of one or the other system has no influence on trade flows, choosing a different system for "internal" and "international" trade has one important consequence: whenever a traveler is crossing a border, a custom officer is there – under the pretext of fighting possible tax evasion – who is entitled to open the traveler's luggage and to go through his belongings, which constitutes a considerable threat on personal property and freedom. Thus, worldwide, citizens are submitted to the arbitrary decisions and the arrogance of state officers, not because they are potential robbers, but because their politicians – who do not understand the principle of international specialization and who believe that internal trade and international trade are of a different nature – have decided on a useless system. From this point of view, the shift to a "tax-included export system" in Europe would be an improvement. However, instead of limiting this change to intra-European relations, why not try to generalize it to the whole world? The only consequence would be on exchange rates: Present exchange rates more or less reflect purchasing power parity (PPP) for tax-excluded prices. The shift to the origin principle would imply relative changes in exchange rates according to the new PPP (with tax-included prices), that is a relative depreciation of the currency (or a lower inflation) in countries with higher VAT rates.

We have, somewhat misleadingly, said above that VAT is paid (or reimbursed) on traded commodities. In fact, we know that the burden of the tax is passed over to the factors of production (that is, to individuals). This means that a higher VAT rate in a country causes a lower real return for factors of production, all other things being held constant. Now, there are a lot of things that may affect the returns achieved by individuals; as we have already seen, a proportional income tax is a perfect substitute for a proportional VAT. Other taxes or even regulations could also be considered as more or less good substitutes for VAT. There is no more reason to reimburse VAT when a commodity is exported, or to harmonize VAT rates between countries, than there is to reimburse or to harmonize income taxes paid by the factors of production who contributed to the production of the exported commodity.[7]

In more general terms, when trade is free the price of a given commodity tends to be the same in different countries. However, it is likely that the structure of costs is not the same in all countries. Two producers can be competitive on the market even if their conditions of production are different. In Chapter 4, we gave the example of a Spanish tomato grower and a Dutch tomato grower who work in different environments, the Spaniard enjoying much more free sunshine. As already stated, it would be absurd to call for a harmonization of competitive conditions and to argue that it would be necessary to oblige Spanish producers to cover their plants with a canvas in order to protect Dutch producers from the unfair competition from sunbeams. The only important thing is to secure competition in the market for commodities, as well as in the market for factors of production.

It is, therefore, completely absurd in a free market economy to try to harmonize the conditions of production, so that all producers could produce with exactly the same structure of costs. And we do not see any difference between the (impossible) harmonization of sunshine conditions and the harmonization of tax conditions, which is so strongly desired. Taxation is only one of the numerous characteristics of the environment to which producers have to adjust, as they do for differences in climate, population or law. There is no more justification for harmonizing one specific tax, such as VAT, than any other part of the production cost. This conclusion is valid both under the destination principle and the origin principle.

One may also add that taxes and regulations are perfect substitutes: Instead of levying taxes to finance specific expenditures, the state can oblige citizens to bear directly the cost of these expenditures. If, for instance, to fight against a given source of pollution the state finances antipollution devices through VAT in country A and it obliges citizens to use them in country B, the mere harmonization of taxes is, in fact, creating a differentiation between countries, although it did not exist before! If ever one wants to harmonize taxes – which is not justified – one would have to harmonize all taxes and all regulations!

In fact, differences between tax rates, such as VAT rates, in various countries merely reflect:

1. Differences in the ratio of the public sector to the private sector.
2. Differences in the tax structure – for instance, between what one calls indirect taxes and direct taxes[8] – or even differences in the mix of taxes and regulations.

If, for instance, the state is larger and less efficient in country A than in country B, it only means that citizens in country A have a lower standard of living. It is a purely internal problem (of shifting the frontier between the public and the private sector) and not an international problem: Producers in country A do not suffer from any specific burden which would make them less competitive in comparison with producers in country B.

The plea in favor of harmonization lies in the dangerous belief that competition is impossible or unfair if the "conditions of competition" are not harmonized. On the contrary, the merits of competition stem from the fact people do not produce under the same conditions. By harmonizing them one kills trade and the benefits of specialization.

1.3 A Monetary Economy with International Immobility of Factors of Production

Our previous conclusions are not at all modified if one shifts from a barter economy to a monetary economy. Let us assume, first, that there is one single currency used in both countries, A and B. By quoting prices in money, one only shifts from a real numeraire to a monetary numeraire, without any change in relative prices. Differences in VAT rates do not create differences in monetary prices for the same commodities: the "law of one price" holds similarly in a barter and in a monetary economy. Contrary to what is usually said, an increase in VAT does not cause an increase in retail prices since monetary prices are determined by the quantity of money: So-called cost-pushed inflation does not exist.

The same conclusions hold if there are several currencies (for instance, one in each country). The law of one price (PPP) still holds if one and the same currency is used as a numeraire in both countries. In other terms, the exchange rate – that is, the relative price between two currencies – makes it possible to shift from one numeraire to another.

Let us assume that the VAT rate increases in country A. There is no reason for prices in currency A to increase if there is no increase in the quantity of money. And if ever the quantity of money increased in A, an adjustment process would take place: Either a change in the exchange rate if there is a flexible rate system or a change in the quantity of money in country B if there is a fixed rate system. In the latter case the desired increase in the quantity of money can be met by a creation of money in country B or by imports of the currency of country A by country B, this currency being converted into national currency by the central bank of country B (since fixed rates exist because a guarantee has been given by the central bank to exchange foreign currencies against the national currency at a fixed price).[9]

Now assume that there is a system initially based on the destination principle. The exchange rate corresponds to the parity between tax-excluded prices. If one shifts to a system based on the origin principle, the exchange rate and/or the general price levels now have to correspond to tax-included prices. If, for instance, the VAT is higher in country A than in country B, the exchange rate of currency A has to depreciate (flexible rates) or the rate of growth of the quantity of money has to be lower in country A than in country B, until the adjustment of prices has occurred (fixed rates). In the case of Europe, the shift to the "origin principle" would imply exchange rate changes (as far as there are countries outside the eurozone) or changes in monetary policies or flows of money between countries according to the relative changes in overall sale prices brought about by the change of VAT system. As regards exchange rate changes, they would be purely cosmetic, particularly if they could be forecast in advance. Those who reject them, such as the EU Commission, consider that harmonization is the only feasible solution.

1.4 Discriminatory Taxes

Let us come back to the case of a closed economy and assume that no taxes exist initially. It may be convenient to use the familiar two-activity (i and j), two-factor (labor and non-human capital) model of (internal) specialization. As factors of production are mobile internally, the marginal rates of return of each one are equalized in both activities, which probably implies different factor intensities in each activity. Each factor is used relatively more in the activity that demands relatively more of it. In the absence of taxes, internal comparative costs are determined by supply and demand conditions. As anyone knows, if countries were to open up to each other, trade would be possible and profitable if internal (isolation) comparative costs differed between countries. The working of the market would set international relative prices in-between internal comparative costs. As we have seen previously, a single tax rate in each country does not modify internal comparative advantages and, therefore, the conditions of international specialization (except for indirect consequences due to structural effects).

However, still with the case of a closed economy, we now relax the assumption according to which taxes are non-discriminatory. As all taxes are ultimately borne by factors of production (or, more precisely, individuals as productive agents), tax discrimination changes the returns achieved by production factors, either directly or indirectly. It is obvious, for instance, that a progressive income tax discriminates against individuals with high incomes. As a consequence, the relative price of the activity that uses relatively more of the highly taxed factor (for instance, high-quality human capital) will increase. But what about differentiated VAT rates?

Assume, for instance, that a higher VAT rate is introduced on activity j than on activity i. Both factors contributing to the production of j will ultimately bear the burden of this increased taxation. However, the factor relatively more intensive in the production of j will suffer relatively more. Equilibrium will be reached again when marginal returns for each factor will be equalized in both activities, but the loss of purchasing power is relatively more important for the factor that is relatively more intensive in the production of the relatively more taxed activity.

In any case, tax discrimination changes internal comparative costs. If ever trade is to take place between two countries, the conditions of international specialization are modified in comparison with the situation in which non-discriminatory taxes would prevail, at least if one uses the origin principle.

If ever the destination principle is used, relative prices are unaffected by the tax discrimination. One may conclude that it is a reason to prefer the destination principle to the origin principle, since it suppresses the effects of tax discrimination on the conditions of international specialization (apart from structural effects caused by the internal discrimination). However, we should rather think that it is one more reason not to have discrimination.

Let us refer, once more, to the experience of European countries and let us take the example of France, in which, for a long time, the VAT rate was higher than the "normal" rate for some commodities, especially cars. It meant that the French factors of production, which were relatively better fitted to the production of cars, were relatively disadvantaged in comparison with other producers. However, there was no relative disadvantage for them as regards external competition (that is, foreign producers of cars and foreign producers of all other commodities) because of the destination principle. If one is to shift from the destination principle to the origin principle, discrimination in comparison with foreign producers is thus introduced into the picture. However, discrimination is always discrimination and there is no reason to hold that it would be justifiable when it concerns different national producers rather than when it concerns national producers vs. foreign producers. Or, in other words, the problem is not one of (international) competitiveness, but one of (nationally imposed) discrimination. Further, considering external trade does not provide us any additional criterion with which to evaluate tax systems.

One specific case of tax discrimination is that of custom duties. Although it is obviously of particular relevance for the study of international problems, we will not develop the corresponding analysis, since it is very well known. The very aim of this sort of discriminatory tax policy is to introduce a difference between internal and external relative prices.[10] However, it may be recalled that the relative advantage thus given to some national individuals is given at the expense of other national (and, possibly, foreign) individuals; and that there is a net loss of resources, which means that the value of the gain obtained by those who benefit is lower that the loss incurred by those who actually pay for it.

Another well-known argument is that of the "optimum tariff," according to which a government could make foreigners to pay for the totality or, at least, the greatest part of the tariff. This would justify tax discrimination, at least from the point of view of the taxing government and its citizens. However, the definition of an optimum tariff structure is practically impossible in this complex world of ours, with innumerable goods and individuals whose reactions to price changes cannot be precisely evaluated. Research done on effective tariffs has also shown that it is very difficult to evaluate the actual effects on relative prices of apparent tariff structures. And, if ever it was possible, could it be morally justified to charge a tax on foreigners who do not benefit from public goods and services produced in the taxing country? Instead of an optimal tariff it would be a "maximum spoliatory tax."

1.5 Factor Mobility

Relaxing the assumption of international factor immobility leads to obvious conclusions. As all taxes are ultimately borne by factors, factors tend to move marginally from nations where they are over-taxed to nations where they are less taxed. Thus, individuals get potential gains and over-taxing states may lose some of their tax base. Ultimately, relative scarcities of factors change until there is an international equalization of after-tax returns.

But individuals do not only consider the amount of taxes they pay. They also take into account the benefits they get from public expenditures. Thus, each factor tends to move marginally from the nation in which it gets the lowest – possibly negative – net (subjective) benefit to the nation in which it gets the highest net benefit. Moreover, the more a factor suffers from tax discrimination, the more it tends to evade to another relative "tax haven." The case of brain drains is explained by an excessively progressive income taxation is a well-known example of this process.

Obviously, actual cases lie in-between the two polar cases of perfect factor mobility and total factor immobility, and the capacity to evade the tax depends on the degree of mobility.

2. NORMATIVE APPROACHES TO INTERNATIONAL TAX PROBLEMS

2.1 Coordination or Competition: An Overview

In the previous section, we distinguished three main categories of situations in which national tax systems are interfering with the international flow of commodities and factors:

1. The first is nothing but a mere aspect of the general interdependence that exists between all individuals. Structural effects belong to this category.

2. The second category is mainly illusory. Some people wrongly believe that taxes which do not affect relative prices have consequences on trade flows, factor movements, the balance of payments, the competitiveness of firms, and so on. These people call for specific measures to suppress or to compensate for these supposed effects.
3. The third is the only category in which international commodity and factor flows are affected by taxes, either directly (protection) or indirectly (tax discriminations), through relative price changes.

Besides, there are diverging views about the role of the state. However, in order to simplify the reasoning we shall cling only to the two polar cases, the benevolent and perfectly informed state on the one hand, and the "Leviathan state" on the other hand.[11]

Those who believe in the benevolent model of state consider that the state is able to define an "optimal" tax system and, more generally, an optimal tax and expenditure system by which it can implement its traditional roles (allocation, distribution and stabilization). Moving from the closed economy model to the open economy model, they may find positive or negative spillovers between countries, which may disturb optimality. According to the quality of their economic reasoning, they may or may not give importance to the illusory effects of the second category. However, the effects of the third category are perfectly acceptable from their point of view, since discriminations and protections can be part of what they consider as an "optimal tax system." Finally, they may add some specific externalities to the model.

Those who believe in the Leviathan model of the state do not care too much about the international effects of taxation, since they do not consider tax and expenditure systems as optimal, so that international considerations may be only of marginal importance in this framework. They care about means to limit the taxing power of the state, such as tax constitutions. However, as Geoffrey Brennan and James Buchanan have strongly stressed, opening national economies, far from introducing undesirable effects, helps to limit the taxing power of states. Tax competition between nations is a substitute for tax constitutions: Individuals flee away from tax hells to tax havens, which may put a pressure on the propensity of states to tax citizens.

To summarize: Those who believe in the benevolent state model also believe that several governments, which are able to define an optimal tax system for each nation, are also able to "coordinate" their tax policies in order to reach a sort of global, optimal tax system. Those who believe in the Leviathan model stress that the coordination of spoliatory tax systems can lead to nothing but to an international spoliatory system.

2.2 The International Coordination of Tax Policies

The theory of international tax coordination can be considered as a direct application of the general theory of public goods. It is assumed that, due to various phenomena – such as economies of scale or externalities with an impossibility to exclude – there are goods that would be produced at "suboptimal" levels if their production were not financed by taxes.[12]

This approach has been especially illustrated by the normative theory of fiscal federalism (see, for instance, Oates [1972]). The optimum size of the producing area being different for different public goods, there is no reason for the national government to monopolize the production of all public goods. It may be efficient to produce some of them at a lower level (regional level), since there is a chance to better adapt the provision of goods to the real needs of those who want them, without incurring a loss because of a smaller scale of production or a risk of free-riding by citizens from other regions. This is the very basis for fiscal federalism.

On the other hand, the optimal area for producing some other public goods may be larger than that of the nation. Protecting the air and the atmosphere is often quoted as such an example: Those who pollute the air are producing negative externalities and, if ever a national government tries to control air pollution, there is a risk of free-riding. Therefore, an international coordination of policies would be justified either under the form of international regulations or so-called "ecological taxes."

The international coordination of tax policies may take several aspects from more or less decentralized processes aiming at "harmonizing" tax policies to the replacement of national tax authorities by one supra-national authority.

Let us then assume that public goods exist and that it is possible to know the optimal size of the area in which each of them ought to be produced ("optimum public good area," of which the traditional discussion of optimum monetary areas is just one specific application). It is likely that the optimum size would be different for all potential public goods. Therefore, existing nations or regions could not be optimal for the production of a great number of them. Instead, the idea of optimal public good areas ought to replace the search for an optimal distribution of public activities between regions, nations and super-nations with a search for functional federalism, whereby any public good activity would be produced in an area at least as large as the optimum size. Now, we do not know these numerous optimal areas and we have to discover them and, moreover, to discover how they change over time. However, we do know, particularly from Hayek's writings, that competition is a process of discovery, so the market ought to be the best way to discover the size of these optimal areas.

Anyhow, those who believe in public goods and in the benevolent model of the state think that it is possible to define optimal public good areas from the outset and, simultaneously, to define optimal tax systems according to the collective targets attributed to the state (allocation, distribution, stabilization). To them, tax coordination between governments is then justified for two main reasons. The first one is the assumed existence of externalities; the other occurs if individuals are mobile, so that the domain of taxation may not coincide with the domain of expenditure. As an example, if a payroll tax is the only tax, one may work in an area where it is low and live in an area where public benefits are high, so that he is a free-rider.

Peggy B. Musgrave (1991) is a typical critic of the tax competition approach and defender of the coordination approach. Quoting the Tiebout (1956) model – which may be considered as an ancestor of the tax competition model – Musgrave writes that: "Local governments are competing for equal-preference individuals by offering a basket of services consistent with their preferences and furnished at least tax cost" and "The size of each jurisdiction is thus determined at the point of lowest average tax cost of providing public services."

Musgrave correctly argues that in such a case there is a tendency for governments to adopt general benefit taxation, where they tax citizens according to the amount of public goods they obtain, since "non-benefit taxes on mobile factors are neither efficient nor sustainable, particularly at the local level." Musgrave is objecting to such a situation, just because she believes that governments must have distributive and stabilization roles and that the financing of such public goods has to be based on "ability-to-pay" taxes and not on benefit taxes. From Musgrave's point of view, a world of benefit taxation is a world of suboptimal taxation. As she says, "If all taxes are reduced to their lowest common denominator or perhaps to zero, inefficiency in the public sector will result as diversity is eliminated and voters' preferences violated."

It is quite true that in a model of perfect mobility each person moves his activities to the place where he gets what he subjectively considers as an optimal mix of public goods and taxation. We would be inclined to think that such a situation ought to be called an optimal situation. But Musgrave – as, maybe, all critics of tax competition – implicitly assumes that some collective optimum situation has to be defined, the one which corresponds to the "voters' preferences"! However, except in the extreme and unrealistic case of unanimity, it is not possible to speak of the "voters' preferences" since there are normally divergent votes. The majority rule does not preclude a collective agreement.

Under the coordination approach, one assumes first an efficient provision of public goods (and distribution policies) in closed economies, next in economies open to each other. Owners of capital, for instance, may evade taxation and no more contribute to taxes, while enjoying public goods. Now, Musgrave correctly points out that in the long run "if all taxes were in the nature of benefit taxes, differentials in tax rates across jurisdictions would have no distorting effects on resources flows" (as anyone would pay exactly for what he gets). But Musgrave objects to this situation, because taxes *are not* just benefit taxes: "The very nature of public goods renders their financing via strict benefit taxation impracticable." Therefore, to avoid this undesirable effect, tax coordination between governments would be necessary, either by jointly preventing tax evasion or by harmonizing tax systems, thus limiting the shift towards benefit taxes, which is the normal outcome of tax competition.

Musgrave does not believe in the competitive model, just because she agrees with the benevolent model of the state, which, in her opinion, could be perfectly implemented in a closed economy and is endangered by openness without coordination. As she writes (1991):

> Once income taxes, property taxes and certain kinds of product taxes, rather than strictly benefit taxes, are used, and even more so as redistributional programs are accounted for, the benign role of fiscal competition breaks down. As taxes are bid down, the level of public services now becomes sub-optimal and the equity of the tax structure will deteriorate as governments seek to maintain their revenue positions by shifting the burden of taxation away from the mobile factor (usually capital) and towards the less mobile factors (labor and land), and away from wealthy residents and towards the less wealthy (and less mobile) [. . .] It is evident that "forces of competition" cannot secure an orderly – efficient and equitable – arrangement of public finances in open economies. The analogy to competition in the private sector does not hold.

Thus, critics of tax competition assume that the tax system and the expenditure system are optimal in the closed economy, so that tax competition leads to suboptimal systems because of tax evasion. However, if people are evading these systems, is it not precisely because they do not consider them as optimal? They were tax slaves in the closed economy, and they now have the opportunity to evade slavery. To say that the closed economy tax system was "efficient" is misleading: In which sense one may call "efficient" a system that is not preferred by all members of the community?

Musgrave considers that the mobility of factors "brings to the fore the problem of exercising 'source entitlement' by the jurisdiction in which the labor or capital income is earned. This also calls for coordinating measures to avoid erosion of the entitlement principle through fiscal competition."

But why would "source entitlement" be justified? Is there any justification for residence or citizenship to be the criterion for tax allegiance?

What is in fact put on the fore is the arbitrary nature of the state. In the opinion of critics of tax competition all jurisdictions are considered as entitled to get revenues independently from services rendered (for instance, to residents) and they consider as suboptimal any situation in which this absolute and arbitrary power of the jurisdiction is alleviated! Thus, it has to be underlined that the case for tax coordination – whether under the form of harmonization, coordination of policies against tax evasion or creation of international taxes – mainly consists in the development of a state cartel to continue tax exploitation of citizens.

Let us give some more attention to two specific proposals, tax harmonization and supra-national taxation.

2.3 Tax Harmonization

As already stressed, tax harmonization is widely considered as wishful for European integration. We also stressed that the harmonization of VAT rates, for instance, is absolutely meaningless. But what about other taxes, such as those that discriminate against a specific factor of production?

Let us take the case in which capital movements are free and the taxation of capital income is different in various countries. We may assume, first, that a government provides services to capital (for instance, safety or communication services), so that a capital income tax is a sort of user tax. Thus, it may happen that taxes on capital income are low in one country, but firms must pay to use roads, to educate their staff, to get security services, and so on. In another country there is a public provision of these services, but taxes are high. When choosing where to locate their activities, owners of capital take these bundles of benefits and taxes into consideration, not just specific taxes.

In this sense, there is an international equalization of returns, which does not correspond to what is usually called an "optimal allocation" (from the point of view of an external observer who is assumed to have a perfect knowledge of all costs and benefits) but to some subjective optimum: Whenever there is competition, individuals can choose specific bundles of positives and negatives, so that there is equalization of *their own* marginal utilities all over the different possible locations.

Thus, the diversity of capital income taxes may only be the counterpart of the diversity in the services given by various governments to capital owners. To be sure, governments sell complex goods and it is difficult to evaluate the part benefiting to capital owners. However, given the fact that information is so poor, there is no a priori reason to believe that an administrative process of harmonization would imply convergence to a situation in which there would be a better correspondence between taxes and benefits.

Let us assume now that public expenditures mainly benefit citizens and contribute to their general welfare (public goods) or specific needs (distribution policy) and that an existing capital income tax cannot be analyzed as a user charge. According to the usual view, there is a risk of capital flight and a need for harmonization in order to obtain a better allocation of capital and a "fair" distribution of the burden of taxation.

In an integrated market in which capital and commodities are mobile, there is normally an after-tax equalization of returns, as well as an equalization of commodity prices. This means that, if ever the rate of a capital income tax, such as the corporate income tax, is increased in a country, commodity prices and after-tax rates of return being determined from outside, the burden of the tax is shifted to the less mobile factors, such as wage earners. Thus, they pay the tax indirectly under the form of lower returns, instead of paying it more explicitly (for instance, under the form of an income tax or VAT). Under certain conditions, corporate income tax, income tax or VAT are equivalent to tax production factors. But the actual after-tax return of a production factor depends on its relative international mobility.

Anyhow, there is no more reason to harmonize capital income taxes than income taxes or VAT rates. Moreover, the diversity of rates for the corporate income tax – or any capital income tax – does not create a distortion in the allocation of capital as far as the burden of taxation is shifted to other factors of production. Once more we do not know exactly to what extent various factors of production are mobile and to what extent tax shifts occur. However, this lack of information is not a justification for harmonization, quite the contrary.

This raises the problem of the place of taxation. As an example, let us take the case in which all taxes serve to finance distributive activities. It seems that it would not be fair that some citizens avoid paying tax by emigrating to other countries. However, if the only aim of public expenditures and taxes was to determine changes in income distribution, the taxation system ought to be designed so that *individuals* would have to pay for other individuals. Therefore, any justification for taxes such as corporate income taxes or interest income taxes disappears: It is meaningless to ask capital or capital income to pay for the welfare of some individuals, since they are not endowed with will and mind. If public policy aims at distribution, one ought not to tax specific *activities* but to tax *individuals*: The very reason for what appears as a tax evasion is that the tax structure does not correspond precisely to the assumed role of the state. One does not correct this built-in error by harmonizing taxes. In fact, such a tax system exists because it is easier for a politician to tax activities and firms than to tax individuals: The tax is less visible and less burdensome. It makes tax illusion possible. However, in fact, it is wrong to believe that firms pay taxes. As aforementioned, firms are sets of contracts and contracts do not think, act and pay taxes. Only those who make the contracts are thinking, acting and paying taxes. It means that taxes assumed to be paid by firms are, in fact, shifted to the owners of firms or other individuals, such as wage earners.

More generally, the tax structure in a country ought to correspond to the expenditure structure: For instance, the ratio of "personal taxation" to "activity taxation" ought to correspond to the ratio between distribution expenditures and allocation expenditures. To simplify, if, for instance, in country A, one half of expenditures were supposed to be made for distributive reasons and one half to produce safety services for capital, a personal tax (lump-sum tax or income tax) ought to represent one half of total taxes, and a capital tax the other half. In such a case, there would not be any reason for capital flights. The personal tax would allow the distribution policy between individuals located in a given country, whereas the capital income tax would correspond to a user charge.

If such a correspondence between expenditures and taxes did exist in European tax systems – different countries being characterized by different mixes of distribution and allocation policies – the sole harmonization of capital income taxes would introduce distortions between the expenditure side and the revenue side. As we do not know to what extent the structure of taxation corresponds to the structure of expenditure in present EU countries, no general plea in favor of harmonization can be justified. And, if ever we had reason to believe that the structure of public expenditures and the structure of taxation did not correspond, the solution would not be harmonization, but tax reform in each country.

Arguments in favor of harmonization implicitly assume that existing tax systems are optimal, so that, for instance, an increase in the mobility of capital would cause undesirable capital flows if tax rates were not harmonized, or highly progressive income tax systems would cause an undesirable migration of the most taxed people.

However, existing tax systems are not optimal and they include a lot of discriminations. Thus, many European tax systems are over-taxing savings and capital. Therefore, the "average" tax structure ought not to be the norm towards which all national tax systems have to converge. The only valid criterion for tax reform is to adopt a better tax structure in each country.

Many of the taxes usually considered as candidates for harmonization are not justified in the sense that they introduce specific discriminations. It is the case, for instance, with the corporate income taxes when there are no equivalent tax credits for the payment of the income tax; with the income tax, its progressivity and the double taxation of savings it implies; and so on. These taxes would have to be modified or suppressed, for internal reasons, *with or without* the present process of European integration. But, one does not suppress distortions by harmonizing them. *If a tax is nonsensical, it is no less so because it is generalized and harmonized.*

In fact, the plea in favor of harmonization mainly stems from authorities, which, for a long time, could tax captive sources of revenue (due to exchange controls and other similar policy measures) and which regret that the process of liberalization in Europe has suppressed this situation of "tax slavery." In order to maintain at least a part of their power to despoil captive resources, they try to suggest that other countries make a pace towards their own tax structure.

The problem we are discussing is similar to that of protection. As it has long been demonstrated, there is no justification for protection and it is a costly way of levying resources. When protection is suppressed, the state loses tax revenue and there is a reshuffling of trade flows, which could be labeled a "commodity flight," using a term parallel to capital flight. However, the citizens benefit from these changes in trade flows and tax systems (even if one assumes that a fairer and more "efficient" tax was to replace the former custom duties, so that total public revenues would be unchanged). Similarly, the liberalization of capital flows and the increased mobility of people imply a possible loss of revenue for the state and a gain for the citizens, since they can obtain higher returns for their savings or their work. In fact, tax evasion can often be considered as a substitute for the suppression of a "bad" tax.

It is generally possible to find ways to diminish or to suppress discrimination. Thus, a general expenditure tax would be one way to suppress the double taxation of savings caused by the income tax.[13] Meanwhile, it would solve the problem of tax evasion. In such a case, it would not matter for a government whether savings would be invested in its country or abroad, since there would be an incentive for the taxpayer to declare the savings invested abroad. Savers would not be penalized for looking for the best allocation of their resources.

Tax coordination between countries, or tax harmonization, appears as necessary in tax systems that are not optimal. The less discrimination in a tax system, the less necessary tax coordination appears to be. Thus, the replacement of an income tax by a general expenditure tax would suppress the double taxation of savings and would make the exchange of information between tax administrations useless, since people would have an incentive to declare their investments abroad. Whenever a tax system is not optimal (from the point of view of citizens), individuals try to do tax evasion and the authorities have to fight against it. In such a second-best world, tax coordination and harmonization may appear as desirable. But it would be preferable to simply improve the tax system.

Tax decisions always have to be evaluated according to their own merits and not in comparison with what exists in other countries. Individual producers do not consider the "do-as-your neighbor" criterion as a valid criterion for decisions. In a competitive setting, they adopt their own criteria and they try to do better than others. Why would this do-as-your neighbor criterion become justified, and allow allocative efficiency and social justice, when applied to public decisions? There is no need for tax harmonization, but there is a need for better tax systems.

For the sake of citizens, tax competition is better than tax harmonization, if the state is of the Leviathan type. It may happen that states learn from competition and, being unable to keep their tax slaves, they are marginally transforming themselves from Leviathan states to benevolent states. However, as tax problems are complex, it is not obvious to link capital flight or brain drain to any specific tax, so then it is not certain that tax competition can deeply improve tax systems. However, tax competition and free movement of factors makes it possible for those who suffer from particularly unbearable discriminations to protect themselves, *even if they do not know why they suffer*: They just observe that their standard of living is not satisfactory in comparison with what they feel entitled to.

Europe is a good example of a situation in which there was coexistence of more or less closed countries (at least as regards production factors), and where governments are more or less close to the Leviathan model. The very process of openness and integration induces opinions in favor of tax harmonization and tax centralization (as well as harmonization and centralization of regulations). At the beginning of the common market, Europe could be viewed more or less as a federal organization,[14] as a case of free trade with competition between states. Now Europe is becoming more and more centralized. Contrary to the model of tax federalism, which is based on the assumption of a benevolent state, there was not a shift from a centralized state to a federal structure, but a continuous process of centralization and harmonization, which may be considered as a proof of the fundamentally Leviathan character of the state.

Thus, it is no surprise if the EU is developing from a mere free trade arrangement to an institutional taxing cartel. The ideology of interventionists, so naturally borrowed by governments, pushes towards such an evolution. In some sense, these European developments duplicate what happened in the US, and history may repeat itself on other continents, the ultimate danger being that of an international coordination of tax policies. To this end the experts in interventionism have already discovered new global public goods (clean air, forests, water, and so on).

The emergence of a global Leviathan state is visible in the various proposals for international taxation, which are presently flourishing. Let us take the example of ecological taxes, which are proposed either at the European level or at the world level, in order to limit air pollution. As already mentioned, this is an obvious application of the idea according to which international taxes are a way of limiting negative externalities. It is well known that externalities seem to exist whenever property rights are not well defined (as explained in Coase (1960)). However, it could be objected by the defenders of international ecological taxes that it is impossible to define property rights of air, so that externalities do exist and international taxation is the best way to cope with them.

This statement is debatable. But, in order to avoid a full discussion of the case – which would be too long and too far from the focus of the present chapter – we recall only two remarks which we have already made:

1. If it is true that individuals may suffer from air pollution, why would the governments benefit from ecological taxes instead of the individuals who are the real victims?
2. If property rights are not sufficiently well defined for the time being, better definitions can be discovered. One of the usual and best ways is for victims to sue those who are responsible. Thus, little by little a better appreciation of real risks and (actual or potential) damages can be realized.[15]

CONCLUSION

Too often, people discuss economic policy issues as if governments were perfectly well informed and benevolent. However, politicians – those who decide tax rates – do not aim at achieving "good taxes." What they aim at is to extract the highest possible resources from taxpayers at the least visible cost. They do not understand problems of tax incidence, and they have no incentive to adopt good tax structures.

Therefore, there is no hope that a coordinated process of harmonization between people who do not aim at good tax structures at the national level could bring a "good" harmonized tax structure. The process of harmonization or coordination is, in reality, decided by a collusion of people who, more or less, aim at a *bad* tax structure. Would it not be preferable to make it possible for citizens who, in a given country, benefit from a relatively better tax structure, to keep their relative advantage (that is, their relatively lower level of despoilment)? Despoilment is always despoilment, harmonized despoilment by cooperative actions – that is, by public cartels – is no less despoilment.

No one is inclined to behave "correctly" on all occasions, unless he is pushed by his own interest. Competition is the best way to constrain people, so that their decisions benefit others. Authorities must also be constrained to improve the tax system, either by constitutional rules (preventing, for instance, tax discrimination or the over-taxation of savings) or by competition. When there is tax competition and if they adopt a bad tax system, they lose their tax base. In that sense one cannot say that there is a *risk* of capital flow diversion to less taxed countries. It is a *chance* for the owners of capital. Governments have "tax slaves" and they want to keep them. As capital may be more mobile than labor, governments are more concerned by capital flights than they are by brain drain.

The author of the present work certainly belongs to this category of people who believe in a spontaneous process of harmonization due to tax competition. But competition does not imply that all tax systems would converge towards a single model. There can be different desired mixes of public expenditures and taxes and there are different equivalent tax structures (since different taxes can be ways of levying resources from the same individuals). Contrary to most people, the author is in favor of tax evasion as far as it allows individuals to escape from spoliatory and discriminatory tax systems.

Tax competition may be more powerful in limiting Leviathan states than a tax constitution. However, keeping tax competition also results from a sort of implicit constitution. Are we certain that governments will respect the free movements of goods and people, which are the best ways to check the Leviathan state? If we can understand the role of openness and tax competition, people from the Leviathan governments are also able to understand it. But they have the practical means to oppose it.

International liberalization in recent times has destabilized the taxing power of governments. But they react by colluding under the pretext of harmonizing tax systems or coping with international externalities. It may not be easier to limit despoilment from a cartel of states than it is to limit it within the boundaries of a closed economy. The larger the super-nation (Europe or even the world), the narrower the scope for tax competition. As the mobility of factors becomes greater, governments tend to cartellize in order to harmonize their tax systems or to substitute international taxes for national ones. And they find alibis in false economic theory, consisting of claiming that tax harmonization is necessary to avoid balance-of-payment problems, inefficiencies, inequities or employment problems.

How to protect from the global expansion of Leviathan? As is shown by history, constitutional limits are not sufficient. Ultimately, the only rampart is an ideological one. From this point of view, it is important to destroy all intellectual myths. The belief in public goods is one of the most dangerous. Those who believe that public goods do not exist have to make their point, again and again, without any intellectual compromise. The concept of a public good is so disputable that it appears as a pure intellectual falsification to make people believe that the government is benevolent.

As stressed, there is nothing such as a neutral or non-discriminatory tax. Any tax system is arbitrary. Tax means violence and we have no possibility to compare a world without violence and a world with violence. From this point of view, it is a pure and dangerous fallacy to believe that one may imagine an "optimal tax system."

One may even argue that the idea of tax competition between states is illusory. Competition implies freedom of contract between individuals endowed with free will and reason. Now, the very existence of the state is based on constraint and, therefore, it cannot accept full competition. I am certainly in favor of tax competition; however, I have to recognize that this idea stems from a normative theory of the state, as is the case for the theory of fiscal federalism, and not from a positive theory of the state. It is not in the nature of the state to accept competition from other states. Either it protects itself from other states or it enters into a cartel of states in order to maximize the despoilment of citizens. To fight the Leviathan state, it may not be more efficient to advocate tax competition than "optimal" fiscal federalism. In some sense, both assume a benevolent state, which either wishes to produce any public good at the optimal scale, or to experiment through competition in order to find the best tax and expenditure system.

Thus, to fight the Leviathan state beyond ideological aims, we may be left only with tax revolt. However, the larger the nation, the more difficult the setting of the tax revolt – it can be organized at the level of a small city better than at the level of a big nation or a super-nation. The survival of a federal tax structure in the US may have made possible the beginning of a tax revolt in recent years. But just imagine this European super-state or, even global super-state, towards which some people are pushing. Who would be able to organize any tax revolt? And which tax haven would remain available for individuals?

NOTES

1. The present chapter is mostly adapted from Salin (1994). It also uses parts from the following reports and articles: Salin (1989–91), Salin (1990a) and Salin (1990b).
2. In fact, even in this extreme case, there would be changes in production and consumption, since there are marketable activities that are taxed and other activities that are not (let us call them "leisure"). Therefore, the tax on marketable activities will change the choices of individuals between these activities and leisure.
3. But it could be said that a lump-sum tax, identical for all individuals, is the only non-discriminatory tax, since it does not discriminate between persons. In other words, there is no obvious justification for a proportional tax (and even less for a progressive tax), in comparison with a lump-sum tax.
4. For the time being, we define a public good as a good produced by the state, without referring to the so-called "theory of public goods."
5. There may be a difference between income tax and VAT in the short-run, if the introduction of the tax could not be forecast. In the case of VAT, the owners of the firm had signed contracts, for instance with wage earners, without considering the necessity of paying VAT. When VAT is introduced, they have to bear the whole burden of it. But, little by little, they will re-contract new, lower wages – or they will increase wages less than it could have been possible thanks to improvements in productivity – so that the tax is partly shifted to wage earners.
6. This point has been emphasized by Murray Rothbard (see, for instance, Rothbard [1970]).
7. It is often considered that VAT has to be reimbursed on exports *because* it is a tax on consumption, which is paid by the final consumer. In fact, we have already stressed that VAT is a tax on the income of factors of production and it is because the destination principle has been generally adopted that VAT *seems* to be a tax on consumption!
8. In fact, this distinction, of a purely administrative nature, has no analytical relevance.
9. This transfer of money from one country to the other under fixed rates has been perfectly described by the "monetary approach of the balance of payments" (see Chapter 12)
10. Thus, any tax or regulation policy can be said to be protectionist as far as it introduces such a gap between internal and international *relative* prices. Conversely, a regulation that, for instance, imposes certain norms both to national and foreign producers cannot be considered as protectionist.
11. This distinction is especially made in Brennan and Buchanan (1980).
12. The benevolent state, which introduces "optimal" tax and expenditure systems, may be viewed as a distributive state, a productive state and a stabilizing state. Providing stabilization services, for instance, is generally considered as a typical public good that individuals would be unable to provide. Salin (1990c; 2010) argues against this view.
13. The tax base of the general expenditure tax is similar to that of the present income tax, but taxpayers have the option to deduct savings from their tax base. Salin (2014a) discusses this proposal extensively.
14. It may be preferable to use the word "confederation" rather than "federation."
15. Chapter 6 analyzes this problem more extensively.

8. The case against "tax harmonization"[1]

There is an apparent contradiction in the present world between, on the one hand, the fact that human activities are more and more globalized, whereas, on the other hand, tax systems remain strictly national (or local). For many people such a discrepancy is not acceptable and they argue in favor of more globalized tax systems, which, in their opinion, means either harmonization of taxes or even the creation of world taxes and, at least, some cooperation between national tax administrations. But such claims are based on a false interpretation of what globalization is. In fact, globalization can be defined as competition at the global level. Now, competition does not imply that activities become more and more similar all around the world, quite the contrary. As a "process of discovery," competition causes producers to differentiate one from the other.[2] Therefore, from this very general point of view, if ever, in a globalized world, one would consider that tax systems also have to be globalized, it would imply tax competition and tax differentiation and not tax harmonization or global taxation.

Most often, those who are opposed to tax competition argue that:

1. By creating a "race to the bottom," tax competition compels governments to decrease the total of their revenue and to abandon the production of certain desirable public goods. It is thus assumed that the level of expenditure was already optimal and any decrease in revenue can only be harmful.
2. It is unfair that some taxpayers who benefit from public expenditure can avoid financing it because they have a mobile tax base (they are thus considered as free-riders). In turn, this argument implicitly assumes that the given distribution of the tax burden is fair ("optimal"), so that any departure from this optimal distribution is undesirable. Implicitly, it may be assumed that redistribution of resources is a public good, so that the production of this public good is disturbed whenever someone no longer accepts the place to which he has been allocated by the state in the redistribution process.

Supporters of tax competition consider that competition is always desirable in any private market and there is no *a priori* reason for it to be harmful whenever it exists in public activities. But the 1998 publication by the OECD (a pamphlet entitled *Harmful Tax Competition*) may have given some official credibility to the idea that tax competition might be harmful.

At the end of the twentieth century and beginning of the twenty-first century, technical improvements in transportation and telecommunications, as well as the elimination of many trade barriers and capital controls, reinforced worldwide competition. The increased mobility, not only of goods and services but also of factors of production, was felt as a threat by countries with high tax rates, especially the "old" countries of Europe. They feared that activities and capital might fly away to countries with lower tax rates so that they would be obliged to decrease their own tax rates. Their important level of redistribution – assumed to be made possible by high rate of taxes and social contributions – characteristic of the "European social model" was thus challenged. Therefore, it is not surprising if all efforts to limit or to prevent tax competition have been mostly inspired by these same European countries. The OECD and the European Union are the main instruments of the struggle against tax competition.

As already stressed, it is feared that tax competition leads to diminished tax revenue because of the lower tax rates implied by the race to the bottom, but also that the decrease in tax rates is particularly important in the case of mobile production factors, such as capital. Thus, low taxation countries may attract capital and other countries may be obliged to adopt tax rates on capital income close to zero. But, more and more, it seems that individuals are reacting to tax incentives and that they emigrate from high-taxation countries to countries with lower tax rates (for instance, countries with less progressive income taxes).

Under the pressure of high-taxation countries that fear tax competition, the European Commission steadily tries to set up a European reporting system – so that a government may be able to tax capital incomes obtained in another country by one of its residents – or a "harmonized" system of withholding taxes. But it has not yet really succeeded, mainly because it meets opposition from small countries – some from Central Europe – that attract capital with preferential tax treatments.

Who could have imagined that countries suffering under a communist regime some decades ago would now be models in the promotion of low taxation and tax competition? This is certainly one of the great and most satisfactory ironies of recent history, but the old EU members frequently do not accept it. Thus, in France, Nicolas Sarkozy, when he was a minister of finance, proposed that European subsidies should not be given to those countries engaging in "harmful tax competition." In some sense he was (involuntarily) right, since the countries that adopt low taxation have a better development strategy than just waiting for subsidies. But it is obvious that, to him, not giving subsidies was to be considered as a sanction against governments that did not play to the normal rules of the game.

In spite of the hostility of the old members of the EU, especially France and Germany, more and more countries have implemented important tax reforms. Specifically, a flat tax was introduced in Estonia, and in several other former communist countries later on.

In order to limit capital outflows to these countries with lower tax rates, the EU introduced on 1 July 2005 a directive that implemented a system according to which capital incomes received in a country of the EU by a resident of another country of the EU are automatically declared in order to be taxed in the origin country. Moreover, Swiss authorities have, in principle, accepted to impose a withholding tax on income from capital belonging to citizens of the EU and to pay back part of the revenue to these countries. But it is obvious that capital owners shift their capital to other financial centers and that the EU is trying to obtain similar agreements with countries such as Hong Kong or Singapore. It was always expected that the US would enter into such an agreement. In 2002, the Bush administration rejected a project of the United Nations (UN) in which an international tax organization would have levied and collected taxes across national borders. But, in 2012, there was an agreement between the US and five important European countries to exchange information about capital income received by non-residents.

In the present chapter we will try to determine to what extent and under what conditions tax competition can be considered as "harmful." We first recall some basic principles of tax theory needed for this evaluation of tax competition (Section 1). The role of tax competition is discussed in Section 2 and we conclude in Section 3 with some thoughts about the limits of tax competition.

1. SOME LESSONS FROM TAX THEORY

In order to be able to better evaluate the precise role played by tax competition, it may be useful to recall some basic principles of tax theory. To make things simpler let us assume for the time being that we are in a closed economy. But our final target consists in addressing the following question: To which extent is it legitimate to speak of harmful competition, as OECD does? We already stressed in the introduction of the present chapter that speaking of harmful competition implicitly assumes that a government had designed an optimal tax system in isolation and that international tax competition obliges it to modify it – for instance by decreasing tax rates – so that the system becomes suboptimal.

1.1 The Optimality of a Tax System

What is an optimal tax system? It is clear that it is impossible to evaluate it without referring to the overall public sphere, that is both the expenditure and the revenue sides. Those who believe that the state is both benevolent and well informed implicitly assume that it is producing only so-called public goods that are desired by the population. However, it is well known that such a vision is debatable. In fact, it would be possible to speak of an optimal system only in a case in which:

1. The public goods produced by the state are desired by all individuals without any exception.
2. The public goods' utility to each individual is higher than the utility brought about by the private goods, which could have been produced with the resources devoted to the production of these public goods.
3. The distribution of the tax burden is considered unanimously as the fairest possible one.

In other words, in such a hypothetical case, as no individual would prefer any change from the existing situation, it is optimal for everyone and, therefore, for all. The tax system can be said to be optimal.

It is obvious that such an extreme assumption cannot correspond to any realistic situation. In reality what is called a public good is a good desired by a certain number of individuals who are ready to pay for it or who use public constraint to oblige others to pay totally or partially for it. Thus, the production of public goods and their financing is considered as optimal by some, but as undesirable by others.

If one considers, on the contrary, that the state is neither benevolent nor well informed – it is at the extreme a Leviathan-type state – the tax system cannot be said to be optimal: The state tries to extract a maximum of resources from citizens in order to finance what it has decided to produce. In such a case, if ever tax competition induces governments to reduce tax rates, it does not lead to a situation of suboptimality. Quite the contrary, it makes it possible to better adapt the tax system to the very wishes of the citizens.

1.2 The Distribution of the Tax Burden

An important principle can be derived from tax theory, namely that the burden of taxation is not necessarily borne by those who explicitly pay the taxes (or social contributions) to the tax administration, because taxes can be shifted to other persons. Generally speaking, it can be said that there is only one tax base: the creation of wealth through exchange (except for a tax such as a lump-sum tax, which is completely independent from economic activities). This has two important implications:

1. As there are two traders in any exchange, the burden of taxation is distributed between them. For instance, whenever a wage contract is signed, part of the value created through it can be extracted by the state, but it does not matter whether the state asks for it from the wage earner (who can shift part of the burden to his employer) or the employer (who can shift part of the burden to the wage earner). Now, the precise distribution of the burden is not known, since it is impossible to know the (ever-changing) elasticities of demand and supply curves for all sorts of services and activities. It means that, in reality, it is unrealistic to claim that a government knows who is paying for the public goods it is producing. An "unfair" distribution of the burden of taxation amongst taxpayers may correspond to the apparently "fair" distribution of this burden. From this point of view it is fallacious to pretend that any government can design an "optimal" tax system, so that any tax competition would be "harmful."
2. It follows from this that, for instance, a tax (or a social contribution) on wages or a tax on profits are equivalent: They are levied on the occasion of an exchange and they are shifted one way or the other according to who has to pay them. But one could also demonstrate (see Chapter 7) that an income tax or VAT are absolutely equivalent, which means that contrary to the traditional accepted view, VAT is not a consumption tax but a tax on the income of production factors.

Thus, let us assume a closed country in which the state provides an "optimal" quantity of public goods (if ever such a situation has any meaning). Let us also assume that added value in production is shared 50/50 between profits and wages, and that there is a tax on capital income at a rate of 20 percent and a tax on wages at the same rate. The behavior of the taxpayers would be affected exactly in the same way if ever there was a tax on profits at a rate of 40 percent and no tax on wages. The tax wedge – that is, the gap between the total cost of the employee for the owner of the capital and the net wage of the employee – is exactly the same in both cases.

1.3 Tax Distortions in Present Tax Systems

There is a lot of discrimination in current tax systems. Some is voluntary, some is not. But, given its importance for the current debate, there is one we would like to stress particularly, namely the discrimination against capital or, more precisely, the bias existing in most tax systems against the future and in favor of the present. For a long time it has been tempting for governments to over-tax capital because it was not very mobile internationally due to capital controls. Moreover, there is quite often an ideological bias against capital and it is politically easier to tax capital than wages. But the over-taxation of capital still exists in most tax systems. This is the outcome of an accumulation of various taxes the base of which is either capital itself, its transmission or its income, For instance, in France there is a wealth tax, death duty, a tax on windfall profits, a corporate tax and an income tax on the returns of capital, as well as some other taxes. But the over-taxation of capital is also the consequence of the existence of income tax. In fact, income is composed of two parts: one is consumed, the other saved. A taxpayer who has paid income tax and who decides to consume will pay the tax only once (since the tax base disappears through consumption). The taxpayer who decides to choose the future against the present and who saves will have to pay income tax again on the returns of his savings.

From this point of view, there is an over-taxation of savings and capital. Moreover, as we have recalled, VAT is nothing but an income tax with another name, so what is true for income tax is also true for VAT.[3]

2. THE ROLE OF TAX COMPETITION IN AN OPEN ECONOMY

As most taxes have more or less the same tax base, we have to care not about one specific tax but about the total amount of taxes extracted from the same base. In other words, a potential investor in a country does not consider specifically one tax or the other, but he is concerned about the final profit he can get after having paid all taxes directly (that is, when he is administratively the taxpayer) or indirectly (that is, when those who are the taxpayers from an administrative point of view succeed in shifting part of the burden of taxation upon him). From this point of view, all empirical studies of comparative taxation are useless, since they isolate a single tax and compare its rate in various countries in order to estimate to which extent these countries are more or less attractive. This method is meaningless both because it singles out one tax among all those which are paid on the same tax base, and because it does not take into account possible tax shifts between people. Therefore, instead of focusing on any empirical aspect of tax competition let us rather focus on the logical aspect of the debate.

To this end, let us begin with one remark: from what we recalled in the previous section, most taxes (and social contributions) are paid by factors of production. They are never paid by consumers or by "firms," but by individuals who contribute to the production of wealth through contracts. Therefore, the main problem we have to consider to evaluate the role of tax competition consists in evaluating to what extent production factors react to taxation. From this point of view, the international mobility of production factors plays a crucial role.

2.1 Immobile Production Factors

Let us first assume that production factors are completely immobile internationally, following the traditional Ricardian model. Globalization exists for goods, but not for production factors. Given the fact that taxes are paid by production factors, differences between tax systems and public expenditure systems are without any consequence: Production factors are trapped in a country and the state can extract from them whatever it wishes. If it is a Leviathan state, it will try to maximize its revenues without caring about the level of public goods it is providing. As is well known, even in such a case, different outcomes may exist: If the state is well informed and it knows, for instance, that there is some "Laffer effect," it may prefer a lower tax rate than a higher one and taxpayers are thus in a better situation. If the state looks for a long-run maximization of its revenues, it may care about the effects of taxation on savings and investment and, for instance, it may avoid a double or multiple taxation of savings.

In such a case of complete factor immobility, one may be tempted to say that there is no tax competition as far as production factors cannot react to differences in tax systems by moving from one tax jurisdiction to the other. However, tax competition may play a role according to two different channels: one channel consists of the reaction of production factors to differences in taxation – which is non-existent in this case – and the other consists of the information brought to a country by what happens in another country. Thus, even with a Leviathan state, which is in a position to extract a maximum of wealth from its citizens, the government may learn from other countries that, for instance, there is something such as a Laffer effect. The "discovery process" of competition is then at work.

Now, many people believe that tax competition exists under this assumption of factor immobility, just because they have not accepted the idea that all taxes are paid by production factors. Thus, the majority of people believe that VAT is paid by consumers on their purchases of goods. Therefore, if goods are internationally mobile, they consider that tax competition exists, at least as far as VAT is not reimbursed on exports. In reality, even in such a case prices are set by the international market so that if the VAT rate is higher in one country than in another, it is shifted back to the returns of the production factors. From this point of view a high VAT rate in a country does not mean that producers in this country suffer from a loss of "competitivity" and it cannot be said that tax competition is "harmful," either for producers or for governments, which would be obliged to decrease their VAT rates in order to maintain the competitiveness of national goods, and, therefore, to abandon part of their production of public goods. Tax competition cannot be harmful in such a case simply because there is in fact no competition! Therefore, and contrary to what is usually believed, there is no need to harmonize VAT rates (that is, to claim to suppress tax competition). By the way, there is no more reason to harmonize VAT rates than to harmonize, for instance, income tax rates, since both taxes are equivalent.

2.2 Mobile Production Factors

Let us now assume that all production factors are perfectly mobile. From a Ricardian point of view nations no longer exist in such a case. But they do exist as institutional areas: In each of them there is a state levying taxes and providing public goods. Tax competition exists, since the tax systems may be different in these nations and production factors can move from one area to another, possibly for tax reasons. But to which extent can tax competition be harmful, and to whom?

Now imagine a world with two countries, A and B. In A, taxation makes it possible to produce a "pure and perfect public good," defined as a good that can only be produced by the state (in order to avoid any free-riding behavior) and which makes it possible for each citizen to obtain a higher level of utility than what he could obtain from any other (private) good or service. Also assume, for the time being, that the state is both benevolent and well informed, which means that it produces exactly the desired amount of public goods and that it has implemented an "optimal" tax system. An optimal tax system could be defined as a tax system such that any slight departure from it would not benefit taxpayers, but would prove harmful for at least one of them. In turn, this implies both that there is an "optimal" distribution of the tax burden – that is, a distribution unanimously desired by all taxpayers – and that the state knows perfectly the behavior of taxpayers. Thus, the state has a perfect knowledge of the "Laffer curve" and, being both benevolent and well informed, it chooses the lowest possible tax rate, which makes it possible to finance the "optimal" provision of public goods.

In country B there is no state (so no public good or taxation). Let us assume that taxpayers can move freely from A to B (a perfect mobility of persons). They may move for non-tax reasons, such as because the productivity of labor is higher in B or the way of life is more pleasant. But in the present chapter we are only concerned with the tax reasons for mobility. Here is a case of tax competition, since the tax rate is positive in A and equal to zero in B. Will individuals move from the high-rate country to the low-rate country to benefit from the zero tax rate in B? If they do move for this single reason, it means that they do not consider that what they get from the state for what they pay is worthwhile. In other words, contrary to our initial assumption, the good provided by the state is not a "pure and perfect public good." In such a case harmful tax competition cannot exist. Quite the contrary, tax competition is necessarily profitable since it makes it possible for taxpayers to *reveal* to what extent they consider the good produced by the state as a pure and perfect public good for them.

To be somewhat more precise, within this general framework, we may consider two polar cases: either the cost of producing the public good is proportional to the number of citizens to which it is provided or the production of this public good implies only a fixed cost. In the first case, whenever a citizen leaves country A for B, the remaining citizens do not suffer from his decision since they will still get the public good at the same individual cost. In the second case, the unit cost increases when the number of citizens decreases. However, it cannot be said that the free-riding behavior of some citizens imposes an additional cost to others who thus have to bear a negative externality. The departure of one citizen is certainly harmful for others, and those who argue against tax competition could be tempted to say that tax competition creates a suboptimal situation. But such a statement is incoherent. In fact, saying that the final situation (after the departure of one taxpayer from A) is suboptimal implies that the initial situation was (socially) optimal. But the only case in which one could legitimately label a situation as socially optimal is one in which this situation is considered by *all* individuals as optimal for them. It would only be the case if the state was producing what we have labeled a "pure and perfect public good." But, by definition, the good produced by the state in the initial situation in country A was not a pure and perfect public good since a citizen preferred to emigrate in order not to pay for this good. And the emigration of the citizen who did not agree with the tax and expenditure systems actually transformed them into "optimal" systems . . .

Thus, under present assumptions (perfect factor mobility; benevolent and well-informed state), tax competition cannot be harmful – either the tax system and the expenditure system are optimal and factors have no reason to move or, if ever production factors move from one country to the other, they reveal that the tax system and/or the expenditure system are not optimal. Thus, if production factors move for tax reasons, it means that the existing tax system in a country is harmful and tax competition cannot be harmful, since it makes it possible for people to evade a harmful system and adopt a better one. Tax competition is profitable for citizens (at least those who were over-taxed). It is harmful for the state, but it has been revealed by the very mobility of production factors that it was more of the Leviathan type than of the benevolent type. How could we say that a process that is preventing someone (the state) from being harmful to others be harmful itself?

We may also imagine that the state is benevolent but not well informed. For instance, it does not know about the existence of a "Laffer effect" and it is charging too high a tax rate, although it could be possible to adopt a much lower tax rate without diminishing public revenue. In such a case, tax competition is certainly not harmful, since it makes it possible for taxpayers to move to areas with lower tax rates. But it may also happen that the state lowers the tax rate either because it learns from the experience of other countries or because it tries to avoid the outflow of production factors.

Thus, there is no possibility for competition to be harmful under the assumption of perfect factor mobility, whatever is the assumption concerning the state (benevolent or not, well informed or not). If governments fear tax competition, it cannot be because they fear that they would be obliged to adopt a non-optimal system, but because the system is not optimal and they fear that they would be obliged by tax competition to adopt a system that would be "better" for citizens.

2.3 Partial Factor Mobility

At first glance, it seems that tax competition has more consequences in cases that are in-between those we have just examined (complete immobility or perfect mobility). And it seems that both the OECD and the EU are particularly concerned with the case in which one factor is more mobile than others and it is usually assumed that this factor is capital. In that case, it is felt, capital owners can act as free-riders, avoiding taxation by moving their capital to low-tax countries, but benefiting anyway from the production of public goods in high-tax countries. The relatively greater mobility of capital would imply lower revenue for the state and/or the necessity to shift part of the burden to the immobile factor (labor) with the risk of increasing unemployment. Therefore, it would be fair to harmonize tax rates and/or to exchange information in order to tax capital in its origin country.

However, it is not correct to describe capital as the only mobile factor. Highly educated labor is very mobile and anyone knows that immigration problems met by many developed countries are a clear indication that less educated labor is also mobile (although probably less so than capital).

But the problem is in fact much more complex than it seems to be due to the existence of tax shifts. Ignoring such possibilities, those who care about tax competition focus their attention on taxes such as corporate taxes. They fear that capital moves to countries where corporate taxes are lower or even nil. And, therefore, they make a plea for the harmonization of these taxes or for a mutual surveillance of capital flows. But we know – as recalled in Section 2 – that part of corporate taxes are shifted to wage earners and interest income earners, and that part of the taxes supposed to be paid by wage earners (or interest income earners) is in fact paid by capital owners.

Let us imagine a situation in which both capital and wages are taxed (possibly at the same rate) and in which neither capital nor labor are mobile. As we have seen, it does not matter much whether public revenue is obtained by a corporate tax or a tax on wages (income tax). What matters is the total value of the "tax wedge," which creates a gap between the supply and demand for labor. The relative burden of each production factor depends on the relative elasticities of both curves.

Now assume that capital suddenly becomes mobile (for instance, due to the suppression of capital controls). It is usually considered that a greater part of the tax burden (or the tax wedge) has to be borne by wage earners. However, it is wrong to believe that harmonizing corporate tax rates will be sufficient to avoid this change in the relative distribution of the tax burden. Even if corporate tax rates were the same all over the world, the increased mobility of capital would make it possible for capital owners to get rid of part of the tax burden they previously had to bear, for instance due to the existence of a tax on wages. In other words, capital mobility does make it possible for capital owners not only to avoid high tax rates on capital in the origin country, but, more generally, to avoid over-taxation coming from any sort of tax.

Thus, tax competition certainly has consequences, but not exactly those that are usually considered (when ignoring the possibility of tax shifts). But can we say in that case that tax competition is harmful? The answer we can give to this question is very similar to the one we gave previously: that it cannot be harmful. One reason is that we have to consider both the tax side and the expenditure side. If capital owners benefited in the high-tax country from very valuable public services, they would prefer to keep their capital inside, in spite of the high tax rates. The outflow of capital is a sign that capital owners think they pay too much for what they get. It is, however, true that in spite of the fact they do not pay taxes in the origin country when exporting their capital, they may benefit from some public goods in the origin country.

But the choice is between suppressing capital mobility, suppressing the production of public goods or modifying tax systems in order to better meet the wishes of the taxpayers. From this latter point of view, the priority ought to be the suppression of the most unfair and most harmful discrimination (if one can accept some hierarchy in the "harmfulness" of various taxes).

Two discriminations that exist in many tax systems seem to be particularly harmful: the discrimination against the future, which we have already underlined, and the discrimination against high-income earners (progressive income taxes or wealth taxes). Both of these ought to be suppressed independently from the existence of any tax competition. But tax competition can actually help in inducing governments to suppress them.

As regards the former – discrimination against the future – the outflow of capital from high-tax countries to low-tax countries can be considered as a normal – and even desirable – reaction of taxpayers in a situation of over-taxation, and not as an evasion from an optimal tax system. Therefore, tax competition is not harmful, quite the contrary. The solution to the apparent problem does not consist of harmonizing taxes on capital, in controlling capital flows or in organizing a system of multilateral reporting. It consists in suppressing the over-taxation of capital. Let us give an example. If a "general expenditure tax" were adopted, the taxpayer would declare his income, as he does presently for the income tax, but he would be allowed to deduct the amount of his periodic savings from the tax base. He would pay the tax in the future only as long as the returns from his accumulated savings would be consumed and not saved. Thus, the overtaxation of savings by the income tax would disappear. Under such a system, taxpayers would be induced to declare the amount of savings they are exporting into other countries, since they could thus deduct the exported savings from their tax base (but they would be obliged to declare the returns obtained from these investments in the future as long as they will not be saved). In such a case governments would have to care less about tax competition.

As regards the progressivity of the income tax, it presently induces those who have the highest incomes to emigrate to tax havens. Here again it cannot be said that tax competition is harmful, since it makes possible for some taxpayers to avoid what they rightly consider as an unfair over-taxation of their income. It does not induce any departure from some optimum, quite the contrary.

From both these examples, one cannot deduct a general principle according to which tax competition will always have the consequence of suppressing or decreasing over-taxation, although it seems to be the case in the present world. And we have to admit that the difference of mobility between different production factors may be a subject of concern. However, beyond these practical consequences of tax competition, it is certain that tax competition must be preserved at any rate and without restriction, just because it means freedom of choice for taxpayers.

Moreover, one ought to reverse the usual reasoning. According to it, whenever one factor is internationally mobile, the other factors suffer from an additional burden for two reasons:

1. The marginal productivity of the immobile factors is lowered since they are associated with less of the mobile factor (capital or highly educated individuals).
2. Immobile factors may have to pay more in order for the government to provide the public goods it wants to.

Once more, such a line of reasoning implicitly assumes that the government is benevolent. But if we assume that it is more or less a Leviathan state – which may be a realistic assumption – such a state may be tempted to over-tax immobile factors who can thus be considered as "tax slaves." It has long been the case for in many countries as regards capital, and the temptation of governments to over-tax capital owners was reinforced by the fact that they are less numerous than the owners of human capital (that is, they have less electoral weight). Now, if ever the mobility of this factor is increased, it can escape from its situation of tax slavery.

It is certainly a pity that the owners of the other factor do not have the same opportunity (for instance, low-income wage earners), but no principle could justify any measure designed to prevent a mobile factor benefiting from its position under the pretext that others do not have the same opportunity.

3. THE LIMITS OF TAX COMPETITION

From what is stated in the previous section, it seems that competition plays its role in the field of taxation as it does in private markets: It brings information and it induces people to better meet the needs of others. However, speaking of competition in the case of taxation is somewhat misleading for the following reason. As regards the production of private goods, competition implies both that producers are free to enter into a market and to supply whatever they want, and that consumers are free to choose the goods supplied by any producer. Obviously, competition does not imply perfect knowledge by producers and consumers so that a consumer, for instance, does not necessarily choose at any time the good that would be best fitted to his needs. However, the costs of shifting from one producer to another is rather low in most cases, particularly in our time, as trade barriers have more or less disappeared and information is spread all over the world rapidly and at a negligible cost. Thus, individuals can use their freedom of choice without having to care significantly about their own location.

Taxpayers and recipients of public goods are not in the same situation. They have to be located in a place where an authority benefits from a monopoly power to tax and to distribute public goods. In order to carry on their potential freedom of choice, individuals have to move from one jurisdiction to another, which is very costly (and even quite often prohibited). Meanwhile, given the limited number of jurisdictions (countries) in the world, individuals do not benefit from a great diversity of tax systems and public goods.

On the other hand, there is no freedom of entry on the market for public goods and taxation. For instance, the Icelandic government cannot propose to a Parisian to pay taxes to them and to get public goods from them, instead of being a customer of the French government. Taxation is always an act of constraint implemented by some institution that benefits from a monopoly, the monopoly of legal constraint. Therefore, tax competition would mean "freedom to enter onto the market for legal constraint," which is somewhat contradictory (and which, by the way, is a market that does not exist).

As already stated, tax competition plays its role through two channels. One is the information a government may get from observing tax reforms and experiments in other countries; the other consists of the possible reaction of taxing authorities who observe that their "consumers," the taxpayers, escape from their jurisdiction (either by emigrating, by shifting their wealth or by using tax evasion), which means that the systems the government are providing are not considered as optimal by those concerned. But neither channel works perfectly.

In fact, the causal relations between tax rates and tax systems on the one hand, and economic activity and public revenues on the other hand, are complex, so that the information brought about by tax competition cannot be easily interpreted, contrary to what occurs on a private market where the consumer can more easily evaluate to which extent the good he has purchased corresponds to his needs. The reactions of a government to tax competition also depend on its desire to be more or less benevolent and its capacity to be well informed. Thus, a Leviathan-type government will be less harmful to citizens if it is well informed and if tax competition is a way for it to learn about the existence of a Laffer effect. It may thus adopt tax cuts because it knows from foreign experiences that they may be profitable not only for taxpayers, but also for the government itself.

However, in spite of its shortcomings, tax competition is a powerful instrument to prevent excessive taxation. It is therefore important to fight without any restriction all efforts made by the OECD, EU or any other international organization to limit tax competition.

NOTES

1. The present chapter is based on Salin (2007b).
2. Such an analysis is developed in Chapters 5 and 6.
3. It is quite often suggested in the US that the replacement of the income tax by VAT would make it possible to suppress the over-taxation of savings by income tax. This belief comes from the fact VAT is interpreted as a tax on consumption – which it is not. It is a tax on income and, therefore, on consumption *and* savings. In fact, the very name of the VAT makes it quite clear: It is a tax on value added and, therefore, on the incomes which are the counterpart of the value added. But the interpretation given is misleading. This incorrect interpretation of the very nature of VAT may come from the fact that governments have wrongly decided to reimburse VAT on exports and to ask for payment on imports (whereas there is no reimbursement of the income tax paid by the production factors whose incomes are the counterpart of the exported value of goods and services).

PART III

Monetary integration

9. Monetary union: pleading for another approach[1]

The process of European unification has long been viewed as the replacement of existing nations by a single European super-state, consisting of existing nations. Pro-European activists have been skillful enough to raise the actual process of European unification to the status of a sacred myth that must not be disputed: Those who disagree with the process of integration are accused of not being "European." But there are people who believe in individual liberty and who fear that this liberty would be threatened by an excessive centralization of power.

Thus, as we have already seen, there are two opposing approaches of European integration and it is important to evaluate both of them. The first is prevalent and considers that the political and economic unification of Europe implies a process of harmonization of all sorts of laws, rules, norms, taxes, economic and monetary policies.

The other view considers that economic integration just implies competition, since competition means that all individuals can freely choose their activities all over the integrated area. In fact, a system can be considered as "integrated" as far as all its parts are coherent one with the other and not when all these parts are similar. Moreover, competition is necessary not only between individuals, but also between governments. People learn from their differences and we lose valuable information and efficient incentives whenever individuals are obliged to live in the same environment all over a vast area, as in Europe. Competition between individuals is useful because it induces each individual to do better than others, and competition between governments is useful because, again, it induces each government to do better than others! It can be hoped that under a competitive system of governments, then legislation, tax systems, rules, money production and policies may be better adapted to the real needs of citizens.

In order to evaluate the scope of the competitive approach, it is necessary to understand that a single market does not mean harmonization, but rather the elimination of artificial obstacles to trade. Also, it is useful to know that people from different European nations can benefit from mutual exchange in spite of differences in tax or monetary systems. These ideas are general principles, which have to be applied to all sorts of fields, such as the monetary field this chapter focuses on.

The chapter begins by presenting the usual views about monetary unification (Section 1). It is widely believed that a single currency is necessary in order to have a true single market in Europe. Therefore, we try to clarify the concept of a single market (Section 2) and then evaluate to what extent a single market requires a single currency (Section 3).

1. VIEWS ABOUT MONETARY UNION

Let us go back to a period before the creation of the euro, the beginning of the 1990s, and consider the debate that then prevailed. In so doing, we may shed some light on more recent debates, as we may find the same differences of opinion about the evaluation of the working of the euro system (arguments that are still alive in countries that remained outside of the Eurozone).

"No single market in Europe without a single currency, no single currency without a single European central bank!" This was the predominant view about monetary integration in the 1990s. This view was held by people for whom the ultimate target of European integration consisted of substituting existing nations with one super-nation. It was considered as obvious that the institutional and the monetary areas in Europe should correspond. The supporters of this view thought that the diversity of currencies existing at that time was an obstacle to trade, thus also an obstacle to the creation of the so-called "single market."

Transactions between European countries were more difficult than a country's internal transactions, since it was necessary to shift from one currency to the other whenever trade crossed borders. This view can be labeled as the "cartel-monopoly approach to European integration," since its supporters believed in the virtues of a centralized decision process and they aimed at the creation of a European (public) monopoly in all fields, especially monetary. Thus, before the creation of the euro, the European Monetary System (EMS) was an institutional process trying to create a cartel of European central banks in order to "harmonize" the monetary policies of different European countries.

Some people objected to such a process of monetary integration and to the Maastricht Treaty, without disputing the assumed necessary correspondence between the monetary zone and the political zone. These people can be classified into two categories (which still exist):

1. Those with strong nationalist convictions, therefore opposed to the process of political integration itself. Although they believe in this

coincidence between the monetary zone and the political zone, they oppose the single currency. In other words, they accept the idea according to which integration would mean a supranational system and, therefore, would imply harmonizing taxes, rules and currencies, but they object to a policy target consisting of implementing some European political integration.

2. Those who stress the fact that, historically, political unification has always come before monetary unification. They view money creation as an attribute of "national" sovereignty and, therefore, suggest that one might abandon the target of monetary unification in the short run and work towards a stronger political union.

Thus, all these views share in common the prejudice according to which there is a strong link between the political system and the economic system. They only differ either as regards the desirability of the political union or the precise stages of the political, economic and monetary unification. This cartel-monopoly approach is the most widely accepted and it could therefore be named the official concept of monetary integration. It consists of substituting the multiplicity of currencies and central banks with a single currency and a single central bank (an official monopoly).

But there is also a completely different approach of European integration, which can be named the "competitive approach" and which we personally favor. According to this view, people benefit from the disappearing of frontiers and the enlargement of competition. As regards money, it implies that substituting existing currencies with a single one is not necessary and may even be harmful. Under the competitive approach, European currencies – either those that existed before the creation of the euro or those that are still national currencies, as well as those that could be created in the future – would compete with one another and the market (that is, the money users) would be free to choose the currencies they regard as the best. This process of free selection may lead to the progressive disappearance of all but one currency (or, at least, a small number of them). Now, before exploring both approaches in more detail, it is necessary to address a more general question and to discuss the precise meaning of the concept of "integration" or the "single market."

2. A SINGLE MARKET: WHAT DOES IT MEAN?

To generalize, the whole process of integration in Europe can be conceived from two very different viewpoints: as the development of a cartel of monopolistic public institutions or as the outcome of the free working of markets. As regards the actual process of integration in Europe, its evolution since the creation of the European Community has been characterized by a progressive shift of emphasis from the initial – and satisfactory – concept of a common market to that of a set of common and harmonized policies, which may even be opposite to the initial aim. Does the "single market" – which is assumed to have been implemented since 1992 – consist of a return to the initial impulse or is it something different? An answer to this question is not clear-cut and it seems in fact that governments have focused on the word "single" rather than on the word "market" (which would imply freedom and diversity).

The shift in policy direction has been reinforced by a semantic confusion between two different meanings of the word "integration," namely "integration of markets" and "integration of producers." A market can be considered as integrated as far as there are no "artificial" obstacles to the free choice of producers and consumers. This was, in fact, the aim of the common market: making it possible for Europeans to buy and sell goods all over Europe without having to care about the nationality of partners in trade.

Free trade means the elimination of specific obstacles (such as tariffs or exchange controls), which are applied whenever trade takes place between different (national) areas and not within each of them. From this point of view, the integration of markets aims at reinforcing competition between producers. Now, competition does not necessarily lead to the homogenization of commodities, contrary to what is suggested by the traditional theory of competition. In reality, the consequences and the merits of competition come from the fact it induces each producer to differentiate his production in order to do better than his present and potential competitors. We argue later on that, in some specific cases, competition may lead to a smaller diversification of products, but we may consider as a general principle that increasing competition implies increasing diversification. Therefore, we may suspect at this point that there is some contradiction between the reinforcement of the common market and the present emphasis on "harmonization," common policies or a single currency.

In fact, integration is generally understood as integration of producers, which more or less means cartellization and *not* competition. The aim is either to replace existing producers with a smaller number of them (possibly even a single producer), or it is, at least, to impose the same environment on all of them. But common policies may be – and often are – policies that avoid or limit free competition. The European authorities have been very skillful in creating and maintaining the confusion between the two meanings of the word integration. Thus they meet a more or less obscure feeling of public opinion according to which any agreement, any cooperation, any harmonization – these terms all evoke social harmony – is desirable.

This confusion in language is very close to another, prevalent confusion that exists between "competition" and the "harmonization of the conditions of production." Most people believe that competition is "unfair" when producers are not placed in the same productive environment, which explains the efforts towards the harmonization of regulations and taxes or the creation of a single currency.

In fact, competition implies freedom of choice, on the part of producers as well as consumers, especially the freedom of entry into a market. But it far from implies that all producers should operate in the same environment and should be subject to the same "competitive conditions." Economic theory – particularly the theory of international specialization – brings the fundamental lesson that producers of the same product operating under different conditions have the responsibility, in combining various factors of production, to make allowance for the particular constraints they are subject to, so as to make their products competitive. But integration being usually interpreted only in terms of production and not of markets, the claim for harmonizing competitive conditions has been translated, in every sector, into a search for common European policies, harmonization of taxes and regulations or the creation of a single currency.

The concept of the single market thus seems to mix the notion of a common market – that is, free trade – and the notion of a constructivist effort in favor of the harmonization of the conditions of production. In that sense, the single market, as it is usually interpreted, rests on a fundamental intellectual error.[2] In the monetary field, the problem ought not to be harmonizing money production and monetary systems, but providing for "optimal money." But, there is no rationale for harmonization per se: Why, for instance, should we harmonize towards a possible standard of over-taxation and despoilment? And, similarly, why should we direct monetary integration towards a possible standard of over-production of money?

When aiming at tax harmonization or monetary unification, the EU Commission and its administration, the national governments and the media that support them, are wasting their efforts to reach targets that are completely useless. There was nothing to add to the common market in order to have a single market. From this point of view the single market has already long existed and there was no justification for shifting in the 1990s from a common market to the so-called single market. Another direction could have been taken, namely shifting from a common market to free markets (that is, deregulated markets). In turn, this deregulation could be obtained either through an explicit and centralized process of public decisions or through a more competitive process. The "single market" would not be more single because of harmonization and centralization. But the "single market" would be closer to a market if it were deregulated: the emphasis has to be put on "market" and not on "single." This applies perfectly to the case of monetary integration.

3. A SINGLE MARKET WITHOUT A SINGLE CURRENCY?

As already stressed, it is widely considered that a single market needs a single currency and, therefore, a single central bank. This opinion reflects the more general idea according to which European integration consists of creating a super-nation out of existing nations. The slogan "One nation, one currency, one central bank" is just translated in European terms. The possibility of disconnecting the national zone and the monetary zone is considered as an absurdity.

In fact, we must apply to money the same sort of reasoning as we used for the production and the circulation of commodities. A single market for money is not necessarily a market in which production is cartellized by force (single currency), or in which the conditions of production are harmonized (fixed exchange rates). A single market or an integrated market exists in a given area as far as there is freedom of choice for producers and money users.

A single market for commodities and production factors does not imply a single currency, since the differentiation of currencies is not an obstacle to the free movement of goods, currencies and financial assets. Modern economies are complex social systems, founded on individual specialization and exchange, because they are monetary economies. To play its role as a means of indirect exchange and reserve of value, money does not need to be a homogeneous product, it needs to be a sound currency, meeting the concrete needs of people in the best possible way. Similarly, an exchange economy also relies on systems of communication and telecommunication. But it does not mean that it is necessary to have a single communication or telecommunication system. Only in a centrally planned economy may it be considered as necessary to use a single currency or a single communication system. Thus, the claim for a single currency may be a consequence of the confusion between a single market and a centrally regulated economy, the latter appearing as the aim of many Europeans.

Let us make a comparison. If it were true that it is inconsistent to have a single market without a single currency, would it not be even more valid to stress that there cannot be a single market without a single European language? In fact, it is much more difficult to imagine two traders using different languages than two traders using different currencies. Therefore, how to explain that the slogan "No single market without a single language" is not yet popular? Should we conclude that there is, from this point of view, a dangerous failure of the integration process and that, even before introducing a single currency, we should introduce a single language? Or should we rather conclude that the diversity of languages is not an obstacle to a single market? But why then should we care about a single currency, which is logically less necessary?

Although the creation of a single market – whatever we understand by that – does not justify the existence of a single currency in Europe (or, at least, a system of perfectly substitutable currencies, such as a system of fixed exchange rates), there may be other reasons for the number of currencies to be limited, as we will see in Chapter 10.

NOTES

1. Adapted from a report prepared for the Conference "Europa due modelli a confront," Torino, Comitato Giorgio Rota, 27 November 1993, and from Salin (1990d). I thank Lawrence White for useful remarks on a former version of this latter text. I have used my general view about harmonization – as explained in previous chapters – to express my opposition to a common monetary policy, in the present chapter, as well as, for instance, in Salin (1980) and Salin (1984).
2. The idea according to which it is not desirable to "harmonize" the conditions of production all over Europe has important implications in the field of taxation. For a critical view of tax harmonization see Chapters 7 and 8 of the present book.

10. Can optimum currency areas be determined in Europe?[1]

Trying to determine the "optimum" number of currencies in a given area – such as the European zone or the world – and to evaluate the desirable characteristics of these currencies is certainly an interesting problem from a purely intellectual point of view. But it is also important from a practical point of view, since many people wonder whether the eurozone can be considered as an optimal arrangement. In fact, it is quite common to hear people claim that the euro system will burst because of diverging economic conditions within the eurozone, or even that it ought to burst, which would mean that the eurozone is not an optimal currency area and that one may consider as more efficient to have a different – larger – choice of currencies in Europe. Therefore, the confidence many people had in the single currency may be decreasing, so it is important to try to evaluate the gains and costs of the single currency in Europe and to evaluate whether another monetary organization ought to be considered.

We will first give an overview of traditional approaches to the problem of currency choice (Section 1), then consider some general principles about monetary policy that are useful for the problem of currency choice, since opinions about monetary areas are strongly linked to the kind of monetary analysis one is using (Section 2). In Section 3 we will consider the extent to which the theory of business cycles can shed some light on the problem of currency areas. We will suggest another approach to optimal monetary systems and monetary zones in Section 4.

1. TRADITIONAL APPROACHES TO THE PROBLEM OF CURRENCY CHOICE

In modern times it is widely admitted that monetary policy is an essential attribute of national sovereignty so that each nation must have its own currency, produced under the supervision of a national central bank. For those who hold such ideas, the optimum number of currencies in the world – or in an area such as the European area – is equal to the number of countries (or the number of economic "integrated" zones such as the European Union).

This vague approach to the problem of currency choice finds an explicit application as regards the process of European integration. Those who are strongly in favor of the creation of a European super-state have always pushed towards monetary unification under the form of the creation of a single currency, the euro, produced under the supervision of the European Central Bank (ECB). According to these people – who like to label themselves as "Europeans," although there are other methods of European unification, as we have already seen – monetary integration will favor political unification and the birth of a new European government. They consider that as monetary policy is no longer available as an instrument of economic policy, then political authorities will be obliged to coordinate their economic policies, particularly fiscal policies (which, in fact, they try to do right now).

Two other categories of people were mentioned in Chapter 9: Those who are in favor of the political unification of Europe, but who believe that it has to come before monetary unification; and the "nationalists" (or "sovereignists") who oppose monetary unification because they do not want political integration.

People in all of these three categories ("Europeans," "Political unification first," "nationalists"), in spite of their apparently diverging opinions, share exactly the same views about the role of money and its relation to politics and economic policy. All of them were very vocal before the introduction of the euro, in spite of the fact that another, completely different, approach could have been adopted: the competitive approach to monetary integration. And even now, we may find exactly the same categories of people, for instance in European countries which do not yet belong to the eurozone. But, due to the recent economic and financial crisis, the same ideas find their way in present public debates: It is often claimed that these events bring a proof of the fact that it is not possible to have a monetary union between countries that are economically too different. From this statement, some people conclude that it could be possible – or desirable – that the eurozone bursts, whereas others stress that these difficulties imply that European countries ought to harmonize even more tightly their economic policies in order to facilitate the working of the monetary zone.

Thus, all the traditional approaches we have considered for the time being assume that the optimal number of currencies is equal to the number of countries. Therefore, the only problem one would have to solve as regards Europe is the following: Is Europe a country or is it a set of countries? Or, alternatively: Should Europe be a single country or should it be a federation of countries? Moreover, quite frequently, such statements about the number of currencies in Europe are founded on some rather vague statements about the relations between monetary policies, other economic policies and politics. In order to be able to debate precisely, we must now try to make the underlying economic analysis – if it exists – more explicit. But let us first mention that there are many possible proofs of the rather vague foundation of all these statements. As an example, it is paradoxical that people who consider that there ought to be a coincidence between the national zone and the monetary zone, quite often also consider that it is preferable to have fixed exchange rates between the different national currencies. In fact, if the rules of the game of a system of fixed rates are correctly respected, all currencies participating into such a system are perfect substitutes one for the other so that one ought to consider them as constituting a single currency (in spite of the fact they have different names in the different parts of the international zone). However, the sovereignists may consider that keeping a national currency and a national central bank makes it possible to opt out, thanks to devaluation or re-evaluation. Thus, in spite of the fact a country participates in an international monetary zone, it can potentially recover its "national sovereignty" and keep such an instrument of national economic policy. The optimal number of currencies would thus be equal to one in the zone under consideration, but with the possibility of increasing this number in cases in which it would deem preferable.

In reality it is more than debatable to consider devaluation as a possible policy instrument. It is first debatable from a theoretical point of view: It is considered that devaluation can bring about an "improvement" in the trade balance, thus increasing exports, total demand and production. But the improvement in the trade balance is normally transitory and, moreover, it is an illusion – contrary to what is taught by the fallacious Keynesian theory – that it is possible and necessary to increase total demand. Moreover, using devaluation as a policy tool is also debatable from a moral point of view, since devaluation means that the price of a currency that was assumed to be fixed in terms of another currency is modified arbitrarily by monetary authorities that do not care about the necessity to honor their previous contract.

To give another illustration of the vagueness of traditional ideas about the choice of currency, it is striking that some people say that there are risks of "currency wars" whenever there are different currencies, whereas other people – or sometimes the same people – say that a single currency cannot be compatible with different economic conditions in various countries so that it would be better to have different currencies.

Thus, it is clear that, predominantly, there is usually a link, in traditional approaches, between the problem of the number of currencies and the problem of economic policies and economic adjustment. The optimal number of currencies just depends on the possibility of designing optimal economic policies. And it is interesting to see that it is exactly this same basic assumption which is made, more or less explicitly, in traditional theoretical approaches that go beyond the vague notions we have mentioned until now and that aim at being based on rigorous considerations of economic analysis.

Such is the case with what is labeled the "theory of optimal currency areas" (OCA theory). This theory has first been developed by the pioneering works of Robert Mundell and refined by many other economists. It is interesting to mention that this concept, instead of remaining a game for theoreticians in economic theory, became widely used in all debates that took place in political circles and in public opinion before the introduction of the euro.

Broadly speaking, according to OCA theory an optimal currency area is an area inside which the use of economic policy instruments can be optimal. Inside the zone, exchange rates ought to be fixed or there ought to be a single currency, and exchange rates ought to be flexible with the outside world. Thus the notion of an optimal currency area is linked to the notion of an optimal process of adjustment. Now, the problem consists of defining an optimal process of adjustment and this, in turn, depends on the specific theory of economic policy one is selecting. Therefore, it is not surprising if we can find in the economic literature different views about the definition of an optimal process of adjustment. Robert Mundell gave a particularly important role to the mobility of factors of production. Let us assume, for instance, as Robert Mundell did, that there is a shift of demand from commodities produced by country A to commodities produced by country B. Let us accept such an assumption, although it is rather unrealistic, both because business cycles in our time have a monetary and financial origin, and because it is difficult to imagine how such a real shock – implying that demand shifts away suddenly from all or most of the productions of a country – could occur. Moreover, if we assume as Robert Mundell does, that prices and wages are rigid and cannot decrease in country A to adjust to this new situation because of some institutional characteristics, then adjustment can occur through shifts of factors of production from country A to country B if ever there is a single currency for both countries (or perfectly fixed exchange rates). But, if factors of production are immobile, then adjustment implies a change in exchange rates (which means that it is better to have different currencies in both countries).

Other authors also stress the role of economic openness, of economic diversity, of financial integration, and so on. We will not give a summary of these different analyses, since here we mostly care about the general and common characteristics of all of them. The central statement, as regards the problem with which we are concerned, is the following: Under a system of perfectly fixed exchange rates or under a single currency, countries which are thus monetarily integrated cannot have an independent monetary policy, contrary to what happens with a system of flexible rates. Therefore, to decide whether it is better to have monetary independence or not – which means having the same currency as some other countries or a different one – public authorities would have to assess whether they could get a better process of adjustment by being monetarily independent and using their own monetary policy, or whether they would be in a better situation by importing the monetary policy of other countries.

2. WHAT CAN MONETARY POLICY DO?

The traditional approaches of monetary integration focus on the problem of macroeconomic adjustment to a shock, for instance a demand shock, and they aim at defining the best monetary organization according to the specific characteristics of a country. To that end, we must remember that flexible exchange rates – which means a multiplicity of currencies – imply that monetary authorities are independent, while fixity of exchange rates or a single currency imply that monetary policies are interdependent so that a country loses a part of its capacity to design its economic policy whenever it enters into a monetary union (for the best or the worst). This in turn assumes implicitly that the use of monetary policy can have positive real effects. This is not surprising in the Keynesian tradition since it is assumed – as is commonly believed – that it is possible to stimulate an economy through an expansionary monetary policy. But this is more than debatable. The basic reason for it stems from the "real balance effect." Individuals need money as a reserve of value or as a waiting purchasing power. Money is useful for them as far as it represents a certain purchasing power. Therefore, the demand for money is a demand for real balances and not a demand for nominal balances. Let us assume that, at a given point in time, all individuals in a country have the amount of real money balances that corresponds exactly to what they desire. If ever there is a creation of money, there will be an excess of money. Individuals will try to get rid of their excess balances by demanding goods (against money). The price of goods in terms of money will increase (inflation), which means that the price of money in terms of goods will decrease. Thus, the decreasing price of money will destroy the excess of real balances and, finally, individuals will hold exactly the same amount of real money balances as they had at the beginning (at least if the factors which explain the demand for real balances have not changed). From this point of view the only *macroeconomic effect* of money creation is inflation, without any consequence on production or employment (except for some temporary structural changes which we will consider later on).

As is well known, Milton Friedman has convincingly demonstrated the inflationary effect of money creation. He stressed that money creation could create an illusion in the short run, such as a temporary increase in employment: The so-called "Phillips curve" (that is, the trade-off between inflation and unemployment) could thus exist temporarily, but it could not last, as has been well demonstrated by evidence. However, it is strange that Friedman opposed the process of European unification under the pretext that it was impossible to have a single monetary policy in an area composed of several countries with different characteristics. The reason for this statement may be that Friedman attributed the Great Depression of the 1930s to the very deflationary monetary policy that had been implemented by the US, and he thought that a country could protect itself from such influences by adopting flexible exchange rates.

Now, we believe that monetary policy as well as fiscal policy can only create short-run illusions without being able to create any positive and lasting real effects. Thus, Keynesians favor budget deficits in order to increase total demand and, therefore, employment and production. Without explaining in detail why it is impossible to increase total demand, let us just stress that financing a public deficit necessarily implies a decrease in private consumption and/or investment, which perfectly compensates for the increased public deficit. As regards monetary policy, we have already stressed that it had only nominal effects, at least as far as we consider possible macroeconomic effects (we will mention harmful microeconomic effects later). Thus, in order to determine the optimal number of currencies in Europe, we have to abandon any macroeconomic considerations. We will suggest another approach based on microeconomic foundations later.

3. OPTIMAL CURRENCY AREAS AND THE BUSINESS CYCLE

As already mentioned, the now traditional literature on optimum currency areas was initiated by Robert Mundell (1961). Broadly speaking, an optimum currency area can be defined as an area in which economic adjustment is the best possible. One has to distinguish very precisely this general view of currency areas – which is not without merit – from the specific applications that have been made by Robert Mundell, Peter Kenen (1969), Ronald McKinnon (1969) and other economists. All these contributions suffer from their basic assumptions, which are, more or less explicitly, mainly inspired by Keynesian-type economics, thus making it possible to create a link between real and monetary variables. While keeping, at least for the time being,[2] the general definition of an optimum currency area as an area of optimal adjustment, we intend to explore rapidly the implications of an approach both inspired by the "monetary approach of the balance of payments"[3] and the "Austrian theory of the business cycle."

Under the monetary approach of the balance of payments, the main channel of influence is through the demand for money. The supply of money adjusts itself through the cash balance effect and money flows from the country (or countries) where it is relatively abundant to the country (or countries) where it is relatively scarce. Real and monetary variables play perfectly symmetrical roles: If there is an additional money creation in a country, money is more abundant in this country, all things being equal, and it flows to other countries. If there is a higher rate of growth of income in a country, the demand for money is increased, money becomes relatively scarcer and flows from outside.

The Austrian business cycle theory, developed by Ludwig von Mises and Friedrich Hayek, emphasizes the role of monetary phenomena. The importance given to money rather than to real variables in explaining the business cycle may not be of a theoretical origin, but it rather stems from empirical observation. In our time, there are not many real shocks, as men have freed themselves from the whims of nature. Shocks are rather of a monetary origin, because there is centralization of money production so that one macro-decision in the monetary field can cause a big shock. Moreover, and contrary to real shocks, monetary shocks can be repeated (a steady growth in the quantity of money).

In trying to reconcile the monetary approach of the balance of payments and the Austrian theory of the business cycle, one meets two difficulties:

1. Both theories are not concerned with the same relative price changes: The monetary approach of the balance of payments focuses on the changes in relative prices between tradables and non-tradables.[4] The Austrian theory focuses on changes in relative prices between goods of different ranks, such as raw materials and investment goods, on the one hand, and consumption goods on the other.
2. The concept of a general price level – which is essential in evaluating the changes in demand for money and the corresponding flows of currencies – cannot be clearly identified whenever relative price changes occur.

In spite of these difficulties let us sketch one specific example and its implications for the analysis of possible links between the integration of commodity markets and monetary integration. Let us take the case of a trade zone composed of two countries, a large country, A, and a small one, B. Commodities being highly mobile between both countries, there is a high degree of price contagion: Country B rapidly imports price changes from country A. Now, let us assume that a business cycle takes place in country A. There are relative price changes over the cycle, mainly between raw materials and investment goods on the one hand, and consumption goods on the other.

Let us assume that all these goods are tradables and that country B is specialized in the production of raw materials, the price of which is important to determine the "general price level" and the standard of living of people. Monetary policy and exchange rate policy in country B are unable to cope with this change in relative prices. Country B has to decide whether it prefers to stabilize the monetary prices of raw materials or that of consumption goods. Stabilizing the value of monetary balances in terms of raw materials implies a high variability of the purchasing power of money in terms of consumption goods, and vice versa.

But let us now imagine that tradables are composed only of consumption goods and that investment goods are non-tradables. Let us also assume that capital is not internationally mobile. In the beginning of the cycle there is inflation in country A, the price of consumption goods increases and the price of investment goods increases even more. What happens in country B? If there are fixed rates between both countries (they belong to the same monetary zone), country B rapidly imports the increase in consumption good prices. Can it protect itself from the relative price changes occurring in country A? It depends on its monetary policy and the degree of capital mobility.

As the prices of consumption goods increase, there is an increase in the demand for money in country B and, as is well known from the monetary approach of the balance of payments, either the country has to follow the same expansionary monetary and credit policy or it imports money from outside. In the first case, exactly the same pattern of business cycle takes place in B and A (money creation, increase in credits, initial decrease of the real interest rate, increase in the demand for investment goods, and so on). Country B imports the business cycle of country A in spite of the fact economic integration is imperfect (there is economic integration on consumption good markets, but not on investment good markets and, maybe, even not on capital markets). If monetary authorities in country B do not enter into a more expansionary credit and monetary policy, the additional demand for money is met by inflows of money from country

A (and exports of commodities from B to A). In such a case – as we have assumed that capital is not mobile between A and B – the fluctuations in interest rates and the demand for investment goods which occur in country A do not occur in country B, which, therefore, can more or less isolate itself from country A.

If ever we loosened the assumptions that capital is immobile between both countries and/or that investment goods are non-tradables, there would be a similar business cycle in A and B: There would be price contagion as regards the interest rate and the prices of investment goods between both countries.

Now the important point is that country B cannot protect itself from imported economic instability when it is strongly integrated to country A; that is not only consumption goods, but investment goods and assets are highly mobile. In such a case, country B cannot avoid imported changes in relative prices by deciding exchange rate changes or by adopting a floating rate (and an independent monetary policy). It can avoid importing inflation by revaluing its currency or having a strict monetary policy (and a steady appreciation of its currency), but whatever the exchange regime is, the fluctuations in the real interest rate and in the relative prices of consumption goods and investment goods are the same. Thus, we just arrive to about the same conclusion as before: whenever a country belongs to a trade zone with another country – or, more generally, to a zone in which commodities and production factors are very mobile – it does not imply that it also has to enter into a monetary zone with this same country. Conversely, it cannot isolate itself from economic fluctuations in relative prices by adopting an independent monetary policy via a floating exchange rate system or frequent exchange rate changes, but it may avoid importing the "general" inflation rate.

However, as already stressed, it is difficult to define price stability whenever there are great changes in relative prices, as is the case under an Austrian-type business cycle. In fact, the difficulty arises from the fact one tries to define monetary stability for a group of people – for instance, the residents of a country – who have different definitions of price stability. For someone who is mainly concerned with the prices of raw materials, a currency seems to be stable if ever it maintains its value in terms of these raw materials. Others will rather consider the purchasing power of money in terms of consumption goods.

Our main conclusion had previously been that whenever relative price changes occur, there is no more justification to make a plea for monetary unification than for floating rates. The reason for that is that the needs of those who constitute a "country" are diversified: Some may have an interest in a fixed exchange rate and some others in a changing exchange rate. In order to meet this diversification of needs, it cannot be optimal to have one single national currency that would either fluctuate against other national currencies or be linked to them. In other words there is no basis for a nationalist approach of money. From the fact relative prices are necessarily changing we can only draw one conclusion: the needs of people as regards money being diversified, they have to be supplied not only with a national currency (in a fixed or a floating system), but with a diversity of currencies, which is brought about by currency competition.

By accepting the traditional debate on the relations between the trade zone, the political zone and the monetary zone, whatever is its orientation, one accepts to be trapped in an a priori institutional setting, which assumes that the monetary area necessarily has a national basis. As already stressed, a trade zone is not optimal in comparison with worldwide free trade, a monetary arrangement based on national currencies is not optimal in comparison with currency competition (that is, non-national monetary systems). Under such conditions, there cannot be any decisive argumentation in order to conclude that non-optimal trade zones and non-optimal monetary zones ought to coincide or not.

4. MULTIPLE CURRENCIES AND MONETARY INTEGRATION

It is usually considered that monetary integration means fixed rates – at least during the transition process before the introduction of a single currency – and the traditional questions raised in the literature or in policy forums are: does a group of existing countries constitute an optimal monetary zone? How to increase the fixity of exchange rates between countries in order to improve monetary integration? However, this approach of monetary integration is close to the general approach of economic integration that we have considered as debatable, namely the one according to which integration does not mean a better functioning of markets – and, therefore, a high degree of potential differentiation between competing goods – but a homogenization of productions between different producers (integration of producers and not integration of markets). From this general consideration, the question has to be raised whether monetary integration necessarily implies fixed rates – and, ultimately a single currency – and whether it could correspond to a situation of flexible rates.

Most people believe that flexible rates mean disorder, erratic variations in exchange rates, worldwide or regional instability, and so on. Thus, it seems that flexible rates in Europe are incompatible with the search for a more "orderly" economic system. In addition to the idea that a great diversity of currencies increases transaction costs, these are the rather vague notions that have always inspired efforts towards European integration in the monetary field.

However, we have first to remember the simple fact that the exchange rate is a price, the price of a currency in terms of another currency. Thus, asking whether flexible rates can contribute to a European monetary order is a special application of the more general problem: Do flexible prices contribute to a social order, to optimal situations? Generally speaking, one may suspect that most economists would give a positive answer to this question: the equilibrium relative price of two goods changes constantly, thanks to changes in the determinants of supply and demand, and it has to be reflected in the actual price, for an economic order to prevail. Thus, at least in the specific case in which the monetary authorities of each country can decide arbitrarily the rate of change of the quantity of money they are controlling, the exchange rate changes if anything happens in the supply or the demand for these currencies. Does it make sense, then, to try to peg this price, to adopt a fixed rate system? To be sure, a system in which all the issuers of currency give a convertibility guarantee in terms of the same monetary base (for instance, gold) – so that exchange rates are fixed and there is no arbitrary creation of money – is to be preferred. But in the present world of discretionary national monetary policies, in which currencies cannot be perfect substitutes one to the other, a complete change of perspective is necessary: instead of discussing the special cases in which flexible rates could be acceptable, we ought to stress that flexibility is the norm – on a well-functioning, "integrated" market – and that fixed rates ought to be the exception.

As present national currencies, being claims on distinct organizations, are not perfect substitutes, their relative prices can be fixed only if there is some guarantee of substitutability given by the producers (that is by public monetary authorities). Thus, fixity, in the present state of monetary organization, means public intervention. Therefore, a system of fixed rates (with different currencies) can be compared to any system of price control or price management, such as a system of rent control in which the authorities determine fixed relative prices between different houses, without any consideration for their specific characteristics.

The benefits of differentiation – due to competition – are so obvious in all fields of economic activity that there must be serious reasons for limiting differentiation in the monetary field. The only justifications for such a limitation, which we could imagine, would stem from situations in which a gain could be obtained by substituting one single producer for a number of them or by coordinating the activities of several producers. Such cases are met in fields such as telecommunications, transportation, and so on.

They result, as already stressed, from economies of scale, economies of scope (economies of joint production) or externalities. Those are the only possible reasons for abandoning differentiation of currencies – therefore, flexible rates – and for adopting either a single currency or, at least, fixed rates (that is, perfect substitutability between currencies).

We may accept the general idea that there are such phenomena in the production of money, even if we cannot know exactly to which extent an optimal size of the production domain does exist. If there was free banking – which excludes the existence of central banks and monetary authorities – and if there were several producers in a European (or global) private monetary cartel, one could imagine that free entry or the potential defection of one member, proposing a better currency, would discipline the cartel. A single currency in one given area, but with several (private) producers, would make it possible to exploit potential economies of scale but, meanwhile, would make "free-riding" and free entry possible so that competition would not be suppressed. Potential flexibility of exchange rates would thus contribute to an international monetary order.

On the contrary, the creation of a European central bank may have introduced the worst solution to the European monetary problem. In fact, one cannot know which is the optimal size of a monetary area, since it is not certain that marginal costs are always decreasing, when the monetary zone becomes larger, and since the creation of a – necessarily public – monopoly prevents potential competition in money creation. If ever the European central bank producing a single currency is proposing a "bad" currency, such as a depreciating currency, Europeans may have no option to use a better currency. *Europeans do not need a single currency; they need good currencies* (or, possibly, one good currency). History repeats itself and it has taught us that whenever a government is supplying a bad currency, it obliges citizens to use it through exchange controls or legal tender laws. From this point of view, the existence of a single European currency is a risk for Europeans, as long as they cannot be absolutely certain that European monetary authorities will not abuse their power and will not impose an over-production of money. In other words, the only cause of monetary disorders can be found not in the existence of flexible exchange rates (that is, competition), but in the existence of national monopolies in money production. The aim of European monetary integration has been the creation of a European monopoly in the production of money: It reduces competition and it creates a risk of monetary instability.

A European monetary order does not imply a single currency or fixed rates, if the optimal size of a monetary area is not Europe. But it certainly implies freedom of choice for money-holders, as well as potential and actual differentiation of activities inside the existing banking systems, and processes for adjustment to changing conditions. Needless to say, free competition is the best solution, since competition induces producers to improve their products. In the case of money, competition induces money-producers to limit or to avoid inflation and monetary instability. However, even if perfect free banking seems to be unrealistic for the time being, partial moves towards more freedom in some activities is desirable and, at least, competition between existing national money-producers may limit their propensity to inflate.

Thus, the plea in favor of a single currency in Europe is justified by considering one characteristic of money – the dimension of the monetary zone – while forgetting the other most important one, its purchasing power. However, the practical problem is that we do not know to which extent economies of scale and externalities do exist in the production of money and in various financial activities, so that we cannot decide *a priori* what ought to be the optimal dimension of a monetary zone. Thus, there is no reason to believe that it is optimal to have a single currency in Europe. If there was free competition between banking systems, at least between existing banking systems and the existing currencies they issue, the possible existence of economies of scale would be revealed by the working of the market: one currency or a couple of currencies would gradually replace all others. In that sense the only way towards a real process of European monetary integration would be that of free banking and flexible rates between competing currencies. The free choice of people would make it possible to determine which currencies are the best from the point of view of those who use them, both as regards the dimension of the monetary zone and the capacity to maintain the purchasing power of money. It also means that monetary integration could have prevailed in Europe for many years (even before 1999 when the euro was introduced), if ever it had only been decided that exchange controls and legal tender laws were abolished.

Fixed rates between currencies issued by national and public cartels of banks correspond to the creation of a public cartel and the disappearing of competition. The existence of such cartels can be explained, similarly to that of any other public organization, by the working of the political market. Instability in such cartels is the necessary consequence of the politicization of decisions. The experience of the European Monetary System (EMS) – before the creation of the euro – has given clear examples thereof. Exchange rates were supposed to be fixed between European currencies, but parity changes were accepted. The designers of the EMS had been clever enough to define their system as an "adjustable" system (although a system ought to be based on intangible rules), which meant that the system was supposed to work well when exchange rates were fixed, and it was supposed to work well when they changed!

Let us stress again: a true economic integration rests on the discipline of competition (integration of markets and not of producers). Thus, badly managed firms have to disappear. In the present world, badly managed monetary systems benefit from international monetary cooperation under the pretense that they have a "need of reserves" or a "need of credit." A lot of technocratic and harmful devices are invented every year to protect badly managed monetary institutions, at the European level as well as at the global level via the International Monetary Fund (IMF). As a consequence, money users do not benefit from an optimal provision of money.

NOTES

1. The present chapter has used parts of different articles and reports: Salin (2011a); a report entitled "Trade Zones and Monetary Zones: To Link or not to Link?", prepared for the Mont Pèlerin Society General Meeting, Vienna, 8–13 September 1996; and a report prepared for the Conference "Europa due modelli a confronto", Torino, Comitato Giorgio Rota, 27 November 1993.
2. We suggest another approach of optimum currency areas in Chapter 10.
3. Robert Mundell was the path-breaking author of this theory. Contrary to his former theoretical contribution to the theory of optimal currency areas, it is, happily, not Keynesian.
4. Under the extreme version of this approach non-tradables do not exist, so that there is a "perfect" contagion effect between foreign prices and national prices, whenever the exchange rate is fixed.

11. A competitive approach to monetary integration[1]

For the time being, the euro is the legal currency in 17 countries of the eurozone. These countries joined the eurozone at different dates, but they all had to comply with the "Maastricht criteria"[2] before they could perform the great jump consisting of replacing overnight their national currency with the European currency. As some other countries may be considering the opportunity to join the eurozone, it may be useful to evaluate the official path to monetary integration that has been used in the past by present members of the eurozone (Section 1).

We then propose another approach of the process towards monetary integration, which takes into consideration microeconomic criteria instead of the macroeconomic criteria of the "Maastricht approach" (Section 2). Section 3 stresses the advantages of a competitive approach to monetary integration.

1. LESSONS FROM THE PAST

As already stressed, the process towards monetary integration has been viewed in the past as a system of fixed rates (the European Monetary System, EMS) which would pave the way to the substitution of the existing national currencies and central banks with a single currency and a single central bank. The traditional approach to monetary integration in Europe thus aimed at constituting a cartel of central banks and monetary authorities and, ultimately, a European public monopoly, instead of an increased freedom of choice for producers and consumers (we call this approach the "cartel-monopoly" approach).

This traditional approach is coherent with the usual approach of European integration, namely harmonization of regulations and taxes, centralization of decisions, common policies and forced cartellization. This approach is quite the reverse of another, which consists of reinforcing competition between European producers and, therefore, favoring the diversification of activities.

In fact, as regards monetary problems, European citizens did not really need a single currency, but sound currencies, which means non-inflationary currencies. It is true that substituting one single currency for several currencies decreases transaction costs and risk costs. But it also implies an increase in the degree of monopolization of money production in Europe, at least if it is not the outcome of a spontaneous market process, but of a process imposed by public authorities.

Monetary authorities, everywhere in the world, are inclined to adopt inflationary policies, either to finance public deficits or to offer voters the illusion of a short run prosperity. Therefore, a sound monetary system implies institutional arrangements in order to impose a discipline on monetary authorities. Competition – that is, freedom of entry on a market and freedom of choice – is the best possible discipline. But let us consider the case of a single central bank in Europe with representatives of the different monetary authorities on the board. Monetary policy is the outcome of painful negotiations between diverging views from governments that are more or less in favor of inflation. And if ever the single currency depreciates rapidly, European citizens have no other option, especially if this currency is protected against the competition of "non-European" currencies.

Speaking of monetary unity, of a single currency, without specifying the rules for monetary management may lead to perverse effects. In fact, it had been decided from the outset that the European Central Bank ought to be independent and have a single target to reach, namely to avoid too high a rate of inflation.

But the existence of a single currency is not the norm according to which monetary arrangements can be evaluated. The main problem in money production is the public monopoly and not the plurality of currencies or the dependence–independence problem: an independent organization works better under competitive situations than when it is a monopoly.

In previous chapters, we have discussed the legitimacy of the view according to which monetary integration meant fixed rates or even a single currency, and we have explained why a single market did not imply a single currency. Having thus discussed the *target* of monetary unification, we turn now to the *process* of monetary integration, still comparing the cartel-monopoly approach and the competitive approach.

As already stressed, it may well happen that a single currency would ultimately prevail on a competitive market. But this process of selection would be gradual and would simply match the concrete needs of money users at the very time they appear.

By contrast, and in spite of what is usually claimed, the cartel-monopoly approach cannot be gradual. Only a deliberate political move can impose a single currency to several monopolistic entities (the former national central banks), and a jump has to be accepted, once and for all, when one shifts to a single currency system. The alleged gradualism of this approach is therefore dubious. It assumes that several institutional changes can "contribute" to the final institutional leap. However, each of these changes implies a brutal breaking in the evolution of monetary systems. The Maastricht approach was ambiguous since it aimed at mixing two different approaches, one in which a once and for all change of system is necessary and one in which the change of system is gradual. But, in reality, there was an institutional discontinuity in this approach.

The official view about monetary integration aimed at substituting one single currency, issued by one single European institution – the European Central Bank – to existing national currencies, issued by different central banks. To pave the way for this change, the Maastricht Treaty made provisions for a stronger and more credible fixity of exchange rates between European currencies, so that they become more widely substitutable one for the other.

Nevertheless, this process implied a drastic change, whenever one shifted from a system – the EMS – in which there were several distinct decision centers to one single decision center. This change is very similar to the one that occurs whenever several firms merge into one single firm. At the very second the merger takes place there is a brutal institutional change: those who make decisions are not the same as before, the decision processes are modified, and so on.

The members of the Maastricht Treaty chose a progressive process, according to which the final target – the single currency – would be reached in three stages, giving this process the appearance of a gradual approach to monetary unification. As a radical institutional change had to take place at the very moment a single currency replaced existing national currencies and a European Central Bank replaced existing national central banks, it could have been decided that this change of system would occur overnight, for instance on the very day all countries had ratified the Treaty. However, such a rapid change would have led to unexpected and dangerous consequences.

In fact, let us consider what happened when the change of system occurred. Lots of contracts had been signed previously and they had been denominated in terms of existing national currencies. On the very day of the change of system, it was easy to convert contracts denominated in any national currency into the new European currency via the exchange rate between both. But let us consider, for instance, lending arrangements. The interest rate that had been previously agreed upon depended on inflationary expectations concerning the corresponding currency. Thus, if monetary unification occurred suddenly between currencies suffering from very different inflation rates, all contracts denominated into these various currencies would be converted into the single European currency, but they would have very different interest rates in spite of the fact the inflation rate would, from now on, be the same all over Europe. This is the reason why it was rightly decided in the Maastricht Treaty that monetary conditions in the various countries had to become more similar before the fusion of all currencies into one. This is the rationale for the convergence criteria concerning interest rates, exchange rates and inflation rates.

However, as experience has clearly shown, it is very difficult to manage a system of fixed exchange rates whenever currencies are produced by different issuers (central banks) that are independent from one another and are assumed to be on an equal footing. Contrary to the "dollar standard," in which all currencies were in fact dependent on the American monetary policy, or – to give another example – the franc zone in which monetary policies in Africa were highly dependent on the French monetary policy (and now on the European monetary policy), the EMS, which was the instrument for monetary unification, had been built as a symmetrical system of independent monetary authorities. It had more or less worked for several years because it was in fact a Deutsche Mark (DM) system, each monetary policy being adjusted to the German monetary policy, in spite of the officially symmetrical character of the system. But the changes in Germany made this link less desirable and the various monetary policies – as well as fiscal policies – were such that convergence was less and less possible.

Thus, the technique of the Maastricht Treaty consisted in easing – via convergence indicators – the shift to the new system by alleviating its possible adverse effects. The Maastricht Treaty made monetary convergence necessary. But convergence is difficult to implement. Another technique would have consisted of adopting a process of monetary unification in which such a convergence of national monetary policies *would have not been necessary*.

2. MICROECONOMIC CRITERIA FOR CHOOSING CURRENCIES IN EUROPE

We have already explained why we must not use macroeconomic criteria – such as the ability to adjust to shocks – to try to evaluate the optimal number of currencies in an area such as the eurozone. But this does not imply that nothing can be said about the problem of the optimal number of currencies in an economic union or in the world at large. In the present section we would like to propose two arguments.

2.1 Money and the Working of Economic Systems

Why we must abandon traditional arguments in favor of the use of monetary policy to obtain some real targets, such as employment or the rate of growth, has already been explained. From this point of view, being independent in designing monetary policy may be of secondary importance. Thus, from a purely macroeconomic point of view, the consequence of an expansionary monetary policy is inflation, which is mainly a nominal problem (but we will stress later on the structural distortions brought about by expansionary monetary policies). However, it is quite true that the more inflation there is, the less efficient an economy is. In fact, money can be considered as a factor of production and the role of money as a waiting purchasing power implies that inflation is an attack against this role. The more inflation there is, the less money is able to play its role, and the less efficient is the economy. What does it imply for the choice of currencies? A country should keep its own currency and, therefore, avoid joining a monetary union, if ever its monetary authorities can be considered as more able than others to preserve the purchasing power of money. This may depend on various factors, among which, for instance, institutional characteristics which may limit the propensity of monetary authorities to create money. On the contrary, it would be preferable for the citizens of a country to enter into a monetary union if ever their monetary authorities were more inclined to accept inflation: entering into a union would limit money creation. However, this does not give us a very precise clue to the problem of currency choice, since the "propensity to inflate" cannot be defined precisely and may be changing rapidly and suddenly.

Now, although it is quite clear that inflation has negative consequences and ought to be avoided, one may consider that the main consequences are the microeconomic or sectoral consequences of money creation. This has been emphasized by the so-called "Austrian theory of the business cycle" developed by Ludwig von Mises and Friedrich Hayek. These authors have pointed out that monetary creation in our time implies a simultaneous creation of credits that do not correspond to voluntary savings. Therefore, by distributing credits and creating money, the banking system is creating illusions that are the main causes of financial crises. In particular, money creation necessarily implies that real interest rates become lower than equilibrium interest rates. Thus, borrowers are induced to ask for credits in order to finance investments that have a too-low rate of return or are too risky and which would have not been decided if equilibrium interest rates had prevailed. As has been stressed by Hayek, there is a lengthening of the process of production. Money creation is the cause of distortion in the structure of production and in the structure of prices. What is the implication of this theory for the problem of currency choice?

Let us consider first that there is a single currency in a zone, such as Europe, or even all over the world. It is clear that the whole world will suffer from the same sorts of distortion. But let us assume now that there are several currencies with different monetary policies and flexible exchange rates. According to the traditional approaches, each country is monetarily independent and can therefore protect itself from the mismanagement of currencies in other countries. But is it really the case if we consider microeconomic consequences of money creation, as we should do?

In order to make the reasoning simpler, let us assume – as we have already done before – that there are two countries in the world, A and B. There is money creation in A and not in B. With flexible exchange rates, currency B will appreciate against currency A and it is true that country B will not import the inflation of A. But, as far as there is international mobility of financial assets, there will be a tendency for *real* interest rates to converge all over the world. Monetary creation in A determines an over-distribution of credits all over the world and distortions in the structure of production and in the structure of prices. A country cannot isolate itself from external influences (except by creating harmful obstacles to international capital flows). This is exactly what we could see during the recent world financial crisis: in spite of the fact that flexible exchange rates were prevailing, the excess of money creation in the US spilled over into the world (and, in fact, was exacerbated by similar monetary policies in other countries). From this point of view there is no clear gain either from joining a monetary zone or from keeping its own national currency. Therefore, we may turn to some other considerations.

2.2 The Role of Money and the Choice of Currencies

As already stressed, the creation of a single market is not a justification for the existence of a single currency in Europe. However, there may be other reasons for the number of currencies to be limited.

The aim to be given to any monetary arrangement ought to be the production of a "sound" currency. A sound currency is one that plays its role, namely to be an "undifferentiated purchasing power." The "moneyness" – or liquidity – of a monetary unit depends on its ability to be exchanged against any other good, at any time and with anybody. The liquidity of money has two components, the stability of its purchasing power (or, even, its increase due to deflation) and the dimension of the zone in which it is circulating.

We more or less know what is a non-inflationary (or a deflationary) currency. But we do not exactly know the optimal dimension of the monetary zone and we may have to discover it from experience. It is obvious that one may gain by increasing the dimension of a monetary area, as far as there are economies of scale and externalities in the production of money. However, the optimal dimension does not necessarily correspond to a single currency in Europe (or in the world). There may be a dimension – narrower than Europe – beyond which the marginal gain from enlarging the zone is negligible.

Thus, the specific characteristics of money production imply that the differentiation of currencies be limited, contrary to our previous argument according to which competition normally creates differentiation. However, it does not mean that one has to control the process of competition in order to avoid an excessive differentiation. Quite the contrary: if gains can be obtained by limiting the number of currencies, competition is the best way to reveal such a situation, since there are always people, in a free system, to extract potential gains. It is therefore likely that, if ever currency competition had prevailed in Europe, the market would have selected a more limited number of currencies than we had before the creation of the euro, and possibly only one of them. However, even if the spontaneous working of the market led to the selection of a single currency, it would not be necessary – and even not desirable – to have a single central bank in Europe.

Rather than imposing a limited number of currencies or a single currency in Europe, it would have been more important – and it is still more important – to think about the institutional structures that would make it possible to obtain sound currencies (or a sound single currency) in Europe. Thinking along such lines makes it possible to explore new approaches to European monetary integration.

From this point of view, we must apply to monetary problems the lessons from general economic theory and, particularly, what we know about competition and monopolies. Monopolies are always bad, because they can impose a burden on customers. But real monopolies are always producers that benefit from a privilege given by public authorities. If there is free entry into a market, there is potential competition from other producers, even if, at a given time, there is only one producer. What is important to assess the competitive nature of a market is not the number of producers but the extent to which freedom of entry exists. In our times, as regards money, it is considered that there must be a monopolistic producer – the central bank – in each country (or each zone, such as the eurozone). No one has the right to compete and to propose another currency than the one produced and controlled by the central bank. This is the very reason why there has never been, in the whole history of mankind, as much inflation and as many monetary/financial crises than has been the case since the creation of public central banks. Historical experience, as well as economic theory, thus make a strong case for competition in currency, which implies the production of private currencies.

Under a system of competitive currencies, each producer is induced to propose a "sound" currency, which means a currency that corresponds the best to what individuals desire when holding money: an exchangeable purchasing power. As already stated, we do not know in advance what the optimal number of currencies in Europe or in the world is (since there is no reason to limit competition to the frontiers of Europe and to consider that there must be a coincidence between the monetary area and the political area). We have to experiment.

However, even if we do not know the optimal number of currencies, there is something we do know, which is the optimum number of central banks: This number is zero. It is zero both because monopolies are harmful and because one of the assumed important roles of a central bank, namely being a "lender of last resort," is particularly dangerous. Whenever such an organization does exist, there is an incentive for banks to take too many risks because they assume that the central bank will bail them out if ever they have a risk of bankruptcy.

As already said, it is likely that the optimal number of currencies that would emerge spontaneously under competitive conditions would be small, because people prefer currencies that can circulate over a very large area, which means that the currency is more liquid. Anyhow, one never knows. Thus, it is striking that there is nowadays a development of "local currencies" (in several countries, particularly in Germany). They are "currencies" – exchangeable, for instance, against euros – which circulate only within the limits of a city or a very small region (and which could be considered as illegal, given the monopoly of the central bank . . .). Why are they accepted? Certainly not because they give a protection against inflation, both because inflation is rather low in most countries right now and because, anyhow, these currencies are defined in terms of public official currencies. But, by accepting this currency people decide voluntarily to purchase goods from sellers who participate into this system, even if they are selling goods at a higher price than others. In other words, these currencies mix two characteristics: being an available purchasing power and subsidizing fellow citizens. This means that the reasons for holding a currency may be complex so that, if ever competition between private currencies was to prevail, there could be different currencies with different characteristics in order to meet the diversified needs of money holders (for instance, currencies with a gold guarantee, or a silver guarantee or currencies defined in terms of treasury bonds or financial assets). Once more, we do not know what the optimal number of currencies is, but we do know that freedom is good and that competition allows the best possible adjustment of production to the needs of customers.

Now, it must also be emphasized that, contrary to what is usually claimed, people need money, but there is no need to *create* money. The reason for that is quite simple, even if it is not generally accepted. We have already mentioned the real balance effect, which means that people react to changes in the quantity of money so that they finally get the desired amount of real money balances. Thus, let us assume that there is only one currency in the world and that it is impossible to create one additional unit of this currency. If there is growth, there will be deflation, a decrease in the money price of commodities, which is desirable since it also means an increase in the purchasing power of money (and we know that money is the more useful the better it maintains or increases its purchasing power). As the productivity gains are not the same in all productions, the prices of commodities with the highest increases in productivity will decrease more rapidly than others, thus causing the necessary changes in relative prices.

The same process will take place if there are several currencies in the world. Probably, each currency would have a different area of circulation. There would not exist any coincidence between the monetary areas and the national areas and different monetary areas would be overlapping. The changes in relative prices would be the same all over the world, as far as competition exists for goods. But there may be some changes in the relative prices of the different currencies, as far as their purchasing power would be defined in terms of different sets of goods. This would only reflect the fact that these currencies are different in the sense that they are viewed as products with different characteristics. The diversity of currencies would not mean a non-optimal monetary organization in the world, quite the contrary. But, in a world in which the quantity of each currency would be perfectly stable, there would be no more arbitrary creation of money and no more distribution of illusory credits, therefore no more monetary and financial crises.

3. A COMPETITIVE APPROACH TO MONETARY INTEGRATION

3.1 A Common Currency or a Single Currency?

As aforementioned, currency competition is an efficient way towards monetary unification. One of the merits of such an approach is that it avoids the difficulties inherent to a process in which there must be a radical change of system overnight. Under the Maastricht Treaty, the assumed convergence of monetary policies produced the feeling that the process was gradual. But gradualism was only apparent. It could not hide the fact that at the very minute the single currency was introduced, other currencies disappeared and all contracts had to be redenominated into the new currency, with the possible adverse effects that have been underlined previously, especially as no one could forecast the monetary policy of the future European Central Bank.

Such a jump in the nature of the system does not exist with the competitive approach. Introducing competition means that European citizens are free to choose which currencies are best fitted to their own personal needs. As Friedrich Hayek has suggested, full competition would also imply that anyone be free to supply a specific currency he might invent.[3] In spite of the merits of this approach, let us limit ourselves to proposals which are more acceptable for European authorities. Competition between existing national currencies is the simplest solution. However, national prejudices may make it difficult for some nationals or their public authorities to accept as a common currency the currency issued in another country. Therefore, the creation of a fiat "European" currency, which would compete with existing currencies, has to be considered. It would have a symbolic aspect, which may be desirable for European activists. It could be acceptable and useful as well for those European countries that are not members of the eurozone as for those which belong to it and which might benefit from the use of a parallel currency.

The advantages of a common (parallel) currency in comparison with a single currency are obvious. Money holders would be free to choose this parallel European currency instead of their own national currency, if ever they could benefit from this substitution. The replacement of existing currencies by a European currency would thus be gradual and it would develop only insofar as it would be desired by those who use money and are concerned by the quality of it. Thus, the parallel currency approach makes it possible to avoid the monetary shock implied by the brutal change of system that exists necessarily under the single currency approach.

The creation of a common currency may be an attractive substitute to the single currency approach, and there is one more important reason for preferring a common currency to a single currency: As already stressed, *we do not know* to which extent Europeans benefit from using a single European currency. In our opinion, the need for such a currency is more limited than is usually stressed, so that a single currency does not bring important gains, and, on the other hand, the development of a common currency would certainly be slow.

In fact, the transactions made by most individuals are "proximity transactions" and for any one of them most transactions can easily be denominated in the same "national" currency without any loss of efficiency (at least if this national currency is not too inflationary). For instance, most people in the UK receive wages in pounds and buy commodities in pounds. They need a foreign (European) currency a few times a year. Even for most firms, transactions denominated in foreign (European) currencies are limited. From this point of view, statistics may be misleading, since they tend to over-estimate the degree of openness of European countries. If, for instance, it is said that trade between one given country and other European countries amounts to 25 percent of its gross national product (GNP), one compares international transactions which may be mostly transactions in intermediate goods with a variable (GNP), which measures the value which is added in production processes and, therefore, excludes intermediate transactions. It means that the ratio of intra-European trade to national trade is much lower than what could be suggested when considering trade/GNP ratios. Thus the benefit from having a common European currency may be rather concentrated and limited. Anyhow, we have to experiment. If such a common currency could be beneficial to some traders, its domain would spontaneously and gradually expand and we may imagine that the common currency might become a single currency after a possibly very long period of time. And we can be certain that it would be selected as a single currency only insofar as it would be a "sound" currency (that is, non-inflationary).

Once more, we may compare money with language. Most Europeans do not need a common European language in their daily life. Only a minority of them have regular contacts beyond their national frontiers. In such cases, a common language is necessary and English emerged spontaneously as being the one most frequently chosen by those who are concerned. However, the same individuals who use this European parallel language are using their national languages, or even regional languages, in order to have relations with their colleagues, family members or trade partners. The same may be optimal with money, namely the use of a common currency for part of commercial and financial activities, and the use of existing currencies within other domains of activity.

As already stressed, two main attributes have to be attached to a currency. A currency is more useful the larger is its area of circulation and the higher is the stability of its purchasing power. The Europeanization of a common currency would meet the first attribute: Circulating all over Europe (and, probably outside Europe), the European common currency would be desirable. But it also has to be a stable currency.

The official plan for a single currency in the Maastricht Treaty was not satisfactory from both these points of view. First, it assumed that the optimal domain of circulation is Europe, although we cannot know it. Second, we have absolutely no guarantee that this currency will not be inflationary. The Maastricht Treaty assumed that it is sufficient to have an independent European central bank in order to obtain monetary stability. This is excessively optimistic: Any independent organization may misuse its independence, since independence means a lack of control.

In order for a common currency to be competitive and to better meet the monetary needs of citizens, it has to be a stable money, for what it means. In fact, we must not forget that the merits of a system such as the gold standard did not come from the fact it made "monetary stability" possible, but that it offered money holders a stable definition of money in terms of a commodity – gold – which had spontaneously emerged as a satisfactory standard of purchasing power, since the changes of relative prices between gold, on the one hand, and other commodities, on the other hand, were slow and limited. In short, a "sound" European currency does not imply a good monetary management, but a good definition of the common currency and institutional arrangements which make people confident in the capacity of the issuer of this currency to honor this definition, namely to be able to convert without limits the units of the common currency into a stable amount of the goods which define them.

How could a common currency be defined? A proposal was made in 1975 by nine European economists in what was called the All Saints' Day Manifesto.[4] They suggested that the European currency be an indexed basket of European currencies. Initially, the common currency would be defined in terms of a weighted basket of currencies, but the number of units of any currency would increase in proportion to the rate of inflation of this same currency. This common currency would thus maintain a sort of "average" purchasing power. Another possibility would be to define the European common currency in terms of gold. In any case, European monetary unification would then mean going back to international monetary stability. The time may have come to substitute a common and stable currency to a single and uncertain currency.

A competitive process of integration is better than a centralized and constructivist process, not only because it lets to the market the choice of the single currency, if any, but also because it creates competition in monetary systems (that is, competing institutional arrangements), possibly producing the same currencies or the single currency; and, beyond, it allows competition for the production of all sorts of monetary and financial services, in which gains from cartellization may be different. This is important since, as we have just seen, the main problem of modern monetary systems and, specifically, of the European monetary system is not the fact that there is not a single currency within a large monetary area – such as Europe – but the fact that they are founded on institutional irresponsibility. Therefore, one has either to design monetary systems in which this irresponsibility is diminished or suppressed or, which is better, to let the market make the selection of the best monetary systems.

3.2 Currency Competition

Various solutions correspond to a more competitive approach than the one generally adopted. A system of free banking, in which anyone would be free to supply a currency and anyone would be free to use any currency, would be the best one, since it would reintroduce responsibility of individual banks. However, it may not be acceptable for the time being, so it may be advisable to discuss other options. We have already discussed the role that could be played by a parallel (or common) currency. But let us now consider the case in which there would be competition between *existing currencies* (one of these being the euro).

Let us make a comparison: The mutual recognition of norms has been accepted in Europe, which means that the norms for a given commodity that are legal in a country have to be accepted by other European countries whenever this commodity is imported. In a similar way, there could be a mutual recognition of currencies. As previously stressed, the flexibility of prices does not mean that there is no single market. In fact, there would be a "common market in currencies." It is quite true that the diversification of currencies impose to money holders the bearing of various costs, such as transaction costs, information costs and risk costs. However, this is the case with all sorts of commodities for which we accept such costs. Diminishing the diversification of goods would decrease these costs, but it would also limit freedom of choice for consumers and incentives to innovate for producers. Transaction costs can thus be considered as equivalent to investment costs: investing in differentiation makes freedom of choice possible. This is true for currencies.

With currency competition, one may expect that, little by little, a currency or a limited number of currencies would be selected by the market as "common currencies." Although we suspect that many existing monetary areas are too small in Europe – maybe with the exception of the eurozone – to extract all possible gains from a large scale of production or economies of standardization, we do not know to what extent this is true and beyond which size significant marginal gains can no more be obtained by decreasing the differentiation of currencies. A competitive process would allow the market to determine the optimal monetary areas. Meanwhile, it would put pressure on central banks not to inflate too much in order to avoid a decreasing role for their currencies. From this point of view, responsibility for monetary management would be distributed among central banks in a more decentralized way and each one would be responsible for its own currency. With central banks having incentives to produce a sound currency, it could happen that inflation rates would be low and exchange rate fluctuations limited, so that it would be largely equivalent for money holders to hold one or the other currency. In such a case the costs of differentiation would be minimized. And if ever a single currency was to replace all existing currencies, the process would be gradual and, therefore, better accepted.

From a practical point of view such a competitive system implies the definitive disappearance of exchange controls or legal tender laws. It also implies possible changes in the organization of monetary systems.

In the present world, a central bank has jurisdiction on commercial banks located in its official area (a nation or the eurozone) and it can impose on them any regulation or try to influence their reserve positions. Let us assume now that Europeans are perfectly free to use any currency for any activity, but that national monetary monopolies still exist, in the sense that a bank would be obliged to issue only the official currency. As the worst currencies would be less and less used, banks issuing these currencies would have to leave the market.

Happily enough, banks are more and more allowed to accept deposits in any other (European) currency. From this point of view, monetary competition is developing within Europe. In the system we are considering – namely freely floating rates and freedom for banks to issue any European currency – an apparent difficulty exists if, for instance, a central bank in country A can impose reserve requirements to the banks belonging to its national system, whereas the banks in other European countries are allowed to issue the currency of country A without having to bear the same requirements, since they are regulated by other central banks.[5] There are several possible solutions to overcome this difficulty, two of which are:

1. Each central bank could be entitled to regulate the activities of all European banks as far as its currency is concerned. Thus, the central bank of country A could oblige all European banks to hold reserves in currency A in proportion to their deposits in this same currency.
2. Another solution would be to accept more deregulation. Each bank would be responsible for guaranteeing the convertibility of the deposits it accepts in any currency. Thus, it participates in different cartels (possibly new ones, if freedom of issuance is accepted). In such a decentralized system, it would be the responsibility of each bank

to make certain that it is able to transfer deposits in terms of any (European) currency and therefore to decide its reserve ratios.

Moreover, one might consider this question not as a difficulty, but as a competitive solution.[6] There would be several competing processes to produce the same currency, as is the case with the Eurodollar. However, in a system which lacks self-regulatory mechanisms, as is the case in present systems, competition between banks could result in more money creation. Limits to money creation in present systems depend on the regulatory powers of the central banks and they may be lightened by competition not between different monetary systems, but inside each monetary system.

3.3 Competition Among Monetary Systems

As already emphasized, a common market – free trade and free choice – does not necessarily imply completely free markets. In the field of taxation, for instance, we have argued that the harmonization of taxes was not necessary because it did not prevent free trade. However, different systems of taxation and public expenditures may be more or less important obstacles for economic activity and one may hope that competition between tax systems would help to select those that better meet the needs of citizens. The same is probably true as regards money.

Competition between currencies – either existing currencies, new public currencies (parallel currency) or private currencies – does not imply a forced harmonization of monetary regulations, but we may expect that the less regulated monetary systems would be able to issue a more desirable currency or to issue one given currency more efficiently, so that it may lead to deregulation of monetary and financial systems. On the contrary, the present European Central Bank is endowed with regulatory powers on the model of other existing national central banks and these powers may be increased under the pretext of creating a banking union. It makes it more difficult to experiment with various means of monetary management and the possible process of deregulation may probably be slowed down.

To a large extent the modern bank is a product of regulations. In a deregulated world, the present roles of a bank – as money issuer, financial intermediary and producer of monetary and financial services – would be scattered between a lot of different firms. Some of them would be specialized in a very specific job, others would link activities that are mainly separated for the time being (for instance, insurance and deposit management), and so on.

To be sure, even with a single currency, it is not necessary to have a single decision center. In a deregulated and decentralized system, each producer gives convertibility guarantees, but each is responsible for that. For instance, let us imagine that two banks issue the same currency, in the sense that they give mutual guarantees of convertibility. However, we may view a currency as a complex good, or – according to the so-called "new theory of consumption" (Lancaster, 1966, 1991) – as a bundle of characteristics. Currencies are claims on different firms, which are differently managed (in a deregulated world), so that the confidence we have in the capacity of different banks to maintain their convertibility guarantees may be different. In other words, although the claims on two different banks benefit from the same convertibility guarantees and are formally considered as substitutable, they are, however, different goods, being claims on different firms. In a deregulated world, there would be continuous efforts to find the best combination of diversity and homogeneity. As perfectly exchangeable means of payments, monetary units have to be as homogeneous as possible, which is made possible by convertibility guarantees and cartel arrangements. However, we also know that there are different – more or less efficient – ways of producing a given good. In a cartel, each participant may try either to be more efficient than the others (that is, to adopt different production processes) or to give different characteristics to its product.

As an example, assume that there are two banks, A and B, in a monetary cartel, their currencies benefiting from convertibility guarantees. However, bank A gives a positive return on demand deposits, but no insurance against the risk of failure, whereas bank B gives no positive return, but a reliable insurance. From this point of view both currencies, although they are convertible one into the other at a fixed price, are not perfect substitutes from the point of view of consumers. Money users do not just demand a convertible currency, they demand currencies with a bundle of characteristics. In this diversified system of free banking, each of them buys the currency that gives the combination of characteristics they prefer. In return, given the characteristics of demand, the producers have to find the precise combination of characteristics which will make it possible for them to give convertibility guarantees to their currencies and to obtain the highest possible profitability. In such a world one gets the "optimal" combination of diversity and homogenization.

One can consider a centralized process of regulation in Europe, as is the case now, in particular with the desired development of the banking union, but competition in regulations and competition between more or less deregulated systems would be still preferable. This may imply that banks would be free to choose their desired reserve ratios, interest rates on deposits and credits, means of insuring deposits, and so on. In order to avoid possible fears about such a process of competition and deregulation, it could be possible to introduce a completely free sector along with existing ones. The consumer would be free to choose one or the other. Thus, the process of integration in Europe would be based not only on a "common market for currencies" (currency competition) but even more on a "common market for monetary and financial systems." We are, anyhow, convinced that thinking about possible changes in monetary systems is far more important that enforcing the present view in favor of centralization.

In the present book we have emphasized that there is no logical link between a single market – whatever it may be – and a single currency. A single market is, therefore, perfectly compatible with a multiplicity of currencies and monetary systems and there are reasons to prefer competitive approaches to monetary integration. But it is also true that there is no reason for limiting monetary integration to the borders of Europe. The optimal size of monetary and financial areas may be larger than Europe for some activities, smaller for others, and one must be cautious about possible risks of Europe becoming a monetary fortress. The time may have come for new initiatives in favor of a worldwide approach, including competition and deregulation.

At this point we can stress that floating rates are not incompatible with monetary integration, if integration is correctly understood as the integration of markets (that is, competition). Therefore, all those who claim that the UK is preventing or slowing down the process of integration in Europe by not joining the eurozone, are, in fact, defenders of a specific approach of integration, which from our point of view is completely wrong. The best contribution the British can make to European integration is not to join the eurozone at some future date, but to reinforce the freedom of choice of consumers and producers and to suppress any possible discrimination between British producers and foreign ones.

As already stated, competition and freedom of activity are the best way to obtain a social order. It is certainly illusory to wait for a perfect worldwide free banking system in the near future. But any liberalization, anywhere in the world, may contribute to the international monetary order, better than any process of coordination would do. Thus, instead of deciding that no differentiation between currencies may exist in Europe – which is the usual way to consider European integration – why not decide that any bank in Europe can adhere to any of the other national monetary cartels (including the euro system)? Other examples of liberalization can be found in one or the other of the numerous roles played by central banks that benefit from strong monopoly positions. For instance, if deposit insurance could be privatized in some countries, it would imply an increased responsibility of banks and a better working of monetary systems. One could imagine that European, or even global, systems of reinsurance could emerge, thus replacing the present public (national or international) safety nets. Or, one could imagine that a free banking sector could be in competition with the legal ones in a country, in Europe or in the world.

Supporting ideas in favor of a better world monetary order is not an easy task. We have to face the misconceptions and the interests of numerous people. There may not be any field in which so many people have such a great interest and in which there are so many wrong ideas. Monetary and financial activities are both complex and important. To help put some order in this complexity we have, however, to repeat continuously some simple ideas founded on sound economic theory and on firm principles concerning human societies.

APPENDIX THERE IS NO "EURO CRISIS"[7]

Contrary to what is claimed daily in the media by politicians and many economists, there is no "euro crisis." The single currency doesn't have to be "saved" or else explode.

The so-called crisis is not a European monetary problem at all, but rather a debt problem in some countries – Greece, Spain and some others – that happen to be members of the eurozone. Specifically, these are public debt problems, stemming from bad budget management by their governments. But there is no logical link between these countries' fiscal situations and the functioning of the euro system. It is worth stressing that the deficits now plaguing these countries were, in large part, justified only a few years ago as necessary to initiate so-called "recovery policies." But it is always an illusion to believe that governments could increase total demand and thereby induce producers to produce more. Governments can only shift resources from those who have created them to those who have not. The present state of affairs in countries that engaged in stimulus blowouts in 2008 and 2009 should serve as proof of the failure of the Keynesian model.

When an individual or a firm is indebted, moreover, they are rightly considered to be responsible for reimbursing their debts, and they either have to spend less or produce more to do so. Their debts are not generally problems to be shifted onto other people who managed their money more cautiously. Why shouldn't the same moral discipline be imposed on governments?

The public debt problem becomes a euro problem only insofar as governments arbitrarily decide that there must be some "European solidarity" inside the eurozone. But how does mutual participation in the same currency logically imply that spendthrift governments should get help from the others? When a state in the US has a debt problem, one never hears that there is a "dollar crisis." There is simply a problem of budget management in that state.

Because European politicians have decided to create an artificial link between national budget problems and the functioning of the euro system, they have now effectively created a "euro crisis." To help out badly managed governments, the ECB is now buying public bonds issued by these governments or supplying liquidity to support their failing banks. In so doing, the ECB is violating its own principles and introducing harmful distortions.

Contrary to what Europeans have been hearing from leaders and pundits over the past few years, a monetary zone can work perfectly well with very different members. The US dollar zone is one example. See also the so-called "franc zone," in which several African countries and France were able to maintain a single currency (with the exception of one devaluation) for decades.

The euro crisis is a pure political construction. It is a splendid opportunity for many politicians to impose some of their longstanding goals on everyone else. For instance, before the introduction of the euro, many politicians who called themselves Europeans considered monetary union a stepping-stone to political union. I was opposed to the euro before its creation, precisely because I feared that the currency's stewards would take this arbitrary link between the monetary system and national policies as a pretense to further centralize political decisions.

Politicians now argue that "saving the euro" will require not only propping up Europe's irresponsible governments, but also centralizing decision-making. This is now the dominant opinion of politicians in Europe, France in particular. There are a few reasons why politicians in Paris might take that view. They might see themselves being in a similar situation as Greece in the near future, so all the schemes to "save the euro" could also be helpful to them shortly. They might also be looking to shift public attention away from France's internal problems and toward the rest of Europe instead. It is easier to complain about what one's neighbors are doing than to tackle problems at home. France needs drastic tax cuts and far-reaching deregulation and labor-market liberalization. Much simpler to get the media worked up about the next euro crisis meeting with Angela Merkel.

Before the creation of the euro, Europeans claimed that the euro would increase growth and stability in Europe. They even went so far as to hire econometricians to claim that the euro's introduction alone would increase gross domestic product (GDP) growth by 1 percent. I did not believe it at the time, and in retrospect it looks even sillier to claim that a monetary change could ever have solved a real economic problem. But now the euro exists and there is no reason not to keep it around. The real solutions to Europe's debt problems lie in tax and expenditure cuts and deregulation, and it's here that national politicians should turn their attention. Pan-European cooperation won't deliver any government from its fiscal or economic crises.

However, keeping the euro does not mean that it may benefit from an absolute monopoly situation into the eurozone. The citizens of the eurozone ought to be free to use another currency if ever they prefer it. And one could even imagine that a new currency – benefiting, for instance, of a gold guarantee – be introduced, a parallel currency which may enter into competition with the euro. Symmetrically, the governments of countries outside the eurozone might accept that the euro competes with existing national currencies. Money holders could thus have a higher freedom of choice and monetary authorities would be prevented from issuing too much money.

NOTES

1. The present chapter has used the following documents: Salin (1990d, 2011a) and the 1993 report mentioned in Chapter 9, note 1.
2. The Maastricht criteria are the following:
    - Price stability: The inflation rate of a given member state must not exceed by more than 1.5 point that of the three best-performing member states in terms of price stability.
    - Government deficit: The annual government deficit must not exceed 3 percent of GDP.
    - Government debt must not exceed 60 percent of GDP.
    - Long-term interest rates must not be more than 2 percent higher than those of the three best-performing member states in terms of price stability.
3. Friedrich Hayek was the first to suggest that monetary integration implied currency competition. See, for instance, Hayek (1976, 1978).
4. "A Currency for Europe," *The Economist*, 1 November 1975.
5. What we call a country here can be the whole eurozone.
6. As was suggested to me by Lawrence White.
7. Except for the last paragraph, this appendix has been previously published under the same title in Salin (2012).

PART IV

Money, finance and economic policies

12. The monetary economics of the Austrian school and the Chicago school[1]

Although we are convinced that "Austrian economics" offer the best approach to economic and social problems, we also believe that it is a fundamental task of economists in our time to try to evaluate to which extent there is some possible convergence between some parts of Austrian economics and other approaches, such as the Chicago school. Comparing extensively the Austrian school and the Chicago school as regards monetary theory would need several books and, obviously, there have already been a lot of articles and books concerning this topic. We have, therefore, to make choices and to focus on some specific aspects of the monetary theories of both schools. Just because they play a crucial role in the foundations of both approaches, we have chosen to focus first on the problem of neutrality and stability of money and, second, on the balance of payments. Moreover, we are mainly concerned with the works of Ludwig von Mises as regards the Austrian school and those of Milton Friedman and Robert Mundell as regards the Chicago school.

1. THE NEUTRALITY AND THE STABILITY OF MONEY

According to Mises, "The notion of a neutral money is no less contradictory than that of a money of stable power" (p. 415).[2] In reality the very reasons why Mises does not accept concepts such as the neutrality of money or the stability of the purchasing power of money is that he considers that the general level of prices is a meaningless concept so that one cannot even measure the so-called "purchasing power" of money. In fact, each individual has his own evaluation of the purchasing power of his cash balances according to the basket of goods relevant for him. By calculating the change in the purchasing power of money via some arbitrary index of prices, a statistician can only give an approximation of the change in the purchasing power of money as it is evaluated by individuals. Moreover,

Mises even considers that the concept of the "quantity of money" is useless.

These statements of Mises are quite understandable. In fact, he considers that relative prices between goods are continuously changing, since individuals are not repeating indefinitely the same actions, but are continuously discovering new actions to be performed. And money, by itself, contributes to these changes, as it makes indirect exchange possible and, therefore, the discovery of new needs, of new specializations. Individuals desire to hold cash balances because money is a potential purchasing power that can be exchanged over time against any other good. However, it is meaningless to try to measure the purchasing power of money in terms of a given basket of commodities, since an individual does not desire the same basket of goods at any time and the basket desired by different individuals at one given time is not the same. Therefore, it is completely arbitrary to define some basket of goods in terms of which one could measure the change in the purchasing power of money and, therefore, the stability of its purchasing power.

Mises – as well as other Austrian economists – also objects to the concept of the general level of prices precisely because the mismanagement of money by central banks in modern times, particularly the over-issue of money against credits, brings changes in relative prices (for instance, between raw materials or investment goods and consumer goods, or between present and future goods), as has been explained in the Austrian theory of business cycles. As Mises considers that these changes in relative prices are more important than the common increase of all prices (inflation) he prefers not to define some arbitrary "level of prices" which would make it possible to measure a rate of inflation.

As regards the quantity of money, one may recall that what Mises calls "money" is the good considered as the most liquid asset by money users (for instance, gold in a system in which individuals hold and exchange gold). In a gold standard system with central banks holding gold and issuing currencies convertible into gold, money would be what is commonly called "base money," that is, the gold stock of central banks. Money has emerged in history because one specific good – for instance, gold – has been selected by individuals as the one which gave them the best monetary services. This good is money and other liquid assets convertible without limits into money are to be labeled "money substitutes." Although money proper is a commodity, it is quite obvious that the use of gold (or silver or any other commodity) in real transactions is costly, in particular because such a currency cannot be split into very small pieces at will.

Therefore, people became used to circulating property rights in gold rather than gold itself. In a 100 percent reserve system, the quantity of such "gold certificates" is exactly the same as the quantity of gold that it represents. Now, in a fractional reserve system, what is called the quantity of money is, in fact, composed of two very different parts: money (that is, gold) and money substitutes. Austrian economists rightly care about the structure of the so-called quantity of money much more than about the mere change in the total quantity of money. In fact, the definition of the "quantity of money" is arbitrary since it sums up two components which have a very different nature and play a very different economic role. The effects of a (spontaneous) increase in the quantity of a money base consisting in gold are completely different from those of an increase in the quantity of money substitutes brought about by the discretionary decisions of money producers.

The Austrian approach to monetary problems is microeconomic and subjective. If ever one is in a pure gold system (100 percent reserve) any individual chooses the quantity of money (the quantity of gold) he wants to hold at any time, given his forecasts about his own activity and the possible evolution of relative prices which are relevant for him and only for him. From the exchange transactions between individuals a given structure of relative prices and money prices emerge at any time. But neither the acting individual nor the potential observer need to know or have the possibility to know the "rate of inflation" or the general evolution of the "purchasing power of money." However, saying that the individual is making his own choices in a given monetary system, does not mean that the economist – as an external observer – has nothing to say about monetary systems and monetary management. As an example, there is a very important debate among Austrian economists between the supporters of a 100 percent reserve system and the supporters of a fractional reserve system.[3] But once a system is adopted (spontaneously or exogenously), individuals make their own choices and one has not to care about the possible outcome of such a system as regards, for instance, the quality of the currency, the evolution of different prices or interest rates, and so on. In other words, Austrian economists care about the processes and not about the results.

On the contrary, mainstream economists – among whom is the Chicago school – care about the end results of the monetary systems they consider and these expected results are criteria for choosing one or the other monetary system, one or the other monetary policy. Thus, the "monetary rule" – according to which a central bank decides in advance the rate of increase of the "quantity of money" or the targeted rate of inflation – is concerned by the outcome of the working of the monetary system. This approach is macroeconomic and it considers aggregate variables – such as the quantity of money and the general level of prices – without giving too much attention to the structure of these variables (relative prices and components of the quantity of money). As far as, for them, the general level of prices and the quantity of money are meaningful concepts – although they are pure constructions of the mind – they have no difficulty in defining the stability of money. Money is stable as far as its purchasing power – defined through some price index – is constant over time (that is, the rate of inflation is equal to zero).

However, there is no reason to consider that such a situation of price stability is optimal and, by the way, an economist such as Milton Friedman does avoid such an error. He rightly considers that individuals care about their real cash balances and not about their nominal cash balances. The less purchasing power a currency is losing over time (the more purchasing power it gets over time) the more useful it is for the money holder. Now, it is costless to produce additional real cash balances, or, more precisely, to increase the ratio of real balances to income or wealth. Thus, if one assumes, for instance, that the demand for money function of each individual remains stable, it just implies that the rate of growth of the nominal quantity of money is lower than the rate of growth of produced goods (that is, there is deflation). And if ever all the demands for money were increasing, the quantity of money being constant, the real cash balance effect would make it possible to meet the needs of money holders through a decrease in money prices. In such a case, individuals decide to hold the more real cash balances the higher is the gain in purchasing power obtained by price deflation. Incidentally, it may be stressed that this means that it is not necessary, in any society, to produce money since the needs of people are necessarily met by the real cash balance effect. Theoretically, it would be "optimal" to obtain an infinite rate of deflation since the real value of cash balances would increase at an infinite rate. But such a situation is impossible. More realistically, it is impossible to go beyond the point at which the rate of deflation is just equal to the real interest rate. If one tried to go beyond that point, no one would find any incentive to invest in any other asset than money, so that the rate of growth would become equal to zero. Thus, a rate of deflation equal to the real rate of interest is "optimal" only as far as it is the best possible rate.

An Austrian economist would disagree not only with the definition of a stable level of price, but also with the very notion of an optimal quantity of money or an optimal rate of growth of the quantity of money (and, even more, with the concept of an optimal rate of inflation–deflation). He would point out that optimality refers to the behavior of an individual and is meaningless when used by an external observer referring to the welfare of a group of individuals. If a monetary system has been selected spontaneously – for instance, a pure gold standard system with 100 percent reserves – the quantity of money held by individuals is optimal since they have freely decided to buy this quantity at the expense of any other use of their resources. This statement holds whatever is the end result of the working of the system, such as whatever the rise or fall in the money prices of goods is. Many Austrian economists refer to the gold standard not because they consider that it is the best possible monetary system according to some criterion, which, in fact, cannot be determined, but because they consider that is has been freely chosen by money holders as the relatively best possible monetary system. More generally, what is important for most Austrian economists is:

1. That the monetary system has emerged spontaneously in the course of history, instead of being designed by some authority.
2. That a specific monetary system being given, there is no possibility for any discretionary monetary policy (for instance, because there is a 100 percent reserve system or, under a fractional reserve system, there are rules forbidding the over-issue of money substitutes).

From this point of view, currency competition ought to be an unavoidable element of any Austrian approach of monetary problems.

Thus, to summarize with some exaggeration, Austrian economics is interested by the free choice of monetary systems, the absence of any monetary policy and the free choice of their money balances by individuals, whereas Chicago economists (and most mainstream economists) focus on the working of existing monetary systems[4] and look for what they consider as the best monetary policy.

So the Austrian approach and the Chicago approach may differ more as regards what deserves to be emphasized than as regards their basic monetary theory (for instance, the analysis of the monetary behavior of individuals). From this point of view, it may be possible to view both of them not as completely opposite approaches but as more or less complementary approaches that could be more or less reconciled. However, these differences would not prevent Austrian economists from discussing the consequences of the working of any monetary system, for instance by evaluating the role of fractional reserves or the policy of a central bank.

In fact, Chicagoans could accept to focus not only on the management of existing monetary systems but to go beyond and to agree with Austrians on the role of currency competition as a way to choose monetary systems. Milton Friedman, for example, had no hostility against currency competition, but he believed that it couldn't play a very significant role. According to him, currency competition exists nowadays, but one does not see any significant shift from one currency to the other, except in the cases of hyper-inflation.[5] In fact, an Austrian may not disagree strongly with this opinion. From what is known as the "regression theorem" of Mises, the use of a currency is the end result of a very long process by which people acquire the knowledge about the information content of prices, which implies that they cannot shift rapidly from one currency to the other.[6]

Conversely, Austrian economists could accept some mainstream concepts such as the quantity of money or the general level of prices, at least as first steps in a chain of reasoning. In fact there would be several justifications for using such concepts – for instance, that of the general level of prices – within the framework of an Austrian approach:

1. A scientific attitude consists in extracting some main features from reality at the expense of a comprehensive description of it. Thus, although Austrian economists are right in stressing that relative prices are continuously changing within an inflationary process, it is also true that all or most monetary prices increase. In order to simplify the analysis, it may be useful to assume (temporarily) that all money prices increase in the same proportion. Thus, whatever the price index one uses, it gives exactly the same measurement of inflation. In reality, each individual has an implicit price index composed of the goods that he may consider as potentially tradable for him. The purchasing power of his cash balances is evaluated via such an implicit price index. As all individuals are different and exchange different goods, each one has a different price index. From this point of view any price index built by an external observer is completely arbitrary. However, it gives some idea of the way money prices react to a change in the quantity of money.
2. The use of such a price index may give some useful information to individuals. Thus, whenever a producer observes that he can increase the money price of the good he is producing, he does not know to which extent this is caused by a change in relative prices or by a change in overall money prices. The price index gives him an idea of the "average" change in money prices. Similarly, thanks to the price index, a wage earner can better evaluate the change in his real wage.[7]
3. For an Austrian economist, business cycles in the modern world are caused by monetary phenomena, namely an excessive increase in the quantity of money substitutes. It creates changes in relative prices (for instance, between investment goods and consumer goods, or between present and future goods). But it also causes an increase in all money prices, which is precisely called inflation and is felt by people as an overall increase in money prices.

4. Using a price index makes it possible to express the change in real cash balances brought about by a change in the quantity of nominal cash balances (m = M/P, in which m is real balances, M is nominal balances and P is the general level of prices).[8] Austrians certainly do not underestimate the importance of the loss of value of real cash balances brought about by inflation. By using a price index we get a simple expression of this phenomenon. In a second step of reasoning we just have to stress that, in reality, all money prices do not increase homothetically and that inflation has not only this global effect on nominal prices, but also a more microeconomic effect on relative prices. As an example, the models proposed by Robert Mundell – to which we refer later on – are using instruments such as the price level or the real quantity of money. They attract attention on important aspects of the reality and, even if they are too global, they are not in contradiction with the core of the Austrian analysis.

Having accepted such concepts as a first step in the chain of reasoning, Austrian economists would now be in a position to add what is specific to their approach, such as the emphasis on the structure of the quantity of money (money and money substitutes), the structure of production and the theory of capital, or the changes in relative prices and interest rates over the business cycle. Moreover, some consensus could also be obtained about the interpretation of the quantity theory of money and about the discussion on the neutrality of money. As regards the quantity theory of money, Mises does stress that there is a nucleus of truth in it, in particular the fact it is a mere application of the general theory of supply and demand. But, according to him, "its shortcoming was that it resorted to a holistic interpretation. It looked at the total supply of money in the Volkswirtschaft and not at the actions of the individual men and firms" (p. 402). And he adds (p. 402):

> Modern monetary theory takes up the thread of the traditional quantity theory as far as it starts from the cognition that changes in the purchasing power of money must be dealt with according to the principles applied to all other market phenomena and that there exists a connection between the changes in the demand for and supply of money on the one hand and those of purchasing power on the other. In this sense one may call the modern theory of money an improved variety of the quantity theory.

Thus, Mises does refer to the purchasing power of money but he avoids giving too precise a definition of what is meant by that.

Now, it can be said that Friedman, for instance, also presented an "improved variety of the quantity theory" in which he explains more explicitly the motives for which individuals want to hold money. His analysis may thus be considered as mostly compatible with the Austrian approach.

As regards the concept of neutrality, several statements can be made, which, in our opinion, are largely acceptable by both the Austrians and the Chicagoans. In particular, in the long run money expansion (or a devaluation) has no real effects, for instance on production and employment. However, this quasi-neutrality of money in the long run would have not been fully accepted by Mises who insists on the fact that money makes indirect exchange possible so that money of lower quality makes human action less easy. This idea may not be very different from another one, which is accepted by Chicagoans (in particular Mundell), namely that, if people forecast the rate of inflation correctly, they demand less real balances and the economic activity of individuals is less efficient. But it is also true that a main difference remains between the Austrians and the Chicagoans: According to the Austrians, an expansionary monetary policy induces over-investment during the boom and as capital goods are mainly specific there is a lasting real effect. Although this over-investment disappears little by little during the bust, it is nevertheless true that, from this point of view, money creation has lasting real effects, which are not considered by other approaches.

In the short run both Austrians and Chicagoans would accept the idea that money expansion has real effects, but they would put the emphasis on different variables, as is revealed by their respective business cycle theories.

Mises takes the example of a production of additional money to finance a public deficit. The structure of demand for real goods changes, since the government demands goods that are different from those demanded by citizens. Therefore, relative prices are not the same at the end of the process. Mises rightly points out that the result depends on the way money enters into the economy. As it cannot be introduced in a "neutral" way, money creation has necessarily real distribution effects.

However, let us assume – once more as a simplifying temporary assumption in the first step of a chain of reasoning – that the demand for and the supply of all goods are stable (the real determinants of demand and supply are not changing). If there is a once and for all public deficit and a once and for all money creation, the economy is going back to what could be called full equilibrium in which the final relative prices are identical to the initial relative prices. From this point of view monetary shocks have no lasting real effects on relative prices. However, Mises does not accept such a conclusion and he writes (p. 410): "The final prices to the establishment of which the market tends after the effects of the increase in the quantity of money have been fully consummated are not equal to the previous final prices multiplied by the same multiplier." To us this seems debatable. It appears more correct to admit that a once and for all expansion of money brings back to a final full equilibrium (according to the traditional quantity theory of money). But, if money expansion is repeated at any time forever, there are steadily different "final" prices.

According to Mises (p. 416): "All plans to render money neutral and stable are contradictory. Money is an element of action and consequently of change." It means that one may make plans only to give a definition to money in terms of some physical good (for instance, gold) and that any monetary prescription, such as the "monetary rule" (namely, a commitment of monetary authorities to a given rate of growth of the quantity of money) is arbitrary. However, if one accepts the idea that it is impossible to define precisely the neutrality and the stability of money, it is nevertheless possible to compare currencies that are more or less stable and neutral. Thus, the Austrian theory of the business cycle gives an example of a situation in which money is particularly "non-neutral."

2. THE BALANCE OF PAYMENTS

According to Mises, "all that cash-induced changes in purchasing power bring about are shifts in the disposition of wealth among different individuals" (p. 417). It is unquestionable that distribution effects are important consequences of any monetary change. And, in some sense, the Austrian theory of the business cycle is a theory of how distribution changes – and, therefore how relative prices change – over time. However, there is also an overall effect, which we have already stressed, namely the decrease (increase) in real cash balances when there is monetary expansion (restriction). By the way, all economists – in particular Austrians and Chicagoans – ought to admit that:

1. The demand for money is a demand for real balances (since money is desired as a purchasing power).
2. The nominal quantity of money is always sufficient, since the real cash balance effect makes it possible for individuals to obtain the amount of real balances they desire, whatever the existing stock of nominal balances in the economy. As Mises puts it (p. 418): "There can never be an excess or a deficiency of money." From that it follows that the best way to produce the desired quantity of money (real balances) is not to produce money (nominal balances).

Even if they fully agree with these statements, it seems that Austrian economists do not give them too much attention and they prefer to focus on other problems, maybe because they do not feel completely at ease with global concepts. But the relation between changes in the quantity of money and the amount of real balances plays a central role in Mundell's theories. From this point of view, Austrian theory and Mundell's theory are more complementary than opposite.

Robert Mundell considers real cash balances as a sort of factor of production. Therefore, the higher the rate of growth of the quantity of money, the higher the rate of inflation and the lower the amount of real cash balances, which implies that the marginal productivity of capital is also lower (capital is associated with a lower level of real balances).

Contrary to the dominant view about the balance of payments – particularly the approaches inspired by some sort of Keynesian economics – Mises and Mundell rightly consider the money item in the balance of payments not as a consequence of what happens in the trade balance and the capital account, but as something desired by individuals and explained by their behavior concerning money. Assuming a two-country model, the money balance in the balance of payments is determined by the relative supplies of and demands for money against commodities and assets in both countries. Mises correctly defines the balance of payment at the microeconomic level when stating that "the confrontation of the money equivalent of all incomings and outgoings of an individual or a group of individuals during any particular period of time is called the balance of payments" (p. 447). He adds, "the balance is always in balance," which means that, contrary to usual ideas and economic policies, *there can never be any balance of payments problem*. This is a necessary and correct consequence both of Mises' and Mundell's approaches. Both are modern versions of the classical price–specie flow theory with slight differences. They are, in fact, specific applications of the general theory of prices and, as such, are not questionable. In fact, the relation between the change in the relative price of two goods, on the one hand, and the changes in the supplies and demands for both these goods, on the other hand, implies, when applied to the case of two currencies, that:

1. Under a system of fixed exchange rates (fixed price) the demands and supplies of currencies adjust to the price.
2. Under a system of flexible rates it is the exchange rate (the price) which adjusts to the changes in quantities.[9]

Now, let us consider the case of a fixed-rate system with fractional reserves and let us assume that there is an expansionary monetary policy (creation of money substitutes not related to the gold base, according to Mises). Mises seems to adopt an adjustment process close to the one which had been analyzed by Hume: the excess of nominal cash balances in one country brings about a change in relative prices between national and foreign goods and, therefore, changes in demands and supplies which create an additional trade deficit.[10] Money pours away from the country with an excessively expansionary monetary policy until cash balances have been redistributed according to the wishes of all individuals. In the process there is inflation and an increase in all nominal cash balances.

The process described by the monetary approach of the balance of payments, as it has been developed by Mundell, does not focus on the changes in prices – except possible changes of the relative prices between tradable goods and non-tradable goods – but on the flows between countries. If there is an excessive creation of money in one country (country A), people try to get rid of these excess cash balances but, by assumption, they cannot globally succeed. The only possibility is to sell these excess balances to individuals in country B and to buy goods and assets from them (trade deficit and capital deficit). As secondary effects, there can be changes in relative prices, since there are changes in production and consumption. Meanwhile, there is an increase in nominal prices and the process goes on until all individuals in both countries have obtained the amount of real cash balances they desire. As money producers in country A lose reserves, they cannot continue their excessively expansionary monetary policy forever. The normal reaction consists in adjusting the quantity of money to the (fixed) exchange rate. To that end, the loss of reserves plays the role of a signal. Contrary to common opinion, it is meaningless to say, for instance, that reserves are insufficient or that a central bank suffers from a loss of reserves: Under a fixed-rate system, the quantity of money has to be adjusted to the balance of payments, that is to the flow of reserves. Both Mises and Mundell would agree on that.

According to Mundell's models, an excessive creation of money in country A has the following consequences:

- A flow of money from A to B (which is wrongly called a balance of payments deficit of country A, because its counterpart is necessarily a deficit in the trade balance and/or the capital balance).
- An inflation in the whole monetary zone of fixed rates.
- A decrease in all real cash balances.
- An increase in the nominal rate of interest, a decrease in the marginal productivity of capital and, therefore, a decrease in the real rate of interest.

This latter aspect is particularly important. It is not considered by Austrian economists, but it could be incorporated without problem into the processes described by them, for instance in the Austrian theory of the business cycle. According to Austrian economists, interest rates are decreasing at the beginning of a business cycle when there is an excessive expansion of money substitutes. But this change is not the same as the one which is considered by Mundell and which is permanent as long as inflation persists. However, both kinds of change in interest rates are compatible. Once more, both approaches are more complementary than conflicting.

The analysis of the working of a flexible rate system is a mere application of the general theory of prices: The exchange rate (the price) adjusts to the evolution of supplies and demands for the concerned currencies. Contrary to the usual prejudice, the change in the exchange rate is not linked to the changes in the trade balance. Here again, the Mises and the Mundell approaches could be reconciled.

3. CONCLUDING REMARKS

As mentioned at the beginning of the chapter, it would be too demanding to try to compare all the aspects of the Austrian and the Chicago approaches of monetary problems and we preferred to focus on some fundamentals of these approaches. However, let us just add some remarks about two topics we have more or less neglected.

The first topic is the choice of a monetary system. As already stressed, modern monetary systems are national, public and hierarchical. Austrians object to all these characteristics and make a plea for different systems. Currency competition, in their opinion, would allow people to select the best systems and they would, most probably, be different from existing systems. Obviously, they would not be national or public since, by definition, there would not be any interference from national governments. As regards the hierarchical characteristic, it is more difficult to imagine the possible outcome and only experience could bring the necessary information. However, considering both the existing historical experiences and economic theory, there are reasons to believe that non-hierarchical systems would emerge. In fact, in a non-hierarchical system, money is produced by a cartel of producers who are, each of them, responsible for maintaining the good quality of their currency (normally by giving convertibility guarantees, for instance in terms of gold or any other commodity). If ever they over-issue money, they bear the risk of bankruptcy, so there is a powerful adjustment process inside the monetary system.

Chicagoans are not much interested by such problems and they prefer to focus on the working of existing monetary systems and on the best policies to be adopted. Thus, they are concerned with the definition of the best monetary rules and, from this point of view, the borders between Chicagoans and other mainstream economists tend to blur. Or they care about the choice of fixed vs. flexible exchange rate systems between monetary systems that are national, public and hierarchical. The theory of optimum currency areas, initiated by Mundell and developed by many Chicago and non-Chicago economists, is part of this research.

Now, if a Chicagoan were asked to imagine monetary systems different from the existing ones, would he not be close to Austrians? And, similarly, if an Austrian were asked to define the best possible monetary policy to be adopted within the context of existing monetary systems, would he not be close to Chicagoans? In spite of his hostility to fiat money, he would probably prefer a monetary rule to a discretionary monetary management by the governor of a central bank.

Obviously, the second important topic, which ought to be considered more fully, is the business cycle. As already mentioned and is well known, the Austrian theory is a theory of capital and a theory of the structure of production, whereas the monetarist theory is more strictly a monetary theory. However, they may be reconciled to some extent. In fact, both theories are monetary theories of the business cycle (and not real theories), they are concerned with the problem of an excessive production of money and they can be interpreted as theories that explain how relative prices are distorted by the errors in information brought about by monetary mismanagement. For Austrians the main distortions are those that concern the rate of interest and the structure of production. For Chicagoans, the main distortions are those that concern wages and consumer prices, but also interest rates. But all these distortions may exist over the business cycle and they may be more or less present in actual sequences.

NOTES

1. Text prepared for the Conference, "The Austrian School of Economics," University of Alberta, The Wirth Institute for Austrian and Central European Studies, Edmonton, Canada, 7–8 October 2005.
2. In the present chapter all quotations from Mises are from Mises (1998).
3. I believe that a fractional reserve system has been freely selected in the past, because it is a simple way to pay for the services offered by the issuers of "gold certificates." Compare with Salin (1998).
4. Modern monetary systems are national, public and hierarchical: A public central bank controls money creation within the frontiers of a nation-state or a group of nation-states. None of these characteristics is necessary – quite the contrary – for the "good" working of a monetary system.

5. However, this apparently limited role of competition may be mainly the consequence of the fact there are legal restrictions to competition, for instance because there are legal tender laws in most countries and because taxes have to be paid with the national currency.
6. We have an illustration of this phenomenon with the euro. A significant number of people have for long needed to convert euro prices in terms of their former national currency in order to understand a price.
7. According to Mises, inflation and deflation are not "praxeological concepts" (p. 419) but only pragmatic concepts if inflation is defined as an increase in nominal prices and not as an increase in the quantity of money. However, as already stated, each individual has his own implicit price index, which is an evaluation of the "personal" rate of inflation and his demand for money depends on his own expected rate of inflation. In that sense, inflation at the microeconomic level is a praxeological concept, if it is defined as the estimated change in the purchasing power of the cash balances held by an individual.
8. One may have the feeling that the fundamental distinction between real and nominal balances is not always clearly done by Mises, just because he dares not use the usual concepts. However, he implicitly uses, for instance, the concept of real balances (which implies some notion of the price level). As an example, he mentions "the exchange ratio between money and the vendible goods" (p. 399), which is the general price level (or its reverse).
9. By the way, Mises did not give too much attention to flexible rates. He focused on the working of a gold standard considered as the "normal" monetary system.
10. See Mises (p. 456): "Credit expansion in A makes prices rise, and short term interest rates drop in A, while prices and interest rates in B remain unchanged."

13. From the financial crisis to the debt crises[1]

The financial crisis that began in 2007–2008 has generally been considered as an illustration of the fact that capitalism is fundamentally unstable, which implies that only state interventionism could make it possible to get out of the crisis and to avoid new crises. Moreover, many people have quite often expressed the view that this crisis was a symptom of the immoral nature of capitalism, since greedy bankers have taken too many risks in order to maximize their profits. Although these ideas are widely held, they are radically wrong and one ought to draw a completely different lesson from the recent crisis. In fact, the crisis is a consequence of state interventionism and governments ought to be considered as the only guilty ones. As a consequence, it is obvious that it is not justified to impose more regulations on financial markets.

There are numerous and complex phenomena that played a role in the arrival and the development of the crisis, but one can find a common characteristic in all of them, namely that they are consequences of a lack of capitalism in the modern world. More precisely, there is a major factor of the crisis, which is the monetary policy that has been implemented in the US and in many other countries at the beginning of the twenty-first century. But other factors – which are also linked to state interventionism – could not have played any role without this destabilizing monetary policy.[2] It is unfortunate that most people and governments have misinterpreted the real nature of the crisis so that the policies that have been implemented, far from helping economic recovery, have prevented it and have brought about a new series of economic problems: the debt crises.

1. MONETARY POLICY, THE MAIN CAUSE OF THE CRISIS

The main cause of the recent crisis has been the extraordinary variability of US monetary policy during the first years of the twenty-first century. Now, it is obvious that monetary policy is decided by public monetary authorities and not by markets. Thus, The Federal Reserve System (the

Fed) moved its main interest rate – the so-called federal funds interest rate – from 6.5 percent in 2000 to 1.75 percent at the end of 2001 and 1 percent in 2003. Then there was a slow increase of the rate beginning in 2004, reaching 4.5 percent in 2006. During the whole period of low interest rates and easy financing, the whole world was overcrowded by liquidities, the more so that many central banks decided on very expansionary monetary policies. In order to benefit from this outstanding opportunity for easy profits, financial organizations accepted to lend money to borrowers who were less and less reliable, as was clearly evidenced by the crisis of the "subprimes," which were credits granted to borrowers who did not meet the best criteria of credit-worthiness. When more normal interest rates returned, the excess of the past appeared in full light: the burst of the "financial bubble" occurred.

Now, it may be useful to introduce some remarks about economic theory. In fact, commentators have generally stressed that the crisis has been proof of the validity of John Maynard Keynes' economics vs. the monetarism of Milton Friedman, which is more than debatable. In fact, Keynes has not really explained the causes of economic crises and, if ever he has tried, it is only to be critical of what appeared to him as an excess quantity of savings. In reality, it is exactly the contrary that has happened, since – as we underline below – it is the lack of voluntary savings which is at the root of the crisis. Keynes was mainly interested in designing policies to be implemented whenever there is an economic recession and his prescriptions are not only debatable, they are dangerous, as we will see.

As regards Friedman, he was mainly interested in the link that exists between money creation and inflation, which is legitimate. But his approach, as the one of Keynes, remained an approach in global terms (national income or total demand for Keynes, the quantity of money or the rate of inflation for Friedman). But people have generally forgotten that there is another school of thought, the so-called "Austrian school", the business cycle theory of which has been developed principally by Ludwig von Mises and Friedrich Hayek. Their theory of the business cycle is, in our opinion, the only one that makes it possible to explain the recent crisis, as well as the other economic crises of modern times. The Austrians have stressed that monetary creation necessarily implies, in the monetary systems of our time, a corresponding and artificial creation of credits which are not based on what individuals really want to save, but are created from nothing! Therefore, monetary policy is producing a contradiction between the ratio of savings to consumption desired by individuals and the one that is imposed by monetary authorities under the pretext of stimulating the economy via an excessive distribution of money and credits.

We personally believe that this problem must be linked to another one, which has already been quoted, namely that savings are particularly low in most great countries. Savings remain abundant in some emergent countries, such as China, in which individuals accumulate capital in order to finance their future retirement pensions, their health or education expenditures. These countries have such a high rate of savings that they can even lend resources to countries like the US. But this is not enough to get the amount of investments necessary to reach a sufficiently high rate of growth, so that monetary authorities try to compensate for this lack of savings by the destabilizing creation of money and artificial credits. Now, the reason why individuals save so little is mainly because the tax systems of our time are destroying the incentives to accumulate capital.[3]

In other words, governments have destroyed what is the main feature of a capitalist system, namely a system in which there are legitimate property rights – which is the very foundation of responsibility – and a high propensity to save. So doing, governments are destroying a fundamental characteristic of human beings, since savings are the way by which people are able to obtain future living conditions closer to what they desire. But, instead of making possible a return to a real capitalism, they wrongly believe that they can compensate the lack of voluntary savings via the creation of fake savings. This is the great illusion of our time, which puts a brake on economic growth and constitutes a major factor of economic instability.

In order to create an expansionary monetary policy, monetary authorities impose interest rates much lower than those that would normally be determined on markets. They induce borrowers to finance investments that are not profitable enough or too risky. Let us not forget that the interest rate is the price of time. Distorting the determination of such an important price obviously creates disasters. Let us stress again that monetary policy is made by monetary authorities and it is therefore absurd to pretend that it is the free working of markets that produces monetary instability and creates distortions in productive structures and price structures.

2. THE OTHER CAUSES OF THE ECONOMIC CRISIS

This process of destruction of information (about the normal long-run real interest rate) and of creation of instability has been made worse by three phenomena also linked to state intervention, but which could not have happened without the expansionary monetary policy. These are discussed below.

2.1 The Housing Policy in the United States

Very strong public pressures were made on credit organizations in order for them to agree on granting credits to households who were not normally creditworthy, under the pretext that they would be accused of discriminating between borrowers. This was the origin of the famous "subprime" problem. The Fed itself has produced a manual intended at determining banks' policies, in which it was asked not to use "out of fashion" criteria, among which the ratio between the amount of reimbursement and incomes or the historical recollection of previous credits of those asking credits. The Department of Justice has even sued credit organizations considered as guilty, because they had not accepted to grant credits to would-be borrowers, as if it was not precisely their very professional role to discriminate between those to whom it is possible to grant a credit and those who must not obtain credit! One even came to consider that borrowers gave sufficient guarantees if they promised to participate in programs giving advice to borrowers. This has obviously worsened the problem of "subprimes." Now, as a great part of these credits had variable rates, borrowers met difficulties when interest rates rose again. Thus the state has deliberately cheated people who were not well informed about the working of financial markets and about the risks they might bear.

On the other hand, the two huge suppliers of credit subprime, Fannie May and Freddie Mac – initially created by the American government – benefited from privileged state guarantees, which induced them to take highly excessive risks.

2.2 Regulations

It has often been said that banking and financial deregulations were a major cause of the crisis because they made it possible for banks to take too many risks. On the other hand, it is also said that there is a specific characteristic of financial systems, namely that there would be a "systemic risk," which means that the failure of one or several large banks could create a "domino effect" and the burst of the whole financial system. But it is not at all certain that such a risk prevails more in the financial system than in any other field. In fact there is a real paradox: The policy measures that have been taken under the pretext of avoiding the supposed systemic risk are precisely those that create a systemic risk, particularly because it is considered that one of the main roles of a central bank is to be a "lender of last resort".

In fact, the feeling of responsibility concerning risk is diminished because it is implicitly admitted that public authorities do not allow important bank failures without reacting (which has been largely confirmed in the past by the behavior of monetary authorities in the US and elsewhere, during the recent financial crisis and other previous ones). Indeed, only a part of the banking system was fragile, as it should be obvious from the fact that some banks – which were better managed – could buy those that were failing. Unhappily, whenever monetary and public authorities are saving banks, it reinforces the idea – commonly accepted in our time – that one must not accept bank failures, particularly when banks are very big (the famous "too big to fail"). This does create *irresponsibility*. The following message is implicitly sent to banks: "You can take excessive risks and get a return, but we will save you if ever you have problems. You did earn profits and you distributed them, but when you have the risk of losses, we will save you." This is harmful, because in any activity failures have a fundamental adjustment role.

Moreover, financial regulation has been by itself a source of perverse effects. Such is the case, for instance, of the obligation imposed to banks by the Basel II agreement to maintain a ratio of equity capital equal to 8 percent. Given the very high profit opportunities due to the Fed's policy of low interest rates, banks wanted to develop their credits as much as possible, while respecting the official ratio. To this aim, they looked for possibilities to circumvent regulations – as is always the case – by shifting part of their assets to other organizations, such as investment funds and SIVs (special investment vehicles). Part of the credits granted by banks thus disappeared from their balance sheets, which made it possible for them to increase their credits while apparently respecting the existing regulation.

It is true that one may consider as desirable that equity capital be "sufficient" in comparison with loanable funds. In fact, in the nineteenth century, the equity capital of banks amounted to about 50 to 80 percent of their balance sheet: Bankers were lending funds which belonged to them or which belonged to a limited number of shareholders. The high (and desired) ratio of equity capital did constitute a tremendous guarantee of stability for shareholders as well as for the customers of the banks. At that time bankers were real capitalists – namely, owners of capital – and, as such, they were responsible. In the capitalist world of the nineteenth century – more stable than the present financial world – bank credit was the outcome of decisions taken by the shareholders of banks. In the statist world of our time, it is exactly the contrary: one is imposing arbitrarily a ratio of equity capital which is only formally miming a real capitalist world; but it is at the origin of financial bubbles. Credit organizations maximize the amount of their credits and after that they try, through various manipulations, to get a ratio of equity capital that corresponds to existing regulations. But a regulation that imposes a result will never replace the free play of decisions taken by responsible human beings (which means capitalists). This is why the calls for more regulation of financial markets are more than debatable.

2.3 Governance Problems of Banks

In our time, it has been thought possible to base economic development on credit rather than on equity capital. Moreover, as we have already seen, a great part of this credit comes from an *ex nihilo* creation, namely the expansionary monetary policy, and not from voluntary savings. Simultaneously, the decline of capitalism – which is itself quite often caused by state interventionism – had the consequence that big banks are no longer managed by capitalists (owners of the capital), but by managers who are wage earners and who, having not to bear the risks specifically borne by shareholders, are induced to maximize short-run profits in order to get large bonuses. Therefore, it is not the normal working of capitalism that led to excessive risk taking, but on the contrary, a lack of capitalism. As a consequence, instead of increasing regulations of financial activities, it would be much more preferable to make possible a real return to capitalism via tax and institutional reforms, which would avoid putting a brake on the accumulation of capital and, more precisely, the development of equity capital.

Thus, if one can be critical of financial institutions for having not been more cautious, one has also to understand that such a behavior has been the outcome of the institutional structures of our time. But this also reflects the fact that information can never be perfect: a capitalist system is not perfectly stable, but it is more stable than a centralized public system. Therefore, instead of being critical of a supposed instability of financial capitalism, one ought to be critical of the extraordinary shortcomings of monetary policies. One could also regret that the managers of big banks had not been more lucid and had not better evaluated the risks they were taking in a world in which monetary policy is fundamentally destabilizing. But it is precisely and above all this destabilizing characteristic of monetary policies about which one ought to lament. Therefore, we ought to stop putting a wrong trial on capitalism and on the contrary to look for the best means to free financial markets from state ascendancy.

3. POLICIES AIMING AT COMING OUT OF THE CRISIS

As we have seen, the causes of the crisis have been linked to state interventionism and it is a pity that markets have not been allowed to work normally.

Therefore, solving the crisis can be better done by markets – which are the best way to make adjustments – than by governments. Markets have been disturbed by many various policies, which have introduced very large disequilibria in economic processes and the only way to correct what has happened would be to let markets make the necessary adjustments, which they are able to do. However, one cannot rebuild the past: Disequilibria have been created and one has to bear the consequences. But, unhappily, most policies that have been decided under the pretext of coming out of the crisis have been exactly the contrary of what ought to be done.

As already stressed, for most commentators the only relevant debate was between Keynesians and monetarists, and they considered that Keynesians gave the best explanation of the crisis and of the policies necessary to get out of it. But they were mainly ignorant of the only theory that could explain the crisis, namely the Austrian theory of the business cycle. Contrary to the Keynesian approach – and the monetarist one – this theory does not consider only global variables – such as national income, aggregate demand or the quantity of money – it stresses the importance of structural distortions. By distributing credits of monetary origin that do not correspond to any voluntary savings, monetary authorities induce changes in the allocation of factors of production and in the structure of production, as producers choose production processes of longer duration because of the low interest rates. This is important because it means that the real problems to be solved are structural problems and not problems related to the level of aggregate variables. Having been unable to adopt a correct analysis of the crisis, governments have in fact decided harmful policies. Such is the case with the so-called recovery policies that consist of wasting resources, laxist monetary policies and policies aiming at reinforcing regulations in the financial sector, in spite of the fact this sector is already, globally, one of the most regulated.

3.1 Recovery Policies

The financial crisis, endured in a great number of countries, has caused a slowdown of economic activity, which can be explained by the need to overcome the errors of the past, implying the suppression of distortions introduced in productive structures. But governments have tried to answer to this situation by launching "recovery plans" according to the traditional prescriptions of the Keynesian theory. If ever they had been purely passive, they could have been blamed as far as all citizens have been educated with the idea that public authorities have the essential duty to bring about prosperity and that they can reach this target. It is generally admitted that the modern state has to take care of so-called stabilization policies and growth policies and that no one else – and certainly not "the market" – could do it. However, in spite of these dominant views, the best way to get out of such a crisis would be to rely on adjustment by markets. But political action is both easily understandable and terrible: a politician is, at the limit, totally unconcerned by the fact that recovery measures are efficient or not, since economic phenomena are so complex that in any case public opinion will be unable to appreciate to what extent the decisions taken had played a positive or negative role. How could it be possible in the future to evaluate whether growth would have been more or less important without the economic policies taken previously?

As politicians care only about "doing something," this is easy as they can use a simple rule, inspired by Keynesian economics: In order to stimulate economic activity, one has to increase total demand and the best way of doing this consists of increasing public spending, stimulating consumption or creating new liquidities. Unhappily, these ideas are completely wrong and without any logical relation to the real situation. In fact, in any field one can find a solution to a problem only if one knows its causes. Now, we know that the financial and economic crisis did not stem from a lack of total demand, but from completely different factors, which we have stressed above.

During the whole period of low interest rates, the world was overrun by abundant liquidities and it was easy to finance all sorts of projects that were not actually profitable. This harmful monetary policy has caused deep changes in productive structures. Malinvestment in certain sectors – for instance, housing – became visible when one came back to more realistic monetary conditions. The problem to be solved therefore was not a global problem – which could be solved, for instance, by increasing total demand – but a structural problem.

The economic crisis has the necessary role to restore equilibrium by coming back to the productive structures that would have prevailed without the unstable monetary policies. Thus, failures of firms contribute to this cleaning up by making it possible to put an end to the waste of resources due to bad investment and management choices. Contrary to what one is tempted to think, they have a creative role and not a destructive one. Maintaining the activity of firms that cannot be profitable would only perpetuate wrong choices, while failures make it possible to shift factors of production towards owners and managers who will better know how to use them. This is why the best recovery policy consists in letting markets play their role in economic adjustments.

It is therefore paradoxical and even tragic that the financial and economic crisis be attributed to the free working of markets, although it has been caused by an unstable monetary policy, and that one is waiting for further interventionist measures instead of being confident in the working of markets. Considering the frequent anti-capitalist mentality of public opinion, one can understand that politicians are tempted to claim that they are the only ones able to save the economy. But the victims of such a claim are the citizens. All over the world governments have spent billions of dollars and euros to save failing banks, to help badly managed firms, to artificially increase the purchasing power of people, in spite of the fact they do not know which adjustments are necessary in the productive structure. But, in so doing they do not create any new wealth, quite the contrary: they just shift resources owned by citizens. In order to finance their expenditures, they increase taxes – thus diminishing the purchasing power of people – or they borrow – thus limiting resources available for investment. Therefore, they do not create any additional total demand just because it is logically impossible; but they take out resources from those who have created them and who would have been able to use them in a responsible way, and they grant them to politicians and bureaucrats who decide the use of these resources in an irresponsible way, since they are not using their own resources and they do not bear the consequences of their choices. Thus, there is a waste of resources and, on the other hand, a brake on the adjustments that would make it possible to go back to productive structures coherent with the real wants of people.

3.2 Monetary Policy

Another answer to the economic crisis has consisted of adopting again a very expansionary monetary policy because the crisis implied a decrease in the amount of credits after the great excess of debt that prevailed before. Therefore, firms have more difficulties in financing their investments. Simultaneously, the recovery policies imply a dramatic increase in public debt. How to meet these demands for financing? Since voluntary savings remain insufficient, as already stressed, one takes the way, once more, of monetary creation and the creation of artificial savings. In so doing, one does not solve the real, deep problems, but runs the risk of a new crisis. From this point of view one may be anxious when considering the very laxist monetary policies of many large countries.

3.3 Regulations

Those who claim that the crisis was caused by the fact that markets were free to work without sufficient regulations, obviously draw the conclusion that the financial sector has to be more regulated. This is why there is a lot of new regulations in many countries. These measures are certainly a wrong answer to the crisis, since it was not caused by a lack of regulation, quite the contrary. Therefore, by introducing more regulations, one may diminish the capacity of markets to make adjustments and to play their role in the circulation of savings.

Let us take as an example a problem that has been widely debated, that of the bonuses of traders. It has been said that traders have been induced to take too-risky decisions because, by increasing the amount of deals, they could increase their bonuses. This risk is real, but, on the other hand, bonuses constitute a system of incentives that induces traders to take the best decisions (and this is, by the way, the reason why they were invented). Therefore, it is necessary to make an arbitrage between both contradictory requirements and to find the optimal bonus policy. But there are two ways to do it. In a free system, it is obviously in the interest of the owners of banks to find the optimal mix and to define the best way to determine bonuses. But it is necessary to experiment and to progressively correct the rules according to the experience obtained. Moreover, the rules to be adopted are not necessarily the same ones according to the concerned activities and banks. The great merit of a system of private rules comes from the fact it is evolutionary and diversified. When the bonus policy is decided by a public regulation, it is the same for everyone. One thus lacks the possibility to experiment and to make changes in rules according to the lessons of the past. Moreover, these rules are decided by people who are not responsible, since they do not bear the consequences of their decisions. In fact, they decide more according to the prejudices of public opinion than according to what would allow an optimal working of markets.

4. FROM THE DEBT CRISIS TO AUSTERITY POLICIES

A great number of governments, especially in Europe, have decided on a so-called "austerity policy" in recent years in order to solve or to avoid a "debt crisis" such as the one that has occurred in some countries of the south of Europe. Let us define – at least provisionally – an austerity policy as a policy aiming at reducing the public deficit and, possibly, reducing the amount of public debt.

4.1 The Economic Background of Austerity Policies

The current economic situation of most European countries is the outcome of three different, but inter-related, phenomena:[4]

1. The long-run "eurosclerosis."
2. The recent financial crisis.
3. The debt crisis.

Countries that suffer from "eurosclerosis" are countries in which there has been, for several decades, a low rate of economic growth and a high rate of unemployment.

Such a long-lasting situation may seem strange in countries that are open not only to other European countries but to the whole world; countries with a well-educated labor force and entrepreneurial traditions. Therefore, only one possible explanation can be given to this state of affairs: misguided economic policies prevent individuals from creating wealth as efficiently as they could. More precisely, high levels of taxation and contributions to the welfare state system, as well as innumerable regulations, especially on the labor market, can be considered as the main factors of this situation.

The harmful consequences of taxation[5] are obvious: taxation destroys the incentives to work, to innovate, to save or to invest. In fact there is a double process of destruction. First, the higher the tax rate, the lower the propensity of taxpayers to create wealth. And as most taxes – income tax, VAT, contributions to so-called social welfare systems – are in fact taken off from the same tax base – namely, the value added produced by firms – taxes are a particular deterrent in countries with a high amount of taxation. In particular, the system can be interpreted as if it was told to entrepreneurs: "Invest, produce, hire workers; if you fail, you are responsible and you lose the whole of what you have achieved. But if you are successful, the state will take the greatest part of the wealth you may have created." It may also be emphasized that present tax systems are particularly introducing a bias in the choice between the future and the present. They are dissuading people from saving because of the multiplicity of taxes on capital, the return of capital or the transmission of capital, but also because the income tax or VAT are based not only on resources that are consumed, but also on resources that are saved (that is, those that will be reintroduced into the economic circuit).[6] It is also well known that a pay-as-you-go pension system does not encourage individuals to save as much as they would do with a capitalization system. As there is no growth without accumulation of capital, the tax and welfare systems can be considered as important brakes to growth.

Second, regulations also play a negative role by decreasing the flexibility of markets and introducing an additional degree of risk (since the state can add new and paralyzing regulations at any time and in a completely discretionary way). This is particularly noticeable as regards the labor market.

Thus, entrepreneurs are more reluctant to hire workers as it becomes more difficult to fire them when necessary or desired.

It is in such a context that the financial crisis came about, and it added a further cause of low – or even negative – growth and high unemployment.

4.2 The Role of Savings

As emphasized, in recent years European countries have suffered both from the long-term "eurosclerosis" problem and from the financial crisis. Both phenomena are related to some extent since one can find a common cause of both, namely the lack of voluntary savings. We have already said that modern tax and welfare systems are over-taxing savings in comparison to consumption, thus slowing down the accumulation of capital. But it can also be said that this lack of savings was the deep-rooted cause of the financial crisis. It is true that part of this lack of savings – which is particularly obvious in the US – has been compensated by borrowing from some emergent countries in which the rate of savings is very high (such as China). But this lack of savings may have also caused monetary authorities to choose expansionary monetary policies, thus creating conditions for a business cycle. In a world with abundant voluntary savings, there would be a more rapid accumulation of capital, therefore a higher rate of growth and no incentive for expansionary monetary policies, thus no business cycle. There is then a strong relation between the long-run situation and the business cycle, which also means that policy reforms aiming at restoring the propensity of individuals to save would entail both the end of the business cycle and long-run prosperity.

It is paradoxical that, despite this, people accept without any rigorous analysis the idea that whenever there is an economic crisis governments must apply Keynesian solutions (that is, to increase total demand, in particular consumption and public expenditures). In fact, we know from the Austrian theory of the business cycle that the problem to be solved is not a global problem (in terms of total demand for instance) but a structural problem, which, in fact, can be solved only by letting markets do the necessary adjustments in price structures and productive structures. Moreover, the roots of the financial and economic crisis are exactly the contrary of what Keynesian economists are usually assuming. According to Keynes, unemployment occurs for very specific reasons. He assumed that there was an excess of savings over investment for some unexplained reason (the "animal spirits" of entrepreneurs). In such a case, according to traditional classical economics, the flexibility of interest rates would be the re-equilibrating instrument: a decrease in interest rates induces an increase in investments and a decrease in savings. But, according to Keynesians, such a market adjustment does not take place for very specific (and arbitrarily designed) reasons: They assume that – for some unknown reason – investments become inelastic to interest rates and/or that individuals keep so-called "idle cash reserves," (that is, they keep money cash balances instead of investing them). However, there is no reason to believe that any rational human being might keep useless cash balances (idle cash reserves) instead of spending them for present consumption or future consumption via the purchase of financial assets.

Unfortunately, most governments did adopt Keynesian economic policies under the pretext that they might accelerate economic recovery after the financial and economic crisis. But these spending policies have had quite different consequences: huge deficits, debt crises and no economic recovery. This is not surprising, since it is an illusion to believe that it is possible to increase "aggregate demand" at will, at least if one considers real demand and not nominal demand. Additional real public expenditures are necessarily made at the expense of private expenditures, either if they are financed via taxes or via borrowing. Moreover, there is a loss of efficiency when resources are thus shifted from those who had created them, and are responsible as owners of them, to politicians and bureaucrats who have a very limited responsibility and do not care much about a possible waste of resources. In fact, it may be considered that Keynesian recipes have only been a pretext to justify public deficits, which are always desired by governments, because they make it possible to give voters present benefits, whereas the cost is shifted to the future.

4.3 The Debt Crisis and Austerity Policies

Unfortunately, this future is not far away and it is striking to see that, some months after having launched their huge spending policies, governments are having difficulties in reimbursing their debts, are afraid of the burden of the debt and deem it necessary to adopt so-called austerity policies.[7]

When speaking of austerity, people have the feeling that one enters into a period in which the standard of living of individuals will decrease. In fact, "austerity policy" is just a policy of reducing the government budget deficit. But the very name implies a Keynesian-type approach: It is feared that the reduction of the public budget deficit may decrease total demand and, therefore, decrease production and incomes. Therefore, it would be preferable not to use the term austerity policy but to label it for what it is: "government budget deficit reducing policy."

Given the desirable nature of government budget deficits for Keynesians, why do they care about them and why should they adopt an austerity policy? In fact, they consider that there is a trade-off between two consequences of budget deficits:

1. The positive consequence, in their opinion, comes from the fact it is considered as boosting total demand and the economy.
2. The negative consequence is the fact that financial markets lose confidence in the capacity of the government to reimburse its debt and to pay interest. In such a case, interest rates rise, which increases the burden of the debt and may push the country – or, rather, its government – into a vicious circle of debt increases and interest rate increases. Meanwhile, the national prestige may suffer if public assets are ever downgraded by ratings agencies. Governments also fear that they lose "national independence" in the design of their economic policies if they ever have to accept financing from the International Monetary Fund (IMF) or European institutions.

In the past, it was considered that the main trade-off in designing economic policies was the one made famous by the Phillips curve, the trade-off between unemployment and inflation, until Friedman demonstrated that such a trade-off could exist only in the short-run and that the long-run effects of an expansionary monetary policy were harmful. Now, the fashionable trade-off is between, on the one hand, recovery policy (via a government budget deficit) and, on the other hand, a reduction of the government public deficit, both to get more or less rapidly low interest rates to finance the deficit and to preserve national independence. It is not surprising if there is a hot debate about austerity policies in many European countries, since most people are more or less explicitly Keynesians and this trade-off is very embarrassing for them. Many among them consider that it would be regrettable to "kill growth" by reducing the public deficit in order to comply with the wants of the disliked financial sector.

There is also a contradiction in the present policies supported by Keynesians (and, therefore, most governments). They do not care about the fact that financing the budget deficit implies a shift of financing resources from private investment, because they implicitly and wrongly assume that there is an excess of savings over investment. But, if ever it was the case – which one ought to deny – why would it be necessary to implement an expansionary monetary policy? In fact, such a monetary policy is desired not because people believe that there are not enough cash balances, but because they feel that the corresponding credits, artificially created, make it possible to finance additional investments. But why should it be necessary to create these artificial savings if there are too many savings in the economy?

The Austrian school of economists don't have to solve such problems: There is no trade-off between the budget deficit and some other economic target and their policy recommendations would be quite different, as we will see in the next section.

4.4 Which Austerity Policy and Which Policy Mix?

Following the financial and economic crisis, the policy mix adopted in many countries has been:

- An additional public deficit via increased expenditure.
- An expansionary monetary policy.

Unfortunately, as already stressed, the public deficit is unable to contribute to the economic recovery and it adds new distortions to the structure of production, since the goods and services demanded by the public sector are probably not the same as the ones that would have been desired by the private sector in the absence of this deficit and which may prevail in the long run. As regards the expansionary monetary policy, we do know that it is only a destructive illusion that creates the risk of another business cycle in the future. Therefore, since the main problems are sectoral problems and not global problems (such as a lack of total demand), the best policy mix would be:

- No budget deficit, but letting markets make the necessary adjustments in the structures of production and the structures of prices.
- No money creation.

Regrettably, after the instability introduced by monetary authorities at the beginning of the twenty-first century, due to their expansionary monetary policy public authorities have added a new source of instability created by the variability in their fiscal policies. After the burst of public expenditure, the concern with the public deficit induces unforeseen changes in expenditure, taxation and public borrowing. As a consequence, the instability in interest rates is increased and people are uncertain about the rates of various taxes or the possible creation of new taxes.

The financial and economic crisis is the means by which the economy comes back to the normal long-run structures of production and structures of prices. Similarly, the austerity policy is the means by which a government suppresses the distortions it has introduced in the structures of production and prices via public deficits, which were not sustainable in the long run. Adjustments are always painful, but it is better to accept them or even to desire them rather than postpone the return to equilibrium. It would have been preferable not to have instability in monetary policies and public deficits, but it is impossible to rewrite history. Instead of complaining about the financial and economic crisis or the austerity policy, one ought to complain about the disequilibrium of policies that made them inevitable.

Thus, we are now left with both an economic crisis and a debt crisis and, in order to alleviate the debt crisis, many governments have adopted a so-called austerity policy. However, as is well known, there are two different austerity policies:

1. Decreasing public expenditure (which means austerity for the government and some beneficiaries of public expenditure).
2. Increasing taxes (which means austerity for citizens or at least some of them, such as the richest who have a comparatively lower voting weight).

For a Keynesian, it does not matter much which austerity policy is chosen, since he cares only about the total deficit and not about the consequences of taxes on incentives or the existence of structural distortions. Moreover, as governments usually consider that it is easier to raise taxes than to cut expenditures, they prefer tax increases.

Thus, the favorite policy mix for most governments is:

- An increase in taxes (in particular on high-income taxpayers).
- A small decrease in public expenditure.
- An expansionary monetary policy.

Such a policy mix may lead an economy into a vicious circle, as the increase in taxes may slow down growth, thus reducing public revenue and increasing the public deficit, so that governments may react by deciding an additional increase in taxes.

Contrary to what is usually done, the most efficient policy mix would be the following:

- A huge decrease in public expenditure and welfare payments.
- Tax cuts, in particular by reducing high marginal rates – as it has been steadily recommended by the supporters of "supply-side economics" – and suppressing over-taxation of savings.
- Deregulation (particularly on the labor market).
- No monetary creation.

Such a policy mix would both help solve the long-run eurosclerosis and the exit from the economic and budget crises.

Moreover, European governments of the eurozone are now introducing a "golden rule" for budget management, which would imply that budget deficits be brought back very rapidly to no more than 3 percent of the gross domestic product (GDP), thus re-introducing one of the famous criteria of the Maastricht Treaty. It may be considered that this rule might put a constraint on the temptation of governments to run public deficits. However, it also implies a risk since, because of this rule, a tax-cut policy – which is so highly desirable – may become impossible and governments may even be tempted to increase tax rates in order to comply with the rule in the short run. In fact, whenever there are large tax cuts, public revenues first decrease – so that the government budget deficit increases – during a short period (two to three years) because people need some time to adjust to the new tax rates. Thus the tax base does not increase much during this initial period. But later on the expansionary effect on production makes possible an increase in tax revenue, which compensates even more the decrease in taxes. This process – known as the "Laffer effect" – has occurred in most experiences of large tax cuts, such as the ones made by Ronald Reagan. The pernicious effect of a golden rule has already been experienced with the Maastricht criteria: Several years before the introduction of the euro, governments did not dare to decrease tax rates because they feared a decrease in tax revenues, which would have implied that they did not comply with the public deficit criterion. As a consequence of this obstacle to tax cuts, Europe may long suffer from a situation of steady stagnation. However, it is also true that although a golden rule may have this consequence, it also has the merit of limiting harmful public budget deficits, at least in the long run.

NOTES

1. The present chapter has used parts of two articles: Salin (2011b) and Salin (2013b). The first article has been translated from its original French.
2. These ideas have been explained in detail in Salin (2010).
3. It would be too long to explain, in the present chapter, why most tax systems cause people to choose the present rather than the future (consumption rather than savings). The reasons for this are analyzed in Salin (2014).
4. Even if one may find a lot of similarities as regards the economic situation of most European countries, it is obvious that there are also great differences. We must confess that our statements are mainly inspired by what we know best: the case of France.
5. "Taxation" refers here to the whole set of taxes and contributions of the welfare state system.
6. Contrary to what is usually assumed, VAT is not a tax on consumption, but a tax on

income, as is the so-called income tax. In fact, its name is correct: It is a tax on value added and value added is equal to the sum of all factor incomes. See Chapters 7 and 8 for more on this topic.

7. A specific aspect of this debt crisis is the so-called "euro crisis" (compare with the Appendix in Part III).

14. The future of monetary policies in an online world

The development of e-business in our time has certainly had a deep influence on productive structures. But the increasing role of the internet in trade also could have important consequences in the working of monetary systems. These influences are not yet very visible, although there are already several e-currencies in the world.[1] But they still have a limited role. However, even if one cannot know the specific details of future e-currencies, one may try to determine their main lines. To perform such a task, one must obviously refer to the general theory of money and monetary systems. In fact, one has to take into consideration services offered by money and to try to evaluate how the internet may change the way in which monetary needs are met.

Money is demanded as the good that is the best suited to meet specific needs, those that correspond to the very definition of money. As already mentioned, money can be defined as a "generalized purchasing power;" that is, it can be exchanged (more or less easily) at any time, against anything and with anyone. Therefore, it is money's capacity to be exchanged – its tradability – that gives it value, and which allows it to meet the specific needs of potential traders.

By the way, one can stress that present currencies have a strange characteristic in comparison with previous ones, since they do not have any definition (in terms of some purchasing power). In fact, the currencies which have been used for centuries always had a definition, either because they were commodities (gold, silver, bronze, and so on) that could be exchanged against other commodities according to relative prices easily known by anyone, or because they were given credible exchange guarantees, such as in terms of gold. But such a definition – which survived until March 1968, at least from a purely formal point of view – has disappeared in the present time with the end of the gold convertibility of the dollar. Since then, currencies have had no definition: a pound is a monetary unit produced by the sterling monetary system, controlled by the Bank of England; a euro is a monetary unit produced by the euro system, controlled by the European Central Bank; and so on. But there is no more exchange guarantee against any commodity and the tradability of a currency is no more than an act of faith.

However, with the appearance of e-currencies, we might be concerned again by the role of money, its definition or the ways it is produced. Thus, it may not be by pure chance that some economists go back to an old debate, the one concerning the ways money is issued and, more specifically, the problem of fractional reserves. In fact, it is not an old-fashioned debate, but a modern and important one.

1. MONETARY ACTIVITIES

As a generalized purchasing power, money incorporates two basic characteristics: it makes possible the coincidence between the needs of traders, and it makes possible the transference of purchasing power over time. It is traditionally considered that money plays a third role, that of being a numeraire (a standard of value). In reality, this role is not a necessary component of the definition of money: Any good can play this role and being a numeraire does not give a monetary nature to a good.[2] If the internet had no other consequence than contributing to the creation of a new numeraire, it would not be worthwhile to look after the possible transformations that it could bring to monetary systems. However, in order to really imagine the innovations that the internet could possibly bring, it is important to distinguish several monetary activities that are too often mixed under a general term such as "money creation" or "money production."

1.1 Inventing a Currency

To be sure, the most important invention is certainly that of the "first currency," namely the one that made it possible to shift from a barter economy to a monetary economy. This invention has certainly been one of the most important discoveries in the whole history of humankind, since it made it possible to develop trade and individual specialization. But it is impossible to determine a place and time of birth for this invention. As far as we know, it was not invented by some entrepreneur/innovator, who would surely have spread it over the market and gained profits from it. Currency has certainly developed in a more gradual and spontaneous way. Gains drawn from this invention, instead of being shared between the inventor and the users – as is usually the case for many goods – has thus wholly benefited to the users of money.

Generally speaking, one may consider that monetary innovation has exactly the same characteristics as any other innovation. The profit is the return obtained from innovation and it is quite often possible for the innovator to receive it. But it is particularly difficult in the case of monetary innovation for several reasons. First, any innovation is generally simple in that field, since it is sufficient, in order to create a new currency, either to select a commodity and to give it a monetary role which it has not yet got (one gives, for instance, a monetary role to silver, while until then only gold had been considered as a currency), or to define a new currency by giving an exchange guarantee to monetary units (under the form, for instance, of notes or deposits) against a commodity or a bundle of commodities and, possibly, to give a name to this currency. On the other hand, it is not sufficient to invent a new currency (for instance, a new definition), if it is not perceived as being new and as bringing new advantages which were not available with existing currencies. From this point of view, the inventor of a new currency stumbles against an important obstacle stemming from the fact the use of a currency is cumulative. If a new currency benefits from an excellent definition (it offers an efficient guarantee against any loss of purchasing power in terms of a given bundle of commodities), it is, however, not a true monetary good as long as it has not been held by a sufficient number of people: for example, if I am the only one who holds this "good" currency, it will not give me the exchange services I am expecting. And these services will keep a low value if it is not used by a great number of people, which makes it less desirable.

Therefore, the inventor of a currency has to bear marketing costs. Moreover, it is easy for other persons to imitate him, precisely because the invention of a currency is relatively simple (it just means inventing a definition). Therefore, there is an important risk that a great number of producers of the new currency appear on the market whenever its production could become profitable, which may reduce to zero the part of profits obtained by the initial inventor of this new currency.

Obviously, one might think that, in order to stimulate innovation in this field, it would be wishful that the inventors of new currencies be entitled to get patents. But the very existence of patents is disputable, since it means limiting the freedom to enter into a market, it gives the inventor rights over other persons. In other words, property rights have to be defined when there is scarcity, so that exclusion is possible and necessary. For instance, if ever I own a piece of land, anyone else is excluded from using it. But, if ever I invent a specific production process or a specific good, no one can be deprived from the use of his own mind. At any rate and as we see later on, it is not as easy to be an imitator than it may seem at first sight.

Inventing a currency is still simpler in our time, since one generally admits that it is even not necessary to care about selecting a specific commodity to define money or to give money exchange guarantees against commodities. The inventor of a currency has nothing more to do than choosing a name, and instead of defining this currency he just has to decide who will be allowed to produce it. The euro cannot be defined otherwise than as the euro! And it is a currency not because of its own monetary characteristics, but because of a legal obligation to consider it as a currency. In other words, the patents for inventing new currencies do exist in our time, but they benefit only to public producers. In fact, the only producers who can produce euros are those who are allowed to do so as members of the European monetary cartel (that is, the banks authorized by the national central banks, which are themselves members of the European system of central banks).

Obviously, it is difficult to invent e-currencies according to such schemes, inasmuch as only the governments have the possibility to invent currencies deprived of any definition, and the production and use of which are regulated and protected. But, as regards the private inventor of an e-currency, in order to get a profit, he may have to overcome the obstacles we have just mentioned.

1.2 New Forms of Money

The second monetary activity does not consist of inventing a new currency, but of inventing *new forms of money* for existing currencies, which obviously implies making it easy to exchange one form against another one. It is the case, for instance, when money takes the form of circulating gold coins and one invents gold certificates (quite often called bank notes): instead of letting gold circulate, one uses, as circulating money, property rights on the gold deposited in the vaults of the producer of gold certificates. The same sort of change occurs whenever one is inventing bank deposits or, nowadays, electronic entries.

Inventing new forms of money involves problems very similar to those implied by the invention of a new currency. It is in fact difficult for the inventor to induce or oblige others to recognize his property right on the invention and, therefore, to receive the profits obtained through his innovation. As far as this new form of money is more "efficient" than the previous ones – it is produced at a lower cost and/or it brings additional services – the corresponding gain is shared between the producers and the users of this currency.

1.3 Production of Additional Units

The third monetary activity is the *production of additional units* of an existing currency and this activity must absolutely be distinguished from the previous ones. It does not correspond to any innovation and, strictly speaking, it ought not to be considered as a source of profit (since profit is, strictly speaking, the return obtained from entrepreneurship), but rather as a source of privilege rents, as we will see.

As far as this production is costly, the costs of production have to be borne, which means that the owners of the corresponding resources must receive a return for their productive contribution (for instance, wages for those who print bank notes).[3] But several different assumptions have to be carefully distinguished.

Let us assume that we are in a world in which there is a currency called the "trick," defined by a given weight of gold (for instance, 1 trick = 1 ounce of gold). The producers of this currency have given a convertibility guarantee in terms of gold at a fixed price. Imagine first that the quantity of money in the world – that is, the number of units of tricks, themselves representing property rights on an identical number of ounces of gold – remains absolutely constant over time, for one reason or another.[4] If real growth exists in the world, so that the demand for real cash balances is increasing, this need for additional money units will be met by the real cash balance effect. The additional demand for money necessarily corresponds to an excess supply of commodities.[5] The consequence is an increase in the price of money against commodities (that is, a decrease in the monetary price of commodities, which is generally called a deflation). A steady deflation is certainly the best way to meet the needs of an increasing demand for real cash balances. A constant nominal quantity of money is perfectly compatible with increasing real transactions, since the nominal value of each transaction is diminishing.

In such a case, by assumption, there is no creation of additional nominal cash balances (namely, of tricks). The quantity of tricks initially issued is sufficient to meet all the needs for money, eternally.[6] But obviously, as far as the prices of commodities in terms of tricks are steadily decreasing, it is necessary to issue notes with smaller and smaller denominations (except in the case of a totally electronic currency, such as the bitcoin). The producers of these monetary goods have to be paid in order to cover their costs of production. As already stressed, this does not normally give way to the collection of a profit, but only to the normal reward for productive services. Moreover, it is obvious that the steady decrease in prices does not imply any cost as far as deposit money is concerned: It is no more expensive to record a deposit of 10 tricks than a deposit with a value of one tenth of a trick.

A completely different assumption is the one in which the issuers of money increase the quantity of money (that is, at each period they create additional monetary units). If the rate of growth of the quantity of money is higher than the rate of growth of real goods, there is inflation. Whenever the latter exists, the issuers of money always receive what is often called an "inflation tax." What is the precise nature of this "tax"? This gain obtained by the issuers of money is neither the normal return of a productive activity, nor a profit, nor a rent. It is not a profit since there is neither innovation nor risk-taking. It is no more the normal return of a productive activity, since this production does not create any utility gain for money users. In fact, it is too often forgotten that *it is absolutely not necessary to create additional money units*, to increase the quantity of money, from the time money does exist: *producing additional units of money is an activity that is socially useless and even socially harmful* (since it creates inflation). As we have seen, the least costly means to meet the needs for money cash balances is not creating nominal cash balances – that is, letting deflation increase the real value of existing nominal cash balances as a consequence of the real cash balance effect.

Multiplying nominal cash balances in no way allows money holders to get a higher utility, but quite the contrary since it only implies a transfer of purchasing power from them to the producers of monetary units, because they have to reconstitute, at least partially, the real value of their cash balances.[7] Therefore, it would be incoherent to pretend that the producers of monetary units get a return for services they are assumed to provide to money holders, since these services have a negative value.

In a free economy, a good is produced if potential purchasers consider they can draw services from it. Therefore, how can it be possible that, as far as money is concerned, there is a production of useless services, or even services with a negative value? If it does happen, it necessarily means that the economy is not a free economy. The institutional environment allows producers of monetary units to sell a good for which there ought to be no demand normally. As has been the case, especially in the twentieth century, the establishing of state control over monetary systems has made such a situation possible. In order for an unwanted additional production of monetary units to take place, it is first necessary that monetary policy be possible, which implies that the gold reserves of the producers of monetary units are lower than the total amount of money which has been issued, that there is a fractional reserve system and not a 100 percent reserve system.[8] But this is not sufficient: in fact, it is quite clear that a fractional reserve system is an easy means to pay the producers of monetary units for the services they provide to others, particularly because it is necessary to replace torn notes and to produce monetary units with decreasing denominations whenever there is deflation (see Salin,1998). In order for an excessive, non-desirable production of monetary units to take place, it is necessary that producers benefit from a legal monopoly on a given national territory and that the money users be prevented from using other currencies (through exchange controls, legal tender laws, and so on). The return obtained by the producers of monetary units, as far as it is the result of public constraint, is therefore neither a profit nor a normal return for providing services to others. It is a pure privilege rent.

1.4 The Circulation of Existing Monetary Units

The fourth monetary activity concerns the *circulation of existing monetary units*. This activity, which is logically distinct from the three previous ones, is frequently confused with them, on the one hand because those who are in charge of this activity are firms (banks) that are also in charge of all other activities, particularly the production of monetary units or the transformation from one monetary form to another (notes to deposits and conversely). But one could easily assume that all these different roles be played by different firms. Thus, it could be imagined that one firm gives a convertibility guarantee at a fixed price – for instance, in gold – to monetary units that it issues and that these units be transferred to other firms in charge, for instance, of the management of accounts and the transformation of deposits into notes. But it happens that it is not equally possible to obtain a payment for both kinds of services. Thus, producing monetary units can be profitable because of the possibility to use a fractional reserve system in which the issuer of monetary units receives an interest on credits it delivers, whereas it may be more difficult to get a payment, for instance, for transforming deposits into notes. In such a case, the firm that is completing the monetary transformation may consider that the best way to get a payment consists of selling both services – the production of monetary units and the transformation of monetary units – as joint products.

In modern monetary systems, all these roles are played by banks in a more or less indissociable way. It may be the result of the "normal" complementary nature of these different activities. But it may also be the consequence of specific regulations – which are important in this sector – according to which some firms, called "banks," benefit from a legal privilege to produce these services.

To summarize, "monetary creation" is a vague term, which in fact refers to four distinct activities: inventing a *new currency* (useful if the new currency is perceived as more effective than previous ones, at least for some users); inventing *new forms* of an existing currency, such as notes, deposits, electronic money (useful if these new forms offer valuable services); *producing additional units* of an existing currency (not useful and even a harmful activity); and *circulating existing monetary units* (a useful activity).

For money, as for any other good, profit is a return for innovation, which means it rewards those entrepreneurs who have accepted a risk by launching a new activity. Consequently, profit is normally linked to the *invention* of a new currency, but it can be collected by the innovator either when there is no imitator – which is doubtful – or whenever he can find a way to oblige others to admit his property rights on this innovation, which is difficult. Profit may also stem from the *invention* of new forms of money, but not from the *production* of additional monetary units nor from the circulation of these units (except if one discovers new circulation methods). In these latter cases there is only a normal reward for a productive activity (under the form, for instance, of wages for those who contribute to this production), except if there is a monopoly situation – which is necessarily of public origin – that allows the appearance of monopoly profits, which one ought rather to call privilege rents. Thus, the possible production of units of an existing currency (replacing damaged units or dividing units into smaller denominations) can only be paid, at best, for what is necessary to cover the costs, whenever competition prevails.

2. MONETARY HISTORY AND THE DEBATE ABOUT FRACTIONAL RESERVES

Looking to the past may seem somewhat surprising when evaluating the possible impact of the internet on the future evolution of monetary systems. However, it contributes to a better understanding of the working of monetary systems and, therefore, to a better evaluation of what may happen in the future.

Initially, and for long after its invention, money has taken the form of a commodity (silver or gold coins, but also pieces of textile, shells, salt lumps, and so on). However, the use of such monetary units was the source of some difficulty for money users, especially because low-value transactions were difficult due to the lack of low-denomination instruments. It may be the reason why the circulation of gold or silver coins was replaced by the circulation of property rights on these same metals, since these property titles could easily be split into monetary units of lower value.

It seems that the first notes were issued by English goldsmiths. Those who have been the first to issue such notes and have provided this service to their customers may have received a profit which can be considered as a reward for their invention. But this profit has not taken the form of a direct return (which would have been difficult to implement), but it was obtained through the form of a higher number of customers, attracted by this new free service, but paying for other services.

But notes being used more and more, the issuers lost this indirect source of return. As is the case in all activities, the imitators follow the innovators and, as a result, profit tends towards zero. In order to pay for the production costs of notes (and the costs incurred to keep the gold reserves necessary to maintain convertibility) the issuers of notes have invented a way of getting an indirect return for the service they provide by substituting 100 percent reserves with fractional reserves. Henceforth, monetary expansion became possible; that is, creating new monetary units not against gold, but against credits (which provide an interest to the issuer of money).

But it is necessary to consider precisely what the scope and limits of this monetary expansion are. First, it is obvious that there is a monetary expansion (production of additional monetary units) whenever one shifts from a 100 percent reserve system to a fractional reserve system. But such an expansion cannot go on indefinitely. In fact, at some point of time the issuers of notes reach the desired structure of their balance sheet (that is, a given reserve ratio, a ratio between gold reserves and the total of assets composed of gold and credits). In fact, the more the reserve ratio diminishes, the higher the risk that the gold guarantee of notes becomes unsustainable, and, therefore, the higher the risk that customers fly towards other money issuers or come back to the use of gold and silver coins. Such is the case, at least, if competition prevails between the various money producers and if individuals are free to use coins or notes as they desire. The creation of central banks and their nationalization in the twentieth century has suppressed this essential mechanism of regulation by competition. National monetary monopolies have appeared – these are situations in which public authorities forbid the issuing of currencies that can compete with national currencies and forbid citizens to use any other currency than the national one, without any consideration to its possible bad quality. So fractional reserves are the instrument of a monetary policy that could become expansionary and therefore inflationary, without any limit.

Now, it has to be stressed that what is open to criticism in modern monetary systems is not the existence of fractional reserves *per se*, but the fact that competition does not exist or is limited. It is because monetary monopolies based on legal tender laws and exchange controls exist that monetary policy exists (that is, the possibility to arbitrarily determine the growth of the quantity of money). And the existence of fractional reserves makes this policy possible. It is usually alleged that monetary policy is necessary since money production has to be managed. In fact, monetary policy is not necessary, but it is made possible because monetary monopolies exist. Incidentally, let us mention that, from this point of view, the euro-producing system must not be considered as the outcome of an innovation, but only as the survival of bad and obsolete monetary systems.

But how to evaluate a fractional reserve system when the monetary system is competitive? The importance of this question is enhanced by the fact one may consider that the internet could favor monetary competition. In fact, three main categories of opinion about the working of fractional monetary systems can be distinguished:

1. The first opinion is of economists in favor of fractional reserves and freedom of issue, because it is thus possible to get a sufficient monetary expansion to stimulate economic activity (see Selgin (1988); Selgin and White (1994); White (1999)).
2. Other economists favor 100 percent reserves because the gold convertibility (or convertibility in any commodity) stems from a contract, and it is dishonest to promise the conversion of notes against gold at any time and at a fixed price, without holding the gold stock corresponding to the amount of issued notes (see Rothbard (1991); Hoppe (1994); Hülsmann (1996); Hoppe et al. (1998)).
3. A third category of economists – to which the author of the present book belongs – believe that fractional reserves are useful as an indirect means to pay the issuers of a currency for their services and that, moreover, there is no fraud *vis-à-vis* the money holders as long as the latter have freely accepted that their notes do not benefit from a full 100 percent gold guarantee (compare with Salin (1998)).

Another interesting observation can be drawn from monetary history, namely that whenever competition prevails between money producers, monetary cartels appear. We have previously explained the reasons for this structure, but it may be useful to restate them in order to better evaluate the possible future evolution of e-currencies. In fact, the usefulness of a currency depends on its ability to maintain its purchasing power – which is a justification for defining a currency in terms of real goods – and on the more or less great dimension of its area of circulation. From this latter point of view, if ever a very great number of money producers, totally independent one from the other, were to exist, the area of circulation of each of these currencies would be very limited and its monetary quality – its "moneyness" – would be low. Therefore, there is a need for homogenization, for the substitution of a great number of currencies with a small number. But this target can be obtained either by replacing a great number of money producers by a small number or even a single one, or by introducing coordination procedures between money producers so that their currencies become perfectly substitutable one to the other and, therefore, considered as identical. Such a situation can be called a "monetary cartel." Contrary to the usual idea according to which a cartel of producers aims at creating a monopoly situation in order to extract a "super-profit" from buyers, we believe that, on the contrary, a cartel is an efficient way to meet a specific need of buyers, namely the need for a homogenization of products (see Chapter 3).

The need for homogenization results from the fact that an excessive differentiation of goods imposes on purchasers information costs (about the respective characteristics and qualities of the different goods) and transaction costs (whenever one wants to shift from one good to the other, for instance from one currency to another). These costs are diminished when the number of different goods – for instance, currencies – is limited. Obviously, the optimal number of currencies at one given time depends on information costs and transaction costs. Thus, in an extreme case, if ever transaction and information costs about the relative present and future values of the different currencies were equal to zero, there would not be any inconvenience for money users from having a very great number of currencies at their disposal. However, in the normal case in which these costs are positive, it is preferable to have a more limited number of currencies. But it remains possible that some innovations lead to a decrease in these costs, so that the optimal number of currencies can increase. This could be a possible consequence of e-currencies.

3. THE IMPACT OF THE INTERNET ON THE MONETARY SYSTEMS OF THE FUTURE

Monetary needs to be satisfied will always remain the same, namely those we have just analyzed. Therefore, the question that has to be answered consists of evaluating to what extent the internet might change the way of meeting these needs. The internet can only introduce changes in the practical ways that monetary systems work, and not in their very nature.

First, it is obvious that the internet can lead to a major change insofar as it may lead to the privatization of money and the disappearance of all regulations, since new currencies will not be managed on a territorial and national basis. In other words, public and national monopolies (or international monopolies, as is the case with the euro) will meet the competition of private and non-national currencies. Thus the wish expressed by Friedrich Hayek – who, by arguing in favor of the denationalization of money in 1976, broke an intellectual taboo and stimulated the interest of many economists – could become a reality much more rapidly than forecast.

Several consequences of this denationalization of monetary systems could occur:

1. The end of monetary policy, since it depends on specific regulations and decisions that can only be imposed on monopolistic systems with a national basis.
2. The dismissal of the very notion of a bank, since the monetary activities that have been described above are not necessarily linked together and since – as we will see below – the development of the internet can contribute to this dissociation of roles.
3. The very disappearance of some currencies, since money users may prefer the new private ones. It can even be imagined that it will occur for the euro, in spite of the fact it has been nearly unanimously celebrated as a main achievement of the European Union.

These important changes in the working and the existence of monetary systems are, by themselves, a consequence of the changes the internet may bring to the working of the main monetary activities. Taking account of the distinctions previously made, one may particularly stress the following possible changes.

3.1 Invention of New Currencies

It may first happen that new currencies are invented. Existing currencies are nothing but a kind of aberration in comparison with what has existed during the whole monetary history. As already stressed, since 1968, currencies have no definition in real terms: a pound is a pound, a dollar is a dollar, a euro is an euro, without any convertibility guarantee in terms of any real good. But such an absence of definition is possible only because existing currencies benefit from monopoly positions created by states. From this point of view the new currencies may represent a return to the past, since, in order to be accepted and desired in a competitive environment, they will have to offer purchasing-power guarantees in real terms.[9] One may even imagine that these convertibility guarantees at a fixed price could be given in gold, but many other solutions can be invented, such as a "basket" of commodities or raw materials,[10] but also a "basket" of shares, for instance those that enter the definition of the Dow Jones, or an even more abstract index.

Obviously, one of the difficulties to be overcome in the launching of these new currencies is the way by which the inventor can obtain a profit. In fact, there are launching costs to advertise about the new currency, protecting the property rights of the inventor on his invention is difficult to organize, and the cost of imitation by a potential imitator is very low. Let us just imagine, for instance, that some firm – let us call it Lemon – launches an electronic currency called web-gold-money (WGM) and that it gives a convertibility guarantee in gold (at a price of 1 WGM = 1 ounce of gold). Even if one is confident in the ability of the producer to actually honor his gold convertibility promise, it will be necessary to sell the first units with a discount, since the potential holders of WGM will not be easily induced to hold a currency used by a limited number of people. Little by little, the area of circulation of this currency will develop and it will be more and more desirable, which, in turn, will increase its area of circulation, and so it will be less and less necessary to invest in the financing of the use of this new currency. There is thus a cumulative process in the acceptability of money.

Once the WGM is widely accepted as a currency, it is likely that it will be imitated by other producers who did not have to bear the launch costs of the initial inventor. In fact, it is not difficult to produce and to sell a currency defined in terms of gold. However, an important point has to be stressed. The different units of WGM are characterized not only by the fact they benefit from a gold convertibility guarantee, but also by the fact this guarantee is given by one or the other firm. In fact, one may be more or less confident in the ability of different firms to honor their promises. In other terms, in the process we are imagining, it would be wrong to refer to the creation of the WGM by different firms. What would exist in reality would be the WGM-Lemon (the web-currency issued by the firm Lemon), the WGM-Orange, the WGM-Pineapple, and so on. Even if all of them are formally convertible into gold at the same price of one ounce of gold, these different currencies may not be viewed as perfectly substitutable, as far as people have different degrees of confidence in the capacity of the different firms (Lemon, Orange, Pineapple) to actually maintain gold convertibility at a fixed price. The currencies issued by the less reliable firms – for instance, those that maintain lower gold reserve ratios – are exchanged with a discount.

In order for all these various currencies to be considered as perfectly substitutable, which means in fact that they are one single currency, it is necessary to introduce procedures by which some issuers promise to exchange without limits these currencies one against the other at a fixed price. In other words, a monetary cartel has to be implemented such that, for instance, 1 WGM-Lemon = 1 WGM-Orange = 1 WGM-Pineapple = 1 ounce of gold. Then, and only then, it will be possible to mention the WGM as *one* specific currency and not as a set of currencies formally defined in a similar way. If such a situation prevails, each money producer must then bear the launch costs in order to convince potential money holders that its own currency is at least as good as those produced by its competitors. Moreover, various firm strategies would probably develop during this launch period. Thus, it may happen that the first inventor of the WGM, Lemon, gives convertibility guarantees at fixed price between its own currency and another one, for instance WGM-Orange, and asks for a payment to firm Orange for this service. Thus, it could make its activity profitable, covering its launch costs and receiving a profit as the inventor of the new currency. As regards the Orange firm, it would benefit from this convertibility guarantee given by the Lemon firm.

Obviously, the inventor of a new currency can imagine other ways to get a reward from its invention. Thus, the use of its currency can be linked to the settlement of various transactions made with it, or with those made with the members of a network of which it is a member. More traditionally, and as has already occurred in monetary history, it may exercise other monetary activities, such as producing various forms of money or selling services concerning the circulation of money.

3.2 New Forms of Money and Changes in Circulation Methods

Inventing new forms of money and changes in the circulation methods of an existing currency is certainly characteristic of e-currencies and, more generally, of electronic payment systems (see Dorn (1997)). Generally speaking, the internet makes it possible to significantly decrease transaction costs and information costs. As regards monetary circulation, it certainly implies that the traditional role of banks as turntables to make compensations or to transform one form of money into another will have a decreasing importance, whereas monetary systems will increasingly be organized as spontaneous and changing networks.

But it is also true that such a change would increase risk costs since the responsibility in supplying convertibility guarantees will be diluted. In other words, a monetary system works better the more precisely one can know those who are responsible for defining and guaranteeing a currency. In the cases that have been sketched above, namely those in which there is a cartel of money producers (for instance, those who produce the WGM), each producer is responsible for the convertibility of its own currency in terms of gold. Moreover, procedures exist in order to guarantee the mutual convertibility of currencies.

The system may be asymmetrical if one of the members of the cartel gives convertibility guarantees, in terms of its own money units, to all the money units produced by all the members of the cartel; it is symmetrical if each producer is responsible for maintaining the convertibility of its own currency units in terms of all the others. The existence of these mutual guarantees reinforces the confidence one may have in each of the currencies issued by the members of the cartel.

It can be imagined – as an extreme possibility – that, due to the network working of a monetary system, all those who trade in terms of any currency are producers of this same currency: I buy a book on the internet and, as a counterpart, I deliver a given quantity of money, for instance WGM, which I promise to exchange against gold at a fixed given price. But, as far as money issuers are innumerable, it is costly to get information about the solvability of all participants to the network, which therefore diminishes the confidence one may have in this currency. However, as far as the internet decreases the information costs, without anyhow being able to make them disappear, it would be normal that some people become specialized in offering convertibility guarantees at fixed price, others being only users of the currency thus defined and guaranteed.

3.3 The Optimal Dimension of Monetary Zones

As a consequence of the abovementioned characteristics, the development of e-currencies would certainly modify the *optimal dimension of monetary zones*. Dismissing the traditional definition of the optimal currency area – initiated by Robert Mundell – as an area of optimal adjustment, we have previously defined an optimal monetary zone as one within which the homogenization of monetary units is optimal.

As noted previously, the optimal dimension of a monetary zone is determined by transaction and information costs, *as they are perceived* by those who are concerned, namely money producers and money users. Since these costs are not equal to zero, it cannot be optimal to have an unlimited number of currencies in the world. But it does not imply that it would be optimal to have only one currency in the world (or in Europe, or in Africa). If competition prevails all over the world, individuals reveal, through their choice of currencies, what can be considered as the optimal number of zones and the optimal dimension of each of them. From this point of view, one may perfectly imagine that some people consider it desirable to use a currency with a limited circulation domain, but with a very specific definition that best corresponds to their needs (for instance, in the case already quoted in which people who mainly trade in raw materials use a currency defined in terms of raw materials). Others may wish, on the contrary, to hold a currency benefiting from a very wide circulation.

Anyhow, using the internet allows a reduction in transaction costs and information costs. If, for instance, a currency, M_1, is defined in terms of gold and another currency, M_2, is defined in terms of a basket of shares, it is easy to know the relative price of both these currencies at any time and practically without any cost, but also to know the future evolution of this relative price as it appears on future markets. If monetary needs are diversified, it is therefore easier to meet this diversification of needs via a diversification of currencies.

Thus, as diversifying currencies is less costly due to the internet, then the homogenization of currencies ought to be lower. In other words, the optimal dimension of monetary zones decreases and the optimal number of currencies in the world increases. From this point of view, the possible development of e-currencies may lead to a spontaneous and therefore desirable evolution, which would be the reverse to that imposed on European citizens with the euro. Instead of a decrease in the number of currencies, one may observe an increase in the future. This may also be a reason to soften a remark made previously, when we had underlined that the inventor of a new currency had to bear the risk of a rapid inflow of competitors into his market. In fact, if it were true that diversification could become more desirable, the inventors of new competing currencies would develop at the expense of mere imitators.

Earlier, money was defined as a "generalized purchasing power." But such a definition has to be interpreted from a purely subjective and individual point of view. What makes a currency generally tradable in the opinion of an individual is the capacity of this currency to be exchanged at any time, with the greatest possible number of people, against commodities that are *desirable for him*. The possibility to exchange this currency against other commodities is not a matter of concern. Thus, any individual desires a specific currency to which is attached a capacity to obtain a purchasing power the general character of which is evaluated *by him and only by him*. It is the role of money producers to meet the diversity of needs for a purchasing power, while taking into account the costs of diversification. If they are very high, individuals will have to accept currencies that give generalized services to a great number of people. If the internet makes possible a decrease in the cost of diversification, a higher degree of specificity of currencies becomes possible.

3.4 The Role of Reserves

It has already been stressed that reserves are an instrument for monetary policy whenever monetary systems are monopolistic, and that they are a way to pay the producers of monetary units for their services in competitive systems. Obviously, the first role disappears with the end of national monetary monopolies. But what about the second one? The role of fractional reserves as an indirect means to pay for monetary circulation services diminishes with the decrease in the circulation costs of money. From this point of view, one possible consequence of the development of e-currencies could be a steady increase in reserve ratios, so that one might come closer to 100 percent reserve systems. A lower economic and monetary instability may result, as far as instability is basically the outcome of the variability of the quantity of money, itself linked to the variability of the reserve ratios and, therefore, of monetary policy.

3.5 Possible Changes in Monetary Systems

As emphasized previously, since it is necessary to create confidence in a currency and since information costs can never disappear, even with the techniques of our time, it is very likely that a complete substitution of a network system to the present system organized around some centers of money production will never happen. However, it is still interesting to try to imagine the workings of a system in which transaction and information costs would be negligible in order to evaluate the directions towards which monetary systems could evolve. Transactions could occur in the following way: I buy a book on the internet and I sell, as a counterpart, a claim defined, for instance, in terms of a given basket of shares (those of the Dow Jones, or any other index) or even the promise to deliver one hour of teaching. The circulation of this claim is easier the lower the cost of providing to its successive holders a guarantee according to which I will honor this exchange promise (that is, converting this claim against goods and services).

From this point of view, one might say that whereas the role of money as an available purchasing power remains, its traditional role as an intermediary in exchange would disappear, since the internet makes it possible to act in a way similar to what happens in a barter economy (for instance, trading a book against one teaching hour). However, the seller of the book has probably no direct interest in buying the teaching hour, but he buys it because he knows that the internet makes it possible for him to know to what extent this teaching hour can be exchanged against other goods he desires. In turn, this certainly means that in such a case we would not be in a barter economy, but that, on the contrary, any good and service could potentially become a "money." If the seller of the book can know instantaneously and without cost the price of my teaching hour in terms of the present or future good that he desires, he will accept to buy a property right on one teaching hour, which will become a monetary good. Under such an assumption, specialized money producers would disappear, but other activities would develop (information network organizer, rating firms for traders, and so on). Anyone becoming what is now called a bank would have to decide to what extent he desires to engage in any sort of monetary policy, such as holding fractional reserves. Thus, I buy a book against a currency I am issuing and to which I give an exchange guarantee in terms of a given basket of shares, but I hold only a fraction of this basket, taking the risk of buying the other fraction whenever I am asked to convert the monetary claim I have issued against shares.

Obviously, for reasons already stressed – the existence of positive transaction and information costs – it will be impossible to ever reach such a situation. More probably, some sort of intermediary firms would appear: they would decide their reserve policies and their reserve ratios. But, as far as they will be responsible, these firms will not take the risk of deciding an overproduction of money. Thus, the internet could make it possible to go back to the sort of monetary organizations which prevailed in the eighteenth century, but probably with a greater diversification of currencies and certainly with more efficiency. Due to the internet, a great diversity is possible in the definition of currencies and in the organization of monetary networks and systems.

CONCLUSION

As James Dorn wrote (1999):

> [In markets] liquidity is not the outcome of a personal knowledge about the real value of a guarantee brought by some other person, but of the technical capacity to analyze, select and classify innumerable amounts of anonymous informations. Now, it is this very capacity which is exploding in our time. It opens new opportunities, nearly without limits, which allows a limitation, from a purely statistical point of view, of the risks due to an accumulation of bad claims.

Obviously, one does not know precisely the monetary landscape of the future. It will be determined by competition, as in the case of other network activities (telecommunications, air transportation, and so on). In the case of money, however, competition and the appearance of new organizational schemes have not been made possible by deregulation. It is the technical evolution that will make regulation obsolete and which will allow people to overcome it until it is completely inefficient.

Innovations, by their very nature, cannot be foreseen. However, one may expect, without a great risk of being wrong, the end of the present characteristics of monetary systems, namely their national, public and hierarchical nature. From this point of view, the euro may be viewed, at some point in the future, as a survivor of an obsolete monetary world and its role may fade away.

NOTES

1. The best known is the bitcoin. But it lacks some of the main characteristics of a sound currency.
2. Thus, the SDRs (special drawing rights) created by the International Monetary Fund (IMF) are not a currency since they cannot be generally exchanged against anything, at any time, with anyone, under any circumstance. They are nothing but a numeraire. It means that "inventing" SDRs was a totally absurd activity, since the utility of a numeraire precisely comes from the fact it is single. Creating a new numeraire is not only useless but also harmful.
3. Obviously, innovations may be possible in the production techniques of these monetary units and, therefore, profit opportunities may exist. It is the case, for instance, if someone invents a more efficient machine to produce notes or a safer technique to avoid counterfeiting.
4. It may be the result of regulations, but it is preferable to consider a situation in which the producers of tricks keep reserves in gold equal to the gold value of issued tricks (since they represent property rights on gold) and in which the quantity of gold in the reserves of the issuers of tricks remains constant.
5. Or financial assets. However, to make things simpler without twisting the argument, we prefer to consider only the case in which the additional demand for money corresponds to an additional supply of commodities.
6. There is a good example of such a situation with the bitcoin, since the number of bitcoins has increased regularly, but it has been decided from the beginning that the issue would not go beyond a given number (21 millions of bitcoins about in 2040).
7. Such a production is quite often justified on the grounds that it would be necessary to "finance economic expansion." But such a statement stems from a severe confusion. In fact, to finance growth, what is needed is not a great amount of monetary units, but savings, which is quite different. However, in our time, as monetary units can be produced at will by supplying credits, people think that this monetary production necessarily means an increase in the total amount of available financing. This idea is certainly wrong, as has been shown in particular by Ludwig von Mises and Friedrich Hayek, and as we have already explained.
8. As an extreme case, the reserve ratio becomes equal to zero, which means there are no more reserves and convertibility guarantees. It is obviously the case in our time.
9. This is not the case with the bitcoin. It has no definition, but it has been announced that a limited quantity of units would ever be created. From this point of view, its purchasing power could increase steadily if it was more and more used. But, as far as we can know, it is not really the case, maybe because most people are not confident in the bitcoin since it has no definition in real terms. In reality there is a great variability of the exchange rate of the bitcoin with other currencies. Therefore, in the short run some holders of bitcoins may guess that they can get a profit (for instance, when exchanging their bitcoins for dollars). But as far as the circulation of bitcoins remains limited, at one time or the other, bitcoin holders may wish to exchange their units against other currencies or goods. If most people do it at the same time, the value of the bitcoin drops and it may disappear.
10. A currency defined in terms of a basket of raw materials may not be the most desirable one, since the variability of relative prices of raw materials to other commodities is great, so that the purchasing power of such a currency in terms of these other commodities would be unstable. However, such a currency could be desirable for specific categories of people, such as those who are active on the market for raw materials.

15. The digital divide: policy or competition?[1]

When mentioning "digital divide" one means that there is an unequal access to digital techniques. The gap may exist between individuals belonging to different categories of persons in one nation, or it may exist between different nations, more precisely developed and less developed countries. The gap in the access to digital techniques and the internet may concern the equipment (the existence of networks, the ownership of computers, and so on), the access to software programs or the ability to get the necessary training to use digital techniques.

The present chapter first gives some data from the literature about the digital divide (Section 1). Section 2 debates the central question of the importance of the digital divide in economic development. The chapter ends with some thoughts about the universal access to digital techniques and intellectual property rights.

1. EVALUATING THE DIGITAL DIVIDE

1.1 The Digital Divide Inside a Nation

A tremendous amount of literature has been published, particularly in the US, in order to stress the existence of all sorts of inequalities in the access to digital techniques among different groups of persons. Thus, one could read on Wikipedia (in 2008) that "the concept of the digital divide was originally popularized with regard to the disparity in internet access between rural and urban areas of the United States of America." But it is considered now as "a phenomenon wherein the rich get richer and the poor get poorer, at least with respect to technology, as the gap between the technological haves and have-nots widens."

The journal *IT & Society* is mainly devoted to the digital divide. Here is a sample of findings published by researchers in this journal, just taking as an example volume 1, issue 5 (Summer 2003):

> This article then proceeds to analyze the social, demographic and psychological predictors of Internet users and nonusers. Demographic factors (being white, well educated, and having a high income) are associated with more Internet adoption, as are high levels of trust, social contentment and media use. Controlling for other variables, Hispanics and African-Americans are less likely to be online, as are people who report frequently socializing with family and friends and being members of social groups or clubs. (Lenhart and Horrigan, 2003)

> Gender pervades how people use the Internet. [. . .] Consistent with the earlier literature on gender roles, (the authors) show that women use the Internet more for social reasons, while men use it more for instrumental and solo recreational reasons. Care-giving for children at home limits mothers more than fathers in the use they make of the Internet. (Kennedy et al., 2003)

> As increasing numbers of Americans have gone online, the academic focus has shifted from the digital divide to "digital inequality", in which attention is given to White and Black levels of Internet social support, navigational sophistication, and Internet knowledge – factors which directly facilitate or inhibit Internet use beyond simple access. (Alvarez, 2003)

Reading papers and books about the digital divide brings a particularly striking illustration of the rather sad state of affairs that exists in economics and social sciences. In the present time, doing research in economics may mean two things. First, looking at an ever more complex sophistication of purely formal mathematical models, without any link to the real world (which is not the case as regards "research" on the digital divide). Second, accumulating statistics and doing econometric tests about supposed social and economic problems. In this latter case, the "researcher" has, quite often, an implicit value judgment to illustrate through his statistics and econometrics. He wants to demonstrate, for instance, that blacks and whites, or males and females, or young and old people, in such or such country, at one or the other time, have not the same access to digital techniques. In fact, we could guess such results without having to spend money in order to better know the existence of the gaps, since there is no a priori reason for individuals belonging to different economic, social, racial or national groups to behave exactly in the same way and to use exactly the same goods and services.

Reading this literature, one may have the feeling that, in the modern world, a tremendous amount of money and – which is worse – a tremendous amount of human capital is wasted in order to produce what Jean-François Revel called "the useless knowledge." Is it really important to know that there is a digital divide between males and females, Afro-Americans and Hispanics, inhabitants of cities and villages? We are not at all convinced that it is. In fact, such research is useful for social activists and politicians who are looking for activities on which to spend public money (that is, private money taken by the state). Such research may in fact open the way to public programs aiming at filling the digital gap between communities. In fact, it is inappropriate to label such works and publication as research. Their authors are providing information, not knowledge. However, to be fair, some of them try to give a theoretical justification to their work. And it is because of this effort that we do not stop our chapter right now, just by saying that the digital divide is a concept that should not attract our attention and take our time. Therefore, we will mainly consider these theoretical arguments in the present chapter.

1.2 The Global Digital Divide Between Nations

According to Wikipedia (in 2008):

> The global digital divide is a term used to describe "great disparities in opportunity to access the Internet and the information and educational/business opportunities tied to this access [. . .] between developed and developing countries" [according to Lu (2001)]. Unlike the traditional notion of the "digital divide" between social classes, the "global digital divide" is essentially a geographical division.

Historically, the notion of a "global digital divide" can be traced back to the MacBride Commission Report debated in 1980 at the General Conference of the United Nations Educational, Scientific and Cultural Organization (UNESCO). This organization has tried to promote a new world information order. Concern about the digital divide is just a part of it. More generally it reminds us of slogans that have been fashionable in last decades about "a new international monetary order" or a "new world trade order" or a "new international environment order."

We are, personally, spontaneously suspicious – as many people may be – whenever someone speaks of a "new international order." In fact, one ought to know that centrally designed "order" means the use of constraint, failure to let people reach their own ends and, quite often, even the failure to reach the official ends of the so-called international order. Thus, as far as the so-called digital divide is just one more manifestation of this illusory quest for a designed order, one might just stop here without exploring the subject further. However, the subject is so widely discussed both in academic circles and in political circles and the role of digital techniques is so important in our present world that it may be worthwhile to explore it somewhat further. But it must be clear from the outset that we are skeptical about the digital divide. The claim for a "new international monetary order" assumed that markets are unable to bring about such an international order and that cooperation between governments is needed to regulate markets. Similarly, it is assumed that markets are unable to bring about some international digital order and that government intervention is necessary. In the latter case, order is very loosely defined. In fact, it is quite often considered, more or less explicitly, that there is no international order whenever there is a digital gap between nations or even a widening gap. Thus, according to Elie Abel (1981): "The affluent would be even better informed than they are today; the lower orders could be even less well informed."

Thus, it is implicitly assumed that an international order would mean a world of equal access of citizens in all countries to digital techniques. There would thus be a confusion of terminology between "international digital order" and "international equality in digital techniques." We find in this field the traditional divergences between those who believe in collective rights – which are not, in fact, "rights" but claims over other people and which are to be satisfied by the state – and those who have confidence in spontaneous processes resulting from interactions between individuals using their legitimate property rights. "Is full information access one of our basic rights in post-industrial society, or is it simply a long range goal left to the play of economic and social forces?" (Compaine, 2001, quoting Wilson Dizard).

Alter-globalists usually claim that developed countries are wealthy because they are dominating other countries and are thus able to plunder them, for instance by imposing low prices for raw materials and agricultural commodities. But it would be impossible for them to say that developed countries are extracting digital techniques from poor countries . . . However, leftists have found a way to fall on their feet. They claim that those who have control over digital techniques also have the control of the content, of the information and ideas that are spreading all over the world. Thus, the global digital divide would have the perverse effect of facilitating an intellectual domination of rich countries – particularly the US – on the minds of other people. Filling the digital gap between countries would make it possible for poorer countries to be more independent intellectually and to avoid an "Americanization of the world."

1.3 The Benefits of Digital Techniques

At first sight, fears about the digital divide are over-estimated and one could even take an optimistic view and consider that digital techniques are a powerful means to fill gaps in information, knowledge, income and wealth between individuals belonging to different categories or different countries. Thanks to the internet, for instance, small producers are able to get in touch with the whole world and to sell their products everywhere, whereas in the pre-internet world engaging in international trade was very costly. The internet makes it possible for people located in remote places to get education and health services or to get information from all sorts of publications and libraries to which they could not have access physically. It has long been clear that international exchange (not only trade in commodities and services, but also in assets and information) is a necessary condition for growth, not only because it makes it possible for individuals to specialize, but also because it brings them new information.

Competition is tremendously stimulated by the internet, and as we know from Friedrich Hayek, competition "is a process of discovery." From this point of view, it can be considered that the internet, far from widening the gap between people, is a fantastic potential equalizer, since it makes possible a dramatic cut in the cost of communications.

Now, those who care about the digital divide would just put things upside down. They would say: It is precisely because the internet and digital techniques are a fantastic accelerator of growth in our time that we have to care about the digital divide. Those who are wealthy enough to benefit from all the innovations in digital techniques can thus push their rate of growth, whereas the poorest are left behind because there are obstacles to the access to digital techniques, particularly for those who have less.

It is true that many among those who care about the digital divide would not complain about the mere existence of a gap, but they would insist on the fact that there is or there could be a widening gap or, at least, that the speed at which new techniques disseminate is "too low."

1.4 Material Obstacles

It is obvious that access to digital techniques is costly and that it is a challenge for poor people and poor countries. It is not necessary to elaborate on this and we may just refer to the summary of these material obstacles given by Wikipedia:

> There is the initial problem of actually buying and deploying computers inside developing nations, as well as assorted networking and communications technologies. All these machines require parts, and may have to be regularly maintained by trained technicians. Though much cheaper than in the past, bandwidth must be paid for if peering agreements cannot be negotiated. Users must be trained to use computers efficiently to find information on the Internet. If information is not in the users' native language, it must be translated or the users must be educated to basic proficiency in a language in which information is widely available, like English.

1.5 Intellectual and Human Obstacles

According to some of those who care about the digital divide, the prospective gap is wider than it has ever been in information techniques because the use of computers and the internet implies more complex learning processes. However, there has been in the past a large divide, for instance, in the ability of people to read, so that a high proportion of human beings could not benefit from information brought about, for instance, by newspapers. The degree of literacy has increased over time so that more people have potential access to digital techniques than had been the case in the past for books and newspapers.

2. THE DIGITAL DIVIDE AND ECONOMIC DEVELOPMENT

2.1 The Traditional Arguments for Gap-reducing Policies

It is indisputable that computers and the internet are now important factors of growth and also an instrument for the dissemination of knowledge and practices, even potentially to remote areas. What does it imply? As already stressed, these techniques could be considered as growth equalizers, since they make it possible for everyone all around the world to get access to the same techniques, the same information and the same markets. But those who care about the digital divide disagree with this view. There would be a clear causality running from digital techniques to growth. They consider implicitly that these techniques are nowadays the instrument of growth. Therefore, those who are disadvantaged at the start because, being poor, they have a limited access to digital techniques, cannot reach the level of development of wealthier countries and, even, may have a lower growth rate, so that there is a growing gap in levels of development. In order to legitimate policies aiming at reducing the digital gap, they use some of the assumptions that are now fashionable in economic theory, two of which are described below.

First, there would be externalities in the use of digital techniques, since they do not benefit only to those who use them, but more generally to the whole society. By reducing the digital divide, one would increase the rate of growth and initiate a virtuous circle: more growth means more possibilities to get digital techniques, therefore more growth, and so on.

In fact, this is exactly the traditional argument used by all those who support the theory of endogenous growth. A very similar argument is used, for instance, to legitimate public spending in education. Learning the use of digital techniques is just one aspect of this view. Thus, those who favor public funding of education, because of its externality effects, may also support public funding for digital equipment or education in the use of digital techniques. Moreover, some of them may even assume that individuals are unable to evaluate by themselves the return they may get from education so that the state has to make education compulsory and it has to organize education and to pay for it through taxes. But, all over the world, private schools in less developed countries are educating children more efficiently than public schools. Could it not be the same for education in digital techniques? Why should we assume that individuals, even in the poorest countries, are unable to discover to which extent the use of digital techniques can be useful for them and may initiate a process of development?

Second, it is often argued that there are decreasing costs, at least in some parts of the digital system. It is not the case for computers and even for education, which implies individualized costs. But it is the case as regards, for instance, the use of a network or the use of computer programs. Once an online network has been created, a potentially unlimited number of individuals can use it. Similarly, once a computer program exists, it can be indefinitely duplicated at near-zero cost. In fact, this is just one specific application of a more general problem, namely that once information has been created, it can be duplicated indefinitely at a zero or low cost. From these characteristics, some might be tempted to conclude that these activities are public goods. Traditionally, it is considered that a good or service is a public good if there is no rivalry and no excludability, which seems to be the case in some parts of a digital system. Non-rivalry is actually present: Many people can have access to the internet where there is Wi-Fi, without diminishing its use by anyone; once a computer program has been invented, anyone can use it without undermining the use by others.

However, it may be considered that the most important characteristic of a public good is not non-rivalry, but non-excludability. If ever individual property rights could be defined on a good or service for which there is potential non-rivalry, there would be no reason to produce it through a public system of free provision and funding by tax. However, the very notion of a public good can be debated, since it is impossible to determine any good or service for which non-excludability would necessarily exist because it belongs to the very nature of this good or service. It happens quite often that members of a collectivity – not only at the level of the state, but at the level, for instance, of a condominium – consider that it is not worthwhile to bear the costs of defining property rights, since the benefit would be lower than the cost. Therefore, they decide to give this good or service a characteristic of non-excludability. But changes in techniques may modify such a decision and transform a so-called public good into a private good. Moreover, such changes are much more likely to occur whenever there is no public monopoly. Freedom to enter into a market is a powerful inducement to discover techniques which make possible to lower the cost of defining property rights. From this point of view, public goods do not exist, but collective decisions do. As we see later on, there is no reason to consider that digital techniques are public goods by nature and should be provided by the state.

2.2 Spreading Techniques

As recalled previously, reducing inequalities is one of the common justifications for caring about the digital divide. In fact, and more generally, there are reasons to be satisfied whenever inequalities do exist, since they may be a symptom of a high growth rate, the benefits of which are spreading little by little to everyone. In a static society there may be inequalities, but they are founded on the use of power and they are immutable, which is not the case in a dynamic society, in which everyone has his own chance to improve his standard of living and his techniques.

Thus, in any new activity there is always a small number of people who accept to pay a high price in the beginning in order to benefit from the corresponding services. Then, little by little, the cost of production is decreasing, people get used to the new products and the new techniques, and more and more people benefit from the innovation. It has been the case for cars, telephones, televisions, and so on. Those who were the most inclined to adopt innovations made it possible for new activities to develop and, in some sense, other people benefited from their positive externalities, which means that the existence of externalities does not imply state interventionism.

Why are people speaking of a "digital divide," whereas one has never mentioned a "car divide" or a "telephone divide"? The more cars there are the more communication there is between people, therefore more development, so that more people can buy cars – so the snowball effect does exist. Now, if there is a "car divide," why should not the government fill the gap and distribute cars and driving licenses to everyone in order to stimulate communication and growth, as it is claimed it should do for digital techniques?

The answer is clear-cut: a car is not free and it would thus be provided at the expense of other things. And it would be provided by coercion, which makes it impossible to know to what extent this is the most desirable use of resources. As for the use of cars, there is a learning process to use digital technology and to learn how to get the precise information one desires. But this learning process is not very costly, much less than the learning process to obtain a driver's license. Moreover, not all people need the same abilities. According to one's specific needs, the learning process is more or less important and more or less distributed over time, whereas everyone must have about the same ability to drive a car. It means that educating potential users of digital techniques cannot be decided along some standardized approach. Why not be confident in the capacities of individuals to discover, little by little, which knowledge they best need?

Technical progress also means that techniques are easier and easier to obtain and that the cost of the learning process is steadily decreasing. Thus, it is now possible to get internet or Global Positioning System (GPS) on mobiles at a low cost. In fact, the speed of adjustment of people to the internet is much higher than that which prevailed with steam railways or cars. What is important is not the digital divide at one given point of time, but the speed at which it is reducing. And this speed is high.[2]

One can certainly accelerate the rhythm of introduction of digital techniques, but at what cost? There are optimal speeds for differentiated learning processes and information needs. In fact, knowledge is not an undifferentiated good that one can add to one's life. It *is* life.

Nothing can replace the individual economic calculation by which anyone evaluates costs and benefits. Therefore, it is meaningless to speak of a digital divide from the outside, for instance by deciding that everyone must obtain the same information and have access to the same techniques. In fact, we meet exactly the same prejudice when people want to reduce the digital divide and when they claim that there must be "transparency in information" under the pretext that everyone has a right to get information. Now, as regards, for instance, information about the management of a firm, the needs are not the same for wage earners, members of the board, lenders, small shareholders or important shareholders. The optimal amount of information cannot be defined other than by letting individuals express their needs and bear the costs. It is exactly the same with the digital divide. There is an optimal digital divide for every individual and it is obtained as far as individuals are free to express their needs. In other words, every individual has to choose what their optimal degree of ignorance or optimal degree of information is. Thus, the internet makes it possible for people to save time when looking at some information (and, sometimes, to waste time in a quest for an indefinite amount of information . . .), but the relative price of time is not the same for all.

2.3 Digital Techniques in the Process of Economic Development

According to the *World Report on Information Technologies* by the World Economic Forum, published in April 2008, the more a country is open to the development and the use of information technologies, the higher is its gross national product (GNP) per head. From such a statement of fact, one might be tempted to deduce that, in order to accelerate the growth of poor countries or poor communities, it is necessary – if not sufficient – to develop digital techniques. However, one must not infer any causality from the mere empirical observation of parallel evolutions. Do internet penetration rates determine the rate of growth or does a high rate of growth (explained by other factors, such as the degree of individual freedom and the stability of property rights) determine internet penetration rates? Moreover, information technologies are recent and do not explain the whole history of the development of a country. In fact, the richer a country – thanks to former factors of growth others than information technologies – the more it may spend on information technologies.

Moreover, a high growth rate in a country may reduce its gap with other countries, but most probably it increases the digital divide inside the country, since growth exists because some people are more innovative, get wealthier and, therefore, have more possibilities to use digital techniques. But, bit by bit, imitation effects and the general increase in the standard of life make possible a decrease in the differentiation of penetration rates.

Any society, at any time, has been an information society, since any material production is, in fact, the result of an intellectual process that consists of creating new knowledge. The digital divide is nothing but a manifestation of the "production divide" or rather of the "information divide," which has always existed, since inequalities in the rates of change for getting information have always existed for a lot of reasons. Now, by insisting on the digital divide and by trying to reduce it in order to reduce the inequalities in the standards of life of people in different countries, one takes the risk of duplicating the errors of past development policies.

In industrial societies, it was considered that industry was the main factor of development, so that people shared a prejudice according to which development implied a shift towards industrial activities. Therefore, it was admitted that international aid could bring about the development of poorer economies, just by building factories and transferring technologies. Politicians, development bureaucrats, and businessmen with vested interests in development considered that you just had to invest in industry for a country to develop. In some sense, one was looking at closing the "industrial gap." As could be expected, this approach failed. It failed because the material elements – such as factories – were exogenously brought into less developed countries without any relation to specific human needs and capabilities. In particular, the human, institutional and political environments – not friendly to entrepreneurship – were not ready to sustain a process of development. Closing the industrial gap did not bring about a closing of the development gap.

Similar confusions may be at the root of the ideas concerning the digital divide. It is considered that wealthy people and wealthy countries have better access to the internet and digital techniques. Therefore, in order to fill the gap, one has to give access at no or low cost to low-income people and countries. And thus both will become wealthier. There is a perfect parallel with transfer policies in industrial activities. And there is the same risk of a disillusion. To impulse a process of development, it is not sufficient to distribute computers and to teach people how to use them. There is, in fact, a complex process of interactions between economic development, acquiring techniques, investment and freedom to act.

To be fair, those who campaign in favor of policies to decrease the gap are well aware that it is not sufficient just to invest in equipment (internet highways or computers), but that investment in education is a necessary supplement whenever one is considering the development of information technologies. It is also fair to recognize that the parallel between industry and information techniques is not absolutely perfect, since digital activities are web activities – contrary to industrial activities – which means that individual behaviors are necessarily more interrelated in the development of the concerned techniques. Whereas it is possible to build a factory in a human vacuum and via a centralized process of decision, no one might consider that digital investments are purely technical and material and that they can be developed without any relation to human actions.

Development is definitely not possible without changes in technologies and from this point of view it is not debatable that access to digital techniques is important for development in our time. However, for a process of development to be sustainable there is the need for incentives of individuals to save, to invest, to take risks and to use new technologies . . . Now, if the right incentives do exist, because of a secure system of property rights, then development occurs and with it a self-sustained process of interactions between the development of digital techniques and the general economic development.

Thus, although there is a link between the penetration of digital techniques and the rate of growth of a society, it would be wrong to assume that there is a causality link between the first and the second, which would give strong justification for policies aiming at reducing the digital gap. As already mentioned, many people – particularly in official circles – believe in such a causality. Thus, a Networked Readiness Index has been constructed for 127 countries, using 68 variables, and it seems that there is a high correlation between the ranking of a country in this index and its

Table 15.1 A comparison of the ranking of countries according to the Networked Readiness Index and the Index of Economic Freedom

Country	Ranking in the Networked Readiness Index (2006–2007)	Ranking in the Index of Economic Freedom (2006)
Denmark	1	8
Sweden	2	19
Singapore	3	2
Finland	4	12
Switzerland	5	15
The Netherlands	6	16
US	7	9
Iceland	8	3
UK	9	5
Norway	10	30
Canada	11	12
Hong Kong	12	1
Taiwan	13	37
Japan	14	27
Australia	15	9
Germany	16	19
Austria	17	18
Israel	18	36
Republic of Korea	19	45
Cameroon	113	119
Paraguay	114	109
Mozambique	115	113
Lesotho	116	99
Zimbabwe	117	154
Bangladesh	118	141
Ethiopia	119	133
Angola	120	139
Burundi	121	132
Chad	122	105

Note: Only the first 19 and last 10 countries have been selected. Note that there are only 122 countries in the Network Readiness Index, whereas there are 157 in the Index of Economic Freedom.

ranking according to the level of its GNP per head. Now, we have made a comparison of the ranking of countries according to this Networked Readiness Index and according to the Index of Economic Freedom[3] and it appears that there is a high correlation between the rankings of a country in both tables. Although we do not want to infer from a statistical correlation to a causal relation, one may believe that the real causality is the following one: The freer the inhabitants of a country, the higher their standard of living (or growth rate), and the higher the penetration of digital techniques (which, in turn, may accelerate development).

As Neil Emerick (2003) wrote: "There are many socially desirable goods – such as health, longevity and literacy levels – that correlate highly with the overall level of economic freedom in a country. Internet penetration rate – and therefore communications access – appears to be no exception."

2.4 Education and State-provided Digital Services

There is a risk of spreading internet services without caring for other aspects, namely creating a confusion between information and education. There is a prejudice according to which the most important thing is to be informed so that all people have a right to the same amount of information. People care about the digital divide because they feel that there is not an equal access to information.

But information has no value if it is not related to specific desires and needs. What is important to give to people, particularly to young people, is not information per se, but the reasoning methods that allow them to look for relevant information and to organize it in a coherent way.

Insisting on the digital divide involves the risk of developing a civilization of individuals who would potentially have access to the same unlimited information, but who would be unable to think independently. They would have a huge amount of information, but this information would be completely unstructured. Because it is assumed that we are in the information era, it is widely admitted that everyone has an equal right to get access to this information civilization. But, instead of focusing on this aspect – information society – should we not insist on some other aspects? Information is a means, not an end. All societies have always been knowledge based because the main characteristic of human beings stems from the fact they think and they cannot act without having previously developed a process of thought, as Ludwig von Mises, in particular, stressed in such a convincing way. From this point of view, there is nothing special in the modern world. All societies have always been information societies and knowledge societies. We could define an "information divide" or a "knowledge divide" even in a world without computers and the internet.

As already stressed, those who support the idea of a digital divide and the necessity to adopt policies to reduce it, are close to those who support the theory of endogenous growth. There is certainly a correlation between the level of education of people and the rate of growth of a country. But does it mean that all people must have the same education and that education has to be managed by the state? Certainly not, since in most underdeveloped countries parents are well aware of the profitability of education. And education is better and less costly in private schools whenever a competitive system does exist. This certainly applies to acquiring education in information technologies.

However, the gap-filling policies also raise the very traditional problem of redistribution. Filling the gap cannot be done successfully at zero cost. There is an opportunity cost and someone somewhere has to bear it. As for any government policy, one does not know what would have happened if individuals had been free to use the resources corresponding to the taxes they have to pay in order to finance the digital system developed by the state. Moreover, as Benjamin Compaine (2001) stresses, there is a risk if the state acts precipitously in order to accelerate the pace of introduction of some technology. In fact, technology is changing rapidly and the state may lock citizens in past technologies. It was the case in France with Minitel, a (technically poor) interactive system produced by the telecommunication administration at a time when computers were developing elsewhere. "There is a time for society to see how some technology or combinations of technologies move towards their natural markets and costs" (Campaine, 2001, p. 114). "It may take decades before it is clear that some technologically innovative service or product has the potential to become an actual or near necessity, worthy of some government attention for regulation, subsidy, etc." (ibid., p. 115).

As Neil Emerick stresses (2003, pp. 29–30):

> Finally, the consumers who have to use technologies would be in the best position to decide what works and what does not. Initial uptakes by aggressive first-time users should not send premature signals to government officials keen to employ the latest and greatest. Technology fashions and consumer preferences change quickly, so it is not the domain of government – which should deliberate in its decisions – to try to second-guess which infrastructure is best. Government can "pull" infrastructure through the market by creating demand for universal services, but should not attempt to "push" it through by directly investing in specific technologies.

There is also the paradox in the modern world that governments claim that they must reduce the digital divide, but, meanwhile, they introduce all sorts of devices in their own countries, restricting access to internet or raising the cost of digital equipment and services. Such is the case with licenses for service producers, the granting of a monopoly, or high tax rates and tariffs.

State intervention to reduce the digital divide is legitimized through various arguments, which we have previously debated. Among them is the idea that the marginal cost of providing digital services is very low, at least in some parts of the digital system, so that it would be optimal for the state to provide these services, in spite of all the well-known drawbacks brought about by any state intervention. Now, the fact that the marginal cost may be low or zero does not imply state intervention, as far as price discrimination is possible. We have already stressed that whenever a new product is launched on the market, the wealthiest persons buy it and thus make possible for others to get it at a lower price on a later date. Similarly, a firm may maximize its profits by charging different prices, for instance for programs, in wealthy and poor countries. This is possible only as far as there are techniques preventing those who pay a low price from reselling the product at a higher price. But in a competitive market, producers are keen both to discover the optimal policy of price discrimination and the ways to prevent the existence of undue profits received by those who would resell the products obtained at a low cost.

A market solution also has the advantage of adapting the rate of penetration of digital techniques to the real needs of people. It is utopian to believe that it is possible and desirable to establish perfect equality at any time. The only relevant question consists in determining the optimal rhythm of introduction of new techniques. Only the market – that is, individuals – can do it.

2.5 Private Endeavors

As in any other field, trying to fill an inequality gap is difficult to justify whenever it is made through compulsory transfers based on state coercion, but it is completely justified whenever it depends on voluntary transfers. However, a distinction has to be made. In fact, non-statist transfers are made by two kinds of organizations: associations or firms.

There are many examples of associations aiming at reducing the digital divide, either between different categories of people or between different nations. For instance, in France, an association (Adie, *association pour le droit à l'initiative économique*) has made an agreement with Microsoft to educate potential small entrepreneurs and help them to use computers and the internet. Using Microsoft programs, they learn accounting and simple management techniques, as well as how to use the internet and how to create a website. Another association cooperating with Adie, helps long-run underemployed or handicapped persons to create a firm by selling to them, at a very low cost, programs or computers that are no longer used in large corporations (such as Microsoft).

As regards the role of associations, there is no room for complaint. They have been founded with the explicit goal of filling the digital divide and those who contribute to the activities of the associations, either as donors or as volunteers, do it voluntarily, just because they feel concerned with the digital divide, and they use their own (human or non-human) resources.

Now, some firms are also concerned with the digital divide, especially those that are producing digital products and programs. But the case of firms is different from the one of associations, since, at least in corporations, those who decide the transfers are not necessarily the legitimate owners of the firm. Whatever they transfer belongs to the shareholders and should not be transferred without their explicit agreement. Such transfers are easily admitted, first because few people are strong supporters of property rights and because there is a general prejudice according to which firms have to behave in an "ethical way." However, there is a great ambiguity as regards ethics: People are confused between what they would like and what is actually called ethical. They have been told that there is a digital divide and that it is a moral duty to diminish this digital divide so that any act aiming at this goal seems to be "ethically" founded.

But libertarians do know that there is only one universal duty: respecting property rights. Whenever the managers of a corporation decide to transfer some belongings of the firm to other people, this subjective moral duty conflicts with the universal duty of respecting property and it cannot be accepted. As an individual, anyone can decide to transfer what he owns legitimately and it is our duty to be respectful of his desires, so that we have not to impose any value judgment upon his behavior, as long as he is in turn respectful of others' property rights. Such people can legitimately make transfers to decrease the digital divide, individually or by entering into an association. But a corporation is not entitled to do that. To be sure, the real motivations for transfers by a corporation may be ambiguous. For instance, a firm producing computer programs may consider that it is profitable in the long run to give to some disadvantaged people free or underpriced access to their programs. The marginal cost of producing these programs is about zero and, at any rate, disadvantaged people would not buy them, so that the firms do not lose any market share. But one may guess that these same people will be able to raise their standards of living over time, so that they will become regular customers, inclined to buy the products of the firm they already know.

By the way, this means also that, if ever one wants to reduce the digital divide, it is not necessary to use compulsory methods (public transfers). Instead of relying on debatable so-called moral justifications for transfers, one might rather give some confidence to what economic theory calls a discriminatory monopoly. The firm producing specific computer programs is in a monopoly position as regards these specific programs. As already said, given the fact that marginal costs are zero or low, it can maximize its (long-run) profit by selling its programs at a much reduced (or zero) rate to some people. The characteristics of programs make it particularly relevant, at least if program producers develop techniques which make reselling difficult or even impossible. Anyhow, from a general point of view, it is interesting to notice that we meet here an example of a situation in which there are decreasing costs. According to the traditional theory, the state has to intervene in such a case to avoid the risk that a monopoly extracts a super-profit from customers. We just saw that a profit-seeking organization may well offer a very low price to some "disadvantaged" customers.

3. UNIVERSAL ACCESS TO DIGITAL TECHNIQUES

As already stressed, information has the specific characteristic that, whenever it is produced, it can be duplicated and circulated indefinitely, at almost zero cost. There is a fixed cost – which may be important – as regards the infrastructure. But, once this is built, the use of it is not very costly. From this point of view, the digital divide, at least inside a country, could probably disappear: Once the network is built and information is created, it can be disseminated at a low marginal cost (the only individualized parts are the computer itself, the cost of learning and the cost of time for the user). Because of these characteristics it is tempting to make a plea for free universal access to digital techniques and programs in order to reduce or to suppress the digital divide. The argument is similar to the one used about drugs: as the marginal cost of producing drugs is very low – as is the provision of many digital services – why not give them for free to those who have low incomes or to poor countries? This, obviously, raises the problem of intellectual property rights on which we will now focus our attention.

3.1 Utilitarian and Philosophical Arguments in Favor or Against Intellectual Property Rights

The traditional argument in favor of patents and copyrights is well known. The one who has invented a new technique or a new idea is its creator and – according to an old intellectual tradition – he is therefore the legitimate owner of this technique or this idea. It may be considered that this statement has a deep philosophical foundation. In fact, a man can be considered as free only if he is the owner of his body and his mind. Therefore, he is also the legitimate owner of what has been invented by his brain. Economic goods have always been created and their creation cannot be separated from their creator.

Because this process of ownership is legitimate, it is also efficient. The existence of a property right on a technique or an idea implies the development of incentives to innovate and to invent new techniques and ideas. As far as these property rights are recognized and protected, an inventor gets a return from his inventions. Thus, it seems perfectly logical to extend the traditional view about the creation of property rights to intellectual property.

From a purely utilitarian point of view, it is not clear which way is the best to diminish the digital gap. On the one hand, defining and protecting intellectual property rights stimulates innovation and anyone may benefit, all over the world, from a higher rate of progress in digital techniques and computer programs. On the other hand, as far as the marginal cost of providing, for instance, a computer program is about zero, it seems that it would be "socially" optimal to impose free access for everyone – or, if not, access at a moderate cost – at least for those who suffer from the digital divide.

In fact, in spite of the wide concern about the digital divide, it seems that there is a general tendency in the world to better protect intellectual property rights. Traditionally, patents are defined only for an idea incorporated into a concrete thing. But, more and more, patents are issued to protect ideas (music, computer programs, genes, and so on). From this point of view, the digital divide may be increased as far as more and more money would have to be spent to have access, for instance, to the best computer programs.

Now, if we consider that intellectual property rights are justified not only for utilitarian reasons, but, more deeply, for reasons of principle, these principles ought to predominate and utilitarian reasons would be without any importance: One must not compromise with a principle for any reason. Therefore, it is important to evaluate to which extent the definition and defense of intellectual property rights is a matter of principle.

In fact, there are very strong arguments against intellectual property rights and, therefore, against the existence of patents on computer programs, as discussed below.

Patents create monopolies and exclusion. Defining a property right consists of recognizing that the owner has an exclusive right to use a scarce resource or good (which, by definition, necessarily implies exclusion because of its scarcity). But this exclusive right may be considered as a monopoly defined and protected by the state. Now, whenever a resource is scarce, and exclusion has to be defined, it is legitimate – as we have seen – to attribute the ownership of this resource to the one who has created it. But an idea is not scarce: once it has been invented, it can be duplicated without any limit. In such a case, cannot a patent be considered as a monopoly privilege which may be legitimate, but which is imposing a cost on "society" and which prevents the less affluent from benefiting from an idea, the marginal cost of which is zero?

Thus, there are conflicting effects of patents and copyrights. On the one hand they create incentives to innovate; on the other hand, they create barriers to the intellectual activity of others by limiting the spreading of ideas and techniques the marginal cost of which is zero or low. It is therefore difficult from a utilitarian point of view to make a general case for or against patents and copyrights. It may depend on specific characteristics of the goods and services considered. Let us consider again the case of drugs about which there is a debate much similar to the one about the digital divide. Inequality in the access to health services is often considered as unbearable and many people make a plea for the distribution of drugs at a low price to populations with low incomes. In fact, there is a very high cost of innovation in this field, but once a drug has been invented, the marginal cost of production is usually very low, as is the cost of imitation. If patents did not exist, there would be the risk that no one engages in the search for new drugs, since the return of investments could be very low and even negative. But what is the optimal duration of patents? It cannot be determined in advance, since one does not know the amount of investment and the cost of production of all drugs to be invented in the future. A law determining the duration of patents is thus necessarily arbitrary.

In the field of computer programs there is a further practical difficulty, namely that it is difficult to determine to which extent an idea is really new and has to be protected. In fact, the rate of innovation is so high that any bureaucratic process aimed at determining the originality of a new program or of a new addition to an existing program may be lagging behind the process of innovation, which, by the way, means that patents and copyrights may not be useful.

From a more philosophical point of view, patents and copyrights on ideas raise an important problem: They imply that, once someone has had an idea, others are prevented from discovering the same idea or a similar one. As ideas are not scarce, there is no basis for this process of exclusion, which creates a right of some over the minds of others. It is quite obvious that I own my ideas. But, whenever I choose to express them, I choose to make them some sort of public goods (no exclusion, no rivalry). Thus a patent on an idea, such as software, would mean I have rights on others' brains and thinking. At the extreme, any expression of thought could be patented, preventing any piece of literature.

3.2 Private Protection of Intellectual Property Rights

There are other ways to protect intellectual property rights than patents and copyrights, such as:

- Secrecy on some parts of the process of production (for instance, source codes in the case of Microsoft).
- Contractual means: by forbidding the buyer of a program or a book to sell it, fully or partly, to someone else.
- Technical solutions preventing the buyer of a program from transferring it to someone else.
- Innovation itself. As just mentioned, when the rate of innovation is very high, it is difficult for an imitator to keep in pace with the producer of new ideas. Moreover, a very innovative firm keeps its market for a long time because there is a cost in shifting to another producer or another product. It is particularly true as regards computer programs where there is a snowball effect: Those who are accustomed, for instance, to using Microsoft products prefer to go on with other Microsoft programs. The snowball effect is usually considered as a source of natural monopoly. But it may rather be considered as a sort of natural protection of intellectual property rights.

As is well known, many people (particularly public authorities and courts) object to what they call a "dominant position" of a firm such as Microsoft. They do not claim that *Microsoft* products might be freely given, but, at least, that *Microsoft* be obliged to disclose – or to sell at a moderate price – its source codes, so that any producer be able to offer products compatible with those of Microsoft. In some sense, this is implicitly considered as a means to facilitate the dissemination of computer programs and, therefore, to diminish the digital divide.

But it is in fact paradoxical that public authorities, which are granting all sorts of monopoly privileges to themselves or to those who get patents and copyrights, do not accept a private protection of intellectual property rights! And courts are giving producers property rights on ideas that have been developed by Microsoft, which Microsoft is understandably trying to protect.

It is in fact characteristic that there is competition nowadays, for instance, between proprietary systems – such as Microsoft – and non-proprietary ones, such as Linux. And it is also characteristic that, in spite of being free, Linux does not eliminate Windows. It means that rapid innovation is the best protection of intellectual property rights; and it implies that there is no reason to oblige Microsoft to disclose its codes. The free working of digital systems has the result that people have the possibility to get programs for free. Is not that a spontaneous way to diminish the digital divide?

The best strategy for a program producer is not to invest in patents, but to innovate rapidly. From this point of view, there is a big difference between computer programs and drugs: developing a new drug implies years of research, which is not the case for programs. Moreover, reverse engineering is relatively easy for drugs, since it just means trying to know their chemical composition, whereas it is much more difficult to do reverse engineering to try to discover source codes of programs. It is in the interest of a firm not to invest in reverse engineering and imitation, but to develop its own products.

Moreover, the high speed of innovation in digital activities implies an ever-increasing diversification both of hardware and software. It is pointless to try to avoid any digital divide for any new technique or any new program and product. As already stressed, there is a typical process of market spread in an innovating activity: At the beginning the marginal cost of production is high and the selling price is high. But the wealthiest people who buy the new product make it possible for the producer to improve his production process and to innovate. Little by little the cost and the price go down and the product is more and more available for lower-income customers. In some sense the initial digital divide is a condition for its own disappearance. As for other economic or social problems, relying on spontaneous processes is the best way to solve them. There is no exception for the digital divide.

NOTES

1. Adapted from a report prepared for the Mont Pèlerin Society General meeting, Tokyo, 7–12 September 2008.
2. Thus, it is interesting to notice that Africa, which had the highest internet gap with other continents, has had the highest rate of growth of mobile phones and internet in recent years.
3. The Index of Economic Freedom is published every year by the Heritage Foundation and *The Wall Street Journal*.

PART V

Foundations of economic theory

16. The gap between Austrian economics and the mainstream

There is a strange problem in economics that deserves to be solved or at least to be addressed: the whole of modern economics lies on a common and single foundation, namely the subjective theory of value.[1] However, from this same foundation, several diverging – or even opposite – theories have developed. Now, any scientific approach consists of starting from an assumption (or set of assumptions) and deducting consequences through a logical process of reasoning. If the reasoning is correct – which implies that no additional and more or less specific assumption is added surreptitiously – one might always obtain exactly the same conclusions. In physics, for instance, different theories stem from different assumptions. As an example, one may assume that the sun revolves around the earth or vice versa. But whenever an assumption has been generally adopted, the same consequences are deducted by anyone. Scientific evolution consists of drawing still unknown consequences from the initial set of assumptions or performing a scientific revolution by changing the initial assumptions.

It is not the case in economics, since divergent conclusions are apparently drawn from the same starting assumptions, which necessarily implies that some economists are making one or several errors in their reasoning process and/or that some assumptions are surreptitiously added. Finding these errors or these additional assumptions is therefore a major task or even a major duty for economists, in particular for the Austrian school of economists, who believe that they are the only ones to be faithful to the very foundations of their branch of science. At first glance it seems that the crucial element lies in the shift from the subjective theory of value to the definition of objective and measurable variables. Many economists have scrutinized this problem, but it seems that some more effort could be devoted to it.

1. THE ROTHBARDIAN ATTACK AND ITS SHORTCOMINGS

Murray Rothbard is one of those who have most tried to disentangle what was acceptable and what was not in the existing mainstream economic theory (see Rothbard,1956). Obviously, he was critical of all efforts to introduce some cardinal measurement of utility. But his main attack was the one against indifference curves. He aimed at showing that the traditional apparatus of microeconomics cannot be derived strictly from the basic foundations of economics, but that it implied an additional *ad hoc* assumption, which, by the way, reduces the generality of microeconomics. In fact, the basic assumptions just imply that an individual is rational in the sense that he is able to *act* according to his own goals, to compare the utility for him of different goals and to choose the means that seem the best for him in order to reach the preferred goals. It is only by acting that the individual reveals his preferred choices.

Now, traditional economics, in order to define measurable variables, add a specific assumption, namely that individuals consider all possible sets of goods and services and determine all possible sets that give them the same "amount" of utility, irrespective of any actual action. From this assumption it is possible, for instance, to derive a mathematical equality between the ratio of marginal utilities brought about by two different goods, and the ratio of their prices (that is, their relative price). This equality can exist only as far as one makes the assumption that each individual is characterized by a continuously derivable utility function, which is certainly an ad hoc and unrealistic assumption. It is clear that there is no logical or mathematical error in the reasoning process of mainstream economists.[2] But, according to Rothbard, the problem may lie in the unnecessary and unjustified introduction of an additional assumption (about utility functions).

Bryan Caplan (1999) published an interesting article in which, among other things, he challenges the criticisms addressed by Rothbard to the traditional neoclassical approach. In fact, Caplan is not systematically critical of Austrian economics. He looks for what he considers to be the main disagreements between Austrian and neoclassical economists and he concludes that there is no reason to abandon neoclassical economics, because the main specific Austrian assumptions are either without great importance or not acceptable. Caplan focuses on four main topics. The first two are concerned with the "Austrian alternatives to neoclassical consumer theory" (the concept of indifference and the debate about continuous utility functions vs. discrete value scales); the other two are concerned with "reconstructing welfare economics" ("demonstrated preference, social utility and the coordination norm" on the one hand; "public goods" on the other). Given the purpose of the present chapter, we will focus only on the first two topics of Caplan's article.

Caplan first challenges the argument of Ludwig von Mises and Rothbard according to which "it is impossible for action to demonstrate indifference." He stresses that there is no reason to assume that "all preferences can be revealed in action," since Mises and Rothbard themselves consider that it is legitimate to use introspection to derive meaningful statements in the field of social science. And it is quite true, for instance, that the general statement according to which human beings act rationally is not inferred from human actions, but from a general knowledge of human nature that we can obtain, in particular, through introspection.

In fact, the use of the concept of "indifference" may not be considered as a correct description of the way individuals actually behave, but as a "stylization," an elegant way to present in simple terms a set of complex phenomena. Thus, drawing indifference curves may be considered not as a way to describe real action, but as a way to describe how individuals think and make their decisions. It is also quite true that it is often simpler not to use such a stylization, but in some cases it may help in the understanding of the logic of choice.

To illustrate, let us consider, for instance, the description of an individual's behavior when he has to choose between two goods, *i* and *j*. It is traditional to represent this situation by drawing a graph on which the quantities of each good are measured on each axis and there is a budget constraint, AB, indicating the various sets of goods *i* and *j*, which the individual can choose, given the limitation of his resources. A neoclassical economist would draw indifference curves and he would say: "The choice made by the individual is given by the point – let us call it point C – at which the budget constraint is tangential to an indifference curve." An Austrian economist would just say: "If the individual chooses any point C on the budget constraint AB, although he could have chosen any point on AB, he reveals that point C is preferred to any other possibility," and there is no need for drawing indifference curves. Thus, basically, there is no real discrepancy between these approaches, which both describe correctly the logic of choice. At the utmost, one might say that it is not necessary to always use the complex presentation of indifference curves (why should one complicate what could be simple?).

But the use of indifference curves can also help one visualize a problem, for instance whenever one wants to understand rapidly the effects of some tax change. However, there is also a risk in such a case that one jumps from this legitimate use of abstract instruments (indifference curves) to an illegitimate use. This occurs particularly when an economist enters the realm of quantification. It happens, for instance, when he shifts from purely qualitative concepts – and indifference enters this category – to quantitative ones, such as the concept of income, as stressed below. In short, using or rejecting the concept of indifference seems to be a marginal problem that cannot be at the origin of any great difference between Austrian and

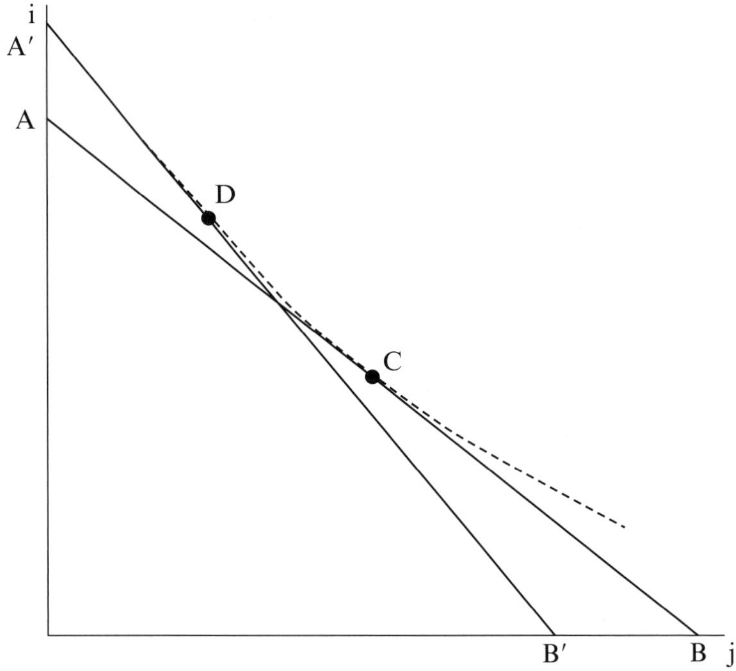

Figure 16.1 Individual preferences and choices

neoclassical economists. And we may accept the answer made by Caplan to Rothbard's attack against the concept of indifference without fearing the disappearance of the distinctive character of Austrian economics.

Agreeing with Rothbard, Walter Block states that (1999, p. 23): "It is an undeniable (for example, praxeological) fact that people act so as to improve their position, not to move from one state of affairs to another, where both are in all respects identical." This is certainly true. By acting, individuals reveal that they prefer the choice they have made to any other action. But is that necessarily and completely inconsistent with indifference curves? Let us consider Figure 16.1 where an indifference curve has been drawn. It is possible to interpret it in the following way: if ever the budget constraint is AB, the individual chooses point C. But, if ever his budget constraint was to shift to A'B' and he was to choose point D, it may happen that he does not feel better or worse in D than in C. The indifference map does not mean that the individual is *actually* indifferent between C and D: By choosing C, the individual reveals that C is his preferred position, given the fact that his actual budget constraint is AB. The choice between C and D is not a relevant one, since it is not actually open to the individual. Thus, the use of indifference curves is perfectly compatible with the statement of Walter Block according to which individuals *actually* always choose by acting (that is, they are not actually indifferent). Therefore, the concept of "indifference" does not mean that the individual may behave as Buridan's ass. It is just an abstract way of representing the logic of choice.

Thus, it is acceptable to consider that Austrian and neoclassical economists may be – but are not necessarily – "fellow travellers," at least until this point in the logical reasoning process at which one uses the concept of indifference. Some Austrians, such as Rothbard or Block, may choose another road before this point, and some beyond this point, without causing any damage to the consistency and uniqueness of the Austrian approach. Should we say that we are "indifferent" between accepting or rejecting the concept of indifference? In some sense, we are. The real discrepancy between the Austrian and the neoclassical approaches – and, obviously, the superiority of the Austrian one – has to be found somewhere else.

Neoclassical economics is derived not only from the concept of indifference, but also from the assumption of continuous (and differentiable) utility functions. Rothbard (1956) is critical – as is Block (1999) – of this assumption, which constitutes one of the main elements in the debate, according to Caplan. This assumption – along with the concept of indifference – is crucial for neoclassical economists, since it makes possible to derive the basic equation according to which the ratio of marginal utilities of two goods is equal to the price ratio of these goods. It is obvious that this equality is meaningless if the indifference concept and the continuity assumption are not accepted. But, by rejecting them, is there not a risk to lose some information and some instrument for a better understanding (although these assumptions can be considered as unrealistic)? In fact one may interpret both these assumptions as a way to make a useful reasoning "at the limit".

Let us assume a world with two commodities, A and B, each of them being constituted by entire units which cannot be divided into smaller pieces. Let us also take the case of an individual who prefers 3 A (3 units of A) to 2 B (2 units of B), and who, moreover, prefers 2 B to 2 A. According to Rothbard, it is not realistic to assume that utility functions are continuous and that the individual may be indifferent between some quantity of A and some quantity of B, since, for instance, the choice (or the "non-choice") between 2.68 A and 2 B cannot be revealed in actual action, because it is materially impossible to desire 2.68 A and because the concept of indifference is meaningless. But when writing that our imaginary individual is indifferent between holding 2.68 A and holding 2 B, we do not mean that he will *actually* express this indifference or make it clear by abstaining from doing any action (which is the very objection made by Rothbard). We just make an abstract statement and we express it in a way which will facilitate the subsequent process of reasoning. Generally speaking, in mathematics, whenever one is reasoning "at the limit", one does not pretend that he is describing something which really exists, but one thus gets the instruments of a better understanding of phenomena.

In other words, any scientific reasoning consists in extracting from a complex reality the features which are characteristic and always present in this reality. Thus, in economics, one does not describe in full details the way individuals behave, but one tries to extract the undebatable characteristics of their behavior and to express them in the most efficient way in order to allow an improvement in reasoning.

Thus, let us imagine that our individual shifts from a situation in which he is facing a choice between 3 A and 2 B (in which case he clearly demonstrates that he prefers 3 A to 2 B) to a situation in which he is facing a choice between 2 A and 2 B (in which case he clearly demonstrates that he prefers 2 B to 2 A). If we imagine that the units of A can be divided into smaller parts (even if they are not concretely in reality), the logic of choices necessarily implies the following preferences:

3 A > 2.99 A
2.99 A > 2.98 A
2.98 A > 2.97 A
etc. . . .

And since 3 A > 2 B et 2 A < 2 B, there may be a certain quantity of A, placed between 2 and 3 units, which the individual considers as giving the same utility as 2 B, which means that he is indifferent. This quantity may not be 2.68 A – as we had assumed – but 2.6785942 A, or any other value (it is obvious that the precise value is not relevant). However, there is no logical necessity or praxeological necessity for this specific situation to exist and one can imagine that the individual "jumps" from one bundle of goods to the other without actually considering the possibility of a situation of indifference. On the other hand, it is also acceptable to assume that the individual may be indifferent between 2.6785942 A and 2 B and this case is compatible with the logic of choices. This means that the traditional approach of microeconomics based on the concept of indifference, although it is not fully incompatible with the logic of choice, has not the character of generality which it pretends to have.

Rothbard does not accept this abstraction of the traditional approach and, therefore, he considers as meaningless some of the traditional microeconomic reasonings, particularly the famous equality between the ratio of marginal utilities and the ratio of prices (and all statements which are derived from it). He may be right in so doing. But one may ask which theoretical construction he is proposing to replace the neoclassical one. And one has to admit that the promised "reconstruction" (in Rothbard, 1956) does not exist. Happily, it seems to us that one ought not to look for the main divergence between Austrian and neoclassical approaches at this point, but beyond. In other words, being an Austrian economist does not imply accepting or rejecting the neoclassical theory of utility, at least if restricting it to the use of indifference curves. As far as he could accept them, in spite of their lack of generality, an Austrian economist could view indifference curves not as a way to describe the actual behavior of human beings, but as a simple way to express it.

Contrary to what is suggested by Rothbard, the famous equality between the ratio of marginal utilities and the price ratio[3] (which we may call "the neoclassical equality" in the present context) does not imply a pretense to measure utilities. What is in fact the real meaning of the statement according to which an individual prefers 3A to 2B? It means that, taking into account the already held quantities of A and B, the utility of 3A is higher than the utility of 2B. If, for instance, in isolation, the individual can obtain 3A or 2B from one working hour, he will choose to use his additional working hour to produce 3A. Here again, there is a reasoning at the limit: at this point, the "internal terms of trade in production" (the marginal rate of transformation) for the individual are equal to 3A/2B. Now, if exchange becomes possible, the individual will compare his internal marginal rate of transformation to the terms of trade on the market. Therefore, he will compare the marginal utility he can obtain by using one working hour to produce a good he may either consume or exchange. Relative market prices are perfectly defined and observable. The behavior of the individual consists in using this information on prices – which is available to anyone – in order to evaluate whether he gets a higher utility from autarky or from exchange. This does not imply a strict equality between the ratio of utilities and the price ratio. But, once again, the neoclassical equality is just the outcome of reasoning at the limit: The individual *tends* toward a situation in which this equality prevails, without possibly reaching it in reality.

Thus, we would be inclined to agree with Caplan in his rejection of Rothbard's attack, which means that Rothbard's objections to the neoclassical analysis – although acceptable – are only of a minor importance. At any rate, if ever one is not convinced by the above arguments, it is nevertheless useful to accept them on a provisional basis just in order to be able to investigate to which extent significant discrepancies between the Austrian and the neoclassical approach still remain. Thus, by putting aside Rothbard's arguments, an Austrian economist accepts to put himself in what could be considered as the worst situation to support the Austrian approach. However, we do believe that it is possible and that, beyond Rothbard's attack against neoclassical economics, there is at least one logical error in the reasoning chain, which makes the neoclassical approach debatable.

2. MISCONCEPTIONS ABOUT VALUE

Let us accept the idea according to which introducing an additional assumption – the existence of continuous utility functions, which makes it possible to write the "neoclassical equality" – cannot be considered as the main explanation of the discrepancies between mainstream economists and Austrian economists. In fact, one could reinterpret the criticism made by Rothbard in the following way: It is not necessary to introduce the abovementioned assumption (about continuous and derivable utility functions) in order to get significant results, for instance as regards the role of prices and the behavior of suppliers and demanders in markets. As this assumption is unrealistic, it is better just to forget it.

Now, it is true that, as far as the role of prices is concerned, mainstream economists and Austrian economists accept supply and demand curves as essential elements of economic analysis. These instruments can be derived from one or the other approach. Both categories of economists agree on the fact a demand curve is decreasing and a supply curve is increasing.[4] Now, prices are observable facts of life and any scientific approach of economics has to take them into consideration and, if possible, to explain how they are determined. The fact that demand is a decreasing function of price is logically derived from the logic of choice.[5] And if ever an economist, just by adding a specific assumption, was to obtain the reverse result, there would be an untenable contradiction so that this specific assumption ought to be abandoned.[6] But if prices are observable and measurable facts, other variables traditionally used by economists and considered as measurable are nothing but an arbitrary construction of external observers. They are not relevant for human action. It is the case for a concept such as income and, more generally, for most accounting variables.

From the subjective theory of value, one can logically deduct the theory of exchange, which is necessarily, eternally and universally true. The theory of exchange leads to a universally understandable and visible concept, that of a market price. In particular, a relative price is an objective and measurable fact of life for both partners in an exchange. The existence of a relative price makes it possible to express the market value of two traded goods. For the concerned traders, as well as for any external observer, the market value of what is sold by an individual is equal to the market value of what he is buying in any act of exchange. It is well known that any trader enjoys a higher level of utility after trade than before trade (since he is rational and he would not have freely traded if he was to lose utility). Thus, we can measure the instruments of action (the market value of traded goods), but we cannot measure the ultimate aim of action (the increase in utility).

To illustrate, let us assume a world with two goods (*A* and *B*) and four individuals (*w*, *x*, *y* and *z*). An equilibrium market relative price between both goods appears on the market from an exchange between *w* and *x* and an exchange between *y* and *z*, both exchanges using the same relative price. Individual *w* understands the meaning of this relative price; he knows how to value the exchange he is doing by using this price. Due to this prevailing price, he knows how many units of good *B* he can obtain in exchange for the one unit of good *A* he is selling. What is meaningful for him is, on the one hand, the market price and, on the other hand, the quantity of good *A* he is disposing of (and, therefore, the quantity of good *B* he obtains). He can play at doing multiplications, for instance by multiplying the number of units he obtains by the price of this good in terms of the other good, taken as a numeraire. Thus he gets what is called the "market exchange value" of his purchase and his sale. Using these market values he can develop his own bookkeeping. Such information can be transmitted to the outside world, but it is not highly useful to the concerned individual who mainly cares about the terms of his transaction: He knows that he can get a certain quantity of good *B* by abandoning a given quantity of good *A*. Moreover, whenever there are a great number of goods and a great number of potential co-contractors, the individual benefits from using money, which facilitates his economic calculus and his choices.

By definition, individual *w* knows that the market value of what he sells is equal to the market value of what he purchases, whatever the quantity he is selling. There is no necessity to look for an empirical test of this basic fact or to express it through some transaction account. In the simplified world we are examining, it is certainly possible to add the value of transactions made by the pair $w-x$ and the value of transactions made by the pair $y-z$, as far as they use a common numeraire. But such an addition is deprived of any meaning. Since evaluating the market value of the transaction made by *w* and *x* is, by itself, without any interest for *w* and *x* (as what is meaningful to them is the gain in utility they are obtaining through exchange), and since it is, similarly, for *y* and *z*, adding both market evaluations is also deprived of any interest. The equality between the market value of the purchase side of a transaction and the market value of the sale side is purely tautological. It is certainly the consequence of human actions, but it does not help us to understand any element of social life. As it is meaningless for the concerned traders, it ought to be a fortiori for an external observer. In fact, the traders do not desire to exchange goods with such or such market values, but goods that have such or such utility for them. Therefore, they do not care, for instance, about some maximization of the market value of their exchanges.

Measuring market values is not related to human action. An external observer can certainly have fun in multiplying quantities by relative prices or by adding several market values,[7] but he ought not to draw any conclusion from these accounting games. All the interesting information is contained in the fact w and x exchange *freely* and benefit from their exchange. That we know a priori, so that the measuring of market values cannot add any additional information. Therefore, it is all the more absurd to add the market values of the exchanges made by the pair $w-x$ and the pair $y-z$. Certainly, adding the market values of what he sells and what he purchases can help an individual to improve his decision-making process. He knows, for instance, that by selling a certain quantity of labor services on the market he can receive a basket of various commodities. But the fact these market prices give him specific information, which he can use efficiently, does not mean that it has some meaning for an external observer.

Market prices are a part of the information an acting individual needs, as is the case for his juridical or climatic environment. But they have a meaning only in relation with individual human decisions and only for the one who uses them and not for an external observer who cannot know the ordinal scale of the preferences of other people. In a complex economy – more complex than the schematic one we referred to previously – the price system makes it possible for an individual to compare a great number of possible exchange actions and, therefore, to choose the ones which are preferable for him. Prices – and money – make economic calculus possible, but economic calculus is necessarily an individual activity. Prices make it possible for an individual to evaluate his relations with others, but this individual economic calculus in no way paves the way for any objective economic calculus. The economic calculus of an individual has nothing in common with the computations done by an external observer who, by so doing, is not developing any economic calculus, but just doing accounting. Now, accounting is not an instrument for understanding, it is nothing but an instrument for individual action.

Shifting from ordinal values to cardinal values is perfectly legitimate (it is exactly what people do when they exchange). But this does not mean that *all* cardinal values are therefore justified, for instance market values for other uses than those concerned by individual economic calculus. Anyone can legitimately maintain his own bookkeeping, but aggregating bookkeepings has no meaning, at least for the very simple reason that a group of individuals does not trade with another group of individuals. Exchange is always individual and, therefore, bookkeeping ought to be, too. This certainly means, for instance, that a "collective" account such as the balance of payments is absolutely meaningless and that publishing it is perfectly useless (and even dangerous). Besides, if a concept which is exogenous to individual economic calculus – that of nation – was not introduced, balance of payments statistics would not exist. What is relevant for an individual is what he is exchanging with other individuals in the world, not knowing the exchanges made with the rest of the world by all the individuals entering a specific category to which he belongs, such as his nation. Such information is not linked to specific human actions.

It is meaningful for an individual to use a price, such as the quantity of a good exchanged against another one, or to measure a market value, since he can thus compare different possible uses of the resources he has created. In so doing, he does not aim at maximizing a measurable variable, such as the price of a good he sells or he purchases, or the value of what he is selling – which can be called his "market income" or his "monetary income." He has interest only in maximizing his utility, which cannot be measured. The measurable variables are only instruments for action. Thus, due to the existence of prices, an individual can choose the best ways to maximize his utility. But a measurable concept such as the concept of monetary income is not fundamentally useful for an individual, although it can be relevant for individual decisions under specific conditions. Thus, an individual may like to know his annual monetary income, because he has a limited number of resources that he can sell (his labor services, for instance), whereas his potential demands are much more diversified. He needs to know the market price of one hour of his work, since working hours are the only things he may sell. Thus he can evaluate what he gets for one hour of work. But he is certainly not interested in maximizing his monetary income, in multiplying his working time by the hourly wage.

But if a concept such as "monetary income" is meaningful for an individual as one element in the process of choice, it becomes completely meaningless whenever one is summing up two such variables – and even more so with a great number of such variables – for instance the monetary income of two (or more) individuals. The sum of two monetary incomes may have an interest and may have a meaning for the entrepreneur who has to pay these incomes and who has to decide on a process of production, but it ought not to be considered as relevant for an external observer. When defining such a variable – for instance, the national income or the total amount of wages paid in a country – an economist or a statistician gives an arbitrary meaning to a concept that in fact loses any meaning and which ought not to be used as an instrument for action. Having no meaning for those who are concerned, these concepts cannot be considered as having any meaning for external observers. Thus, whereas the total amount of wages paid to the wage earners in a firm has a meaning for the owner of this same firm, the total amount of wages paid to wage earners in two different firms has no meaning for the owner of each firm and, therefore, has no meaning for anyone.

Therefore, summing up the wages paid in all the firms that exist on a national territory is also arbitrary. Traditional concepts as the "wage bill" of a nation or the national income of a country are totally deprived of any meaning. Accounting makes it possible for an individual to evaluate whether his exchange activities are profitable or destructive. He needs it as soon as he does not limit himself to pure exchange activities – in which he can evaluate the utility gain of each exchange without needing any accounting – but is doing productive activities that are linked to exchange activities. For instance, the owner of a firm needs to work out several interrelated exchange contracts in order to obtain a final product. He cannot evaluate the utility of one given wage contract without including it in a set of numerous contracts with other wage earners, lenders and providers of goods. Accounting makes it possible for him to better evaluate the specific contribution of a given contract to the final creation of value. As production factors and goods are heterogeneous, prices help the individual to engage in complex economic calculations. And if it appears, for instance, that his entrepreneurial activity is the source of a profit, he is able to compare the value for him of this profit – for example, the quantity of desirable goods he can thus obtain – and the subjective cost of the efforts he has performed to get it. From this point of view it is quite obvious that it is not sufficient for profit to be positive for it to be desired. If the opportunity cost of getting this profit is too high, the corresponding activity will not be undertaken. As a market figure, the amount of profit does not mean anything and does not bring any information to anyone, except to the one who receives it. It is therefore meaningless to add the profit made by different individuals and different firms in a society.

Thus, let us imagine a situation in which a gain received by w has been obtained by an effort (for instance, in terms of working hours) much higher than the gain received by x, in which the monetary profit obtained by w is much lower than the one obtained by x, but in which w is satisfied and considers that his gain is worth the effort, whereas *x* considers that his gain is not sufficient (so that he would have not made the effort, had he known the result). What is the relevance and the value of the information we can get from a mere figure about the global monetary profit of both individuals? It is not worthwhile. On the contrary, the amount of profit obtained by the owners of any firm is interesting information for those who are considering the purchase of its shares.

In any society, relative prices (and monetary prices when money does exist) constitute the only variables that are not only useful but indispensable for individuals. All other so-called economic variables are only *ad hoc* constructions, which may be made for any reason – maybe to further help decision-making, but also just for fun or curiosity – but that are not necessarily useful for human action in any circumstance, even at the individual level. For instance, all those who are supplying or demanding labor services are interested in knowing a specific price, called the wage rate (per unit of time). But it does not imply that they have any interest in knowing their annual income.

Let us take, as an example, the case of an individual who is selling his labor services to several demanders during one period of time (for instance, one year). Each time he is considering the possibility of selling one more hour of work to any demander, by using the price per hour of his labor (in terms of money or commodities) he is in a position to decide whether this marginal effort is worthwhile. But he may not be interested in adding the monetary value of all the working hours he has sold to various people during one year, in order to evaluate something that he would arbitrarily call his annual "income," since choices are only made on the basis of marginal costs and benefits. As a concept such as "income" is not relevant for individual decision-making, it cannot have any relevance for economic theory. And as it is not relevant for individual decision-making, it cannot, *a fortiori*, have any meaning at a more aggregated level.

Let us underline it again: one cannot imagine an exchange economy – a society of human beings – without prices, but one can perfectly imagine a society in which the concept of income does not exist, which means that the concept of income ought not to have any theoretical status in economics. And the same could be said about a number of other variables that are frequently used in economic analysis.

Thus, a major part of traditional economics, which uses such variables, lacks the characteristic of universality, which is one of the main criteria of any scientific approach. This, in our opinion, is the real point of discrepancy between Austrian economics and neoclassical economics. This, moreover, is a reason to believe that Austrian economics are superior or, rather, that Austrian economics are scientific, while the greatest part of neoclassical economics is not. The difference between both approaches is not only a question of choosing between two alternative paradigms. More fundamentally, we believe that a scientific approach of social problems implies abandoning the greatest part of neoclassical economics. One has not to be afraid at accepting such a radical proposal. It is not a scientific attitude to try to explain phenomena that cannot be explained or that do not exist, or to reason with the use of concepts that are *ad hoc* or meaningless constructions without any real relation to actual human behavior.

This discussion also sheds some light on an important problem, namely the existence of the so-called "income effect" of a price change in microeconomics. In Chapter 17 we show that the "income effect" could not have the character of generality attributed to it by all presentations of microeconomics, so that it can be said that the income effect is a myth (from a scientific point of view). Under some very specific circumstances, something similar to the income effect may exist, but the only universal – and, therefore, the only scientific – effect is the "substitution effect." By splitting the effects of a price change into a substitution effect and an income effect, traditional economists mix together a universal concept – that of a relative price – and an ad hoc concept – that of income. They implicitly assume that individuals can simultaneously and consistently try to maximize a subjective variable (utility) and an objective one (income), which cannot be consistent.

Now, one may wonder why so many economists have developed analyses well beyond what is acceptable, which is certainly the case of neoclassical economists, and, even more, of extreme heretics such as Marxists and Keynesians. The state is certainly a main culprit in this story. In order to intervene and, possibly, to find justifications to its interventions, it needs measurable concepts. By the way, let us imagine a society without any state. It is very likely, as already said, that one would even not try to measure the annual income of an individual. At least, it is certain that a concept such as the national income would not exist, since it could not be of any value for any action. But as soon as a state exists, it has to find resources. By definition, it gets them by coercion, since the only justification that can be imagined for the state to exist consists of assuming that it has to provide public goods, which, by assumption, could not be provided by private markets and have necessarily to be financed by taxes. As the state cannot levy units of utility, it has to levy monetary resources (except, possibly, in the case of a lump-sum tax) and it does this from an evaluation of resources in terms of market prices. Measurement of economic variables thus becomes an inescapable instrument of economic policy. One does as if one was measuring something that exists, although the measured variables do not exist.

Price theory is perfectly and rigorously derived from the theory of value (either in the Austrian or the neoclassical version), but it is then diverted from its normal role whenever it is used for anything other than individual action. One acts as though prices were the ultimate value of human actions, which is not the case: They are an instrument for individual action, to be used only in a specific context, for instance by the one who acts and not by the one who is observing. It is certainly inconsistent to assume both that an individual wants to maximize his utility and to assume that he wants to maximize his income. But as soon as one is measuring monetary income – or tradable production – one makes possible the surreptitious substitution of one criterion (utility) by another (income, wealth or production).

This certainly does not mean that one has to stop any scientific effort beyond utility theory and some basic price theory. It just means that Austrians and mainstreamers are certainly diverging beyond a point corresponding to a minimum threshold. The conviction that it is an error to develop economic reasoning based on illegitimate (and mainly measurable) concepts induces Austrians to care more about meaningful concepts such as property rights. But such a choice is not arbitrary; it is not just a question of personal mood, it is a question of scientific logic.

NOTES

1. I thank members of the Jean-Baptiste seminar at University Paris-Dauphine for their comments on a previous version of this text (in particular, Guido Hülsmann, Georges Lane and Alain Wolfelsperger).
2. Obviously, many different economists or streams of thought could be found under the label "mainstream" and it is certainly an arbitrary simplification to speak of *the* mainstream. It implies that we cannot be fully fair with all in the following pages. But we think that it does not undermine the core of our argument.
3. It would be more correct not to mention a price ratio between two goods – the price of each of them being implicitly assumed to be, in fact, the exchange ratio between the corresponding good and some currency, used as a numeraire – but to consider the terms of trade between those two goods.
4. In the absence of the so-called "income effect," which we consider later on. One may assume that mainstream economists consider that the income effect always exists, whereas Austrian economists would be more reluctant. The very reason for this difference in emphasis may stem from their diverging assumptions.
5. Contrary to the traditional presentation of textbooks in microeconomics, there is no need for developing a specific theory to explain supply (theory of the producer), since supply is just the other side of demand: There is no demand without supply, no supply without demand. A rational individual is the happier the more goods he gets (demands) for one unit he supplies, or the fewer goods he has to deliver (supply) in order to get one unit of the desired (demanded) good.

6. The other solution would consist in abandoning the rationality assumption, but it is obvious that nothing can be derived from the unrealistic assumption that individuals are irrational, except the idea that all human events are pure random events.
7. In a free society, individuals are able to use their time and own resources as they like, perhaps to compute the number of clouds per day or to add market values to obtain a sum which they label "national income." But, by so doing, they cannot claim they are doing science or explaining anything. And normally it ought to be difficult or impossible to sell such information that ought not to be useful for anyone. This may be the reason why national accounts are always produced by public offices and not by private firms.

17. The income effect does not exist[1]

It is traditional in microeconomics to state that any price change has consequences that can be split into two different effects, the substitution effect and the income effect.[2] As it is assumed that both effects work in divergent directions, the precise reaction of demand or supply to a relative price change can operate either way: The supply curve is not necessarily upward sloping and the demand curve is not necessarily downward sloping. Thus, the income effect has an important role in traditional microeconomics, as well as in applied economics, since it causes one to think, for instance, that there are "kinked curves." Such curves are particularly assumed to exist as regards the supply of labor. Within a certain range, a decrease in the real wage would not bring about a decrease in the supply of labor, since people want to maintain their income and, therefore, increase their supply of labor. As an important consequence in tax theory, the "Laffer effect"[3] would not exist, at least in a given area (the one in which the supply curve for labor is supposed to be atypical). In such a case, an increase in the tax rate on labor income – that is, a decrease in the real after-tax wage – would create a negative income effect which would be compensated for by working more, whereas the Laffer effect assumes that there is always an inverse relation between the tax rate and productive efforts. Similarly, the income effect would account for a possible increase in the rate of savings when the return on savings is decreasing.

The income effect is supposed to exist because one assumes that the concept of income can be defined in a non-ambiguous way. In fact, this is not true. Whereas it is generally assumed that income can be measured, it has no precise meaning, contrary to the concept of utility which is precise, but does not allow any room for measurement. In the present chapter we show that believing in the income effect is not consistent with the logical theory of utility. In reality the income effect can exist only if one adds a specific assumption. Contrary to the general belief according to which the existence of the income effect is a general principle, it is only a possible consequence of a specific assumption. The substitution effect – consistent with the general theory of utility – is the only general principle.

Let us take as an example the supply curve for the labor of an individual and let us imagine a world in which there are only two goods, leisure and wheat. Time is the only scarce production factor and there is, for instance, no scarcity of land, so that the physical productivity of one hour of labor in terms of wheat is constant. There is a certain relative price between leisure and labor (production of wheat), for instance 1/1 (in one hour can be produced one hour of leisure or one pound of wheat). For this given relative price, an individual wishes a certain sharing of his available time between leisure and the production of wheat. If he does not desire to produce and to consume more wheat, it is just because sacrificing one hour of leisure to get one more pound of wheat is not worthwhile from his own point of view. Now, one is used to defining the income of an individual by the quantity of tradable resources (wheat) he is producing at each period and to exclude his production of leisure services from this concept. But such a notion of income is arbitrary in comparison with the more general concept of satisfaction (or utility): The total satisfaction of the individual is equal to the "sum" of the satisfaction he draws from leisure and the satisfaction he draws from consuming the wheat he has produced. Saying that the desired level of income is equal to y is in fact saying that a maximum satisfaction is obtained when the production of wheat – named income – is equal to y and the production of leisure services is equal to x, knowing that $x + P_x y = \underline{t}$, where P_x is the price of one unit of wheat in terms of hours of leisure and $\underline{t}$ is the available quantity of time, such as 24 hours a day.

Let us assume now that some disease occurs in the production of wheat, so that labor productivity is cut by one half or – what is equivalent – that a tax has been introduced on the production of wheat, so that one can get only half a pound of wheat for one hour of work. The opportunity cost of producing and consuming wheat increases in terms of leisure. The logic of choice would imply that one does not produce as much wheat as before.

Referring to this logic of choice, what could be the meaning of the income effect? It implies that an individual aims at maintaining the level of his income, at least partially (that is, at maintaining his production and consumption of wheat). But it is inconsistent to hold both that the aim of the individual is an income target (a certain amount of y) – so that leisure time would be nothing but an instrument that can be used to reach this income target through a process of transformation – and that the individual aims at maximizing his level of satisfaction (that is, obtaining a certain optimal mix of x and y).

In the above example, it is traditional to say that the individual facing an increase in the opportunity cost of wheat may not decrease his production of wheat – although it is more costly in terms of sacrificing leisure – but may decide to work more. Therefore, the supply curve would be backward sloping.[4] There are more work hours when the return of one hour of work is decreasing. The income effect would thus overcompensate the substitution effect. In fact, one believes in the existence of this effect because one implicitly adds a set of *specific assumptions*, of which no one is absolutely and logically necessary. This is to say that the income effect does not exist as a general phenomenon, but that it is a sort of mathematical illusion in a badly specified world.

What happens in reality? If one assumes that an individual increases his supply of labor when the return on work hours decreases, it is necessarily because one has added surreptitiously an additional assumption (if not, one ought to admit that the substitution effect – which necessarily exists – is the only one to be met). Very likely, it is implicitly assumed that wheat, contrary to leisure, is necessary for one's survival, so that if the substitution effect was the only existing effect there would be a risk for an individual of passing under the subsistence level, which he cannot accept. But that is really saying that there are three goods (or three sources of utility) and not two, namely the pleasure drawn from leisure, the pleasure drawn from consuming wheat, and survival services obtained from wheat consumption. One also assumes implicitly that there is only one possible technology to get survival services, namely wheat production (which is called "income"). But why would there not be another one? As an example, it may happen that the concerned individual does know that he can survive by extracting big roots from the soil, the taste of which he does not like very much, but the nutritive value of which is indisputable. As long as wheat is not expensive (in terms of time) in comparison with roots, he prefers to eat wheat. If the opportunity cost of wheat increases too much, he will certainly consider possible substitutions between wheat, roots and leisure.

It may happen that shifting to another consumption pattern cannot be done immediately, since one has to find the most productive field of roots, or to invent suitable instruments to extract the roots. Therefore, during some period of time, the individual may increase his production of wheat in order to survive and to prepare the change in technology. But this is also saying that the existence of the income effect is due to two specific assumptions: the existence of some subsistence level and the existence of transfer costs when shifting from one activity to another. Now, if the individual could have forecast the relative price change between wheat and leisure, he would certainly not have waited until the last moment, which obliges him to increase his supply of work in order to produce wheat. He would probably have decreased earlier his leisure time in order to prepare the new survival technology. Because of the increasing relative price of wheat to roots there is a substitution effect between these goods, which makes it possible to meet both targets (survival and gastronomic pleasure) in different proportions.

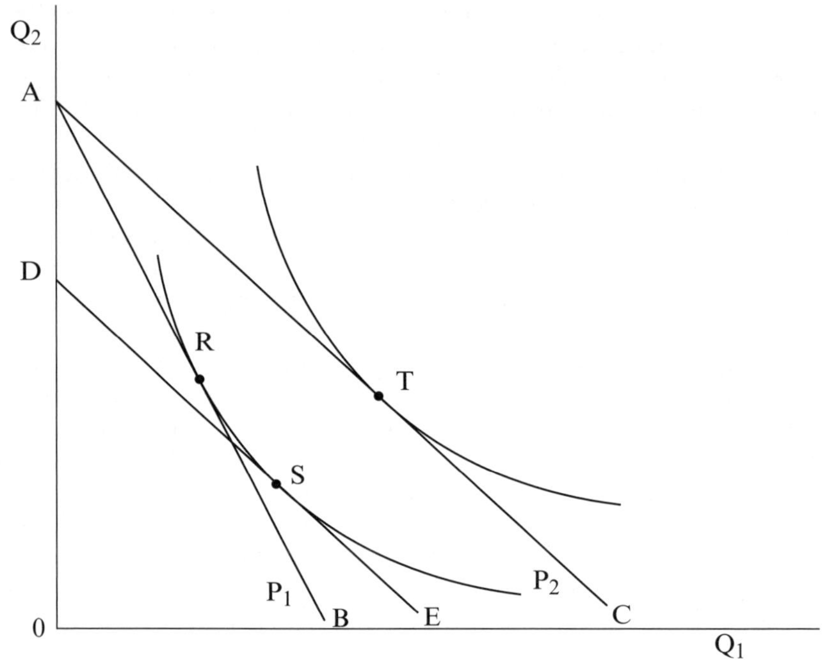

Figure 17.1 Traditional representation of the substitution effect and the income effect

One thinks that there is an income effect only because the model has been badly specified and one has surreptitiously added implicit assumptions that can be interpreted as the introduction of an exogenous event in a world in which there are rigidities of a technical or institutional nature. Choices are then reshuffled and, during a transitory period, what is named the income effect may appear in certain circumstances, as the result of a search for minimizing adjustment costs until the process of change in activities has led to all desired substitutions.

The above remarks can be reconciled with traditional statements of microeconomics. Let us take the traditional figure, which is used to illustrate the existence of both the substitution and the income effects (Figure 17.1).[5] The initial equilibrium position of a "consumer"[6] – who has to choose between two goods, Q_1 and Q_2, for a relative price p_1 – is point R. If the price of Q_1 decreases, the new budget constraint is AC and the equilibrium point becomes T. Now, one can obtain this latter point by a formal splitting of the path from R to T into two paths: The path from R to S represents the substitution effect (pure relative price change, the utility level being maintained constant), and the shift from S to T represents the income effect (the decrease in the price of Q_1 corresponding to a gain in the purchasing power of income). Such a presentation does not help to clarify an important aspect of the problem, namely that the rotation of the budget constraint from AB to AC implicitly assumes that the consumer holds a stock of goods Q_2 equal to OA, so that the relative price change between Q_1 and Q_2 does not modify the position of point A. For a stock of goods Q_2 equal to OA, the individual can obtain a different (higher) quantity of Q_1. On the contrary, if the individual was holding (or producing) good Q_1, it would be point B that would stay at the same place and the budget constraint would then cut the Q_2 axis at a point lower than D. Total utility would thus diminish. The result is perfectly logical: If the individual supplies Q_2 and demands Q_1, a decrease in the relative price of Q_1 (increase in the relative price of Q_2) leads to the transformation of more Q_2 in goods Q_1. The graph can then be interpreted from three different points of view:

1. The relative price change reflects a technological change. Thus, with the same quantity of work, OA, an individual can obtain a greater quantity of wheat (OC instead of OB). The figure then does not represent the choices of the abstract "consumer" of textbooks, but the choices of the individual who *acts* (for instance, Robinson alone on his island). If the productivity of labor is increasing, the individual will produce more wheat. In Figure 17.2, OA represents the number of available hours by day, namely 24 hours. When the relative price is p_1, the amount of work is equal to AV, the quantity of leisure to OV and the quantity of wheat produced to OZ. When the price of wheat in terms of work hours shifts to p_2, work increases (AU), leisure decreases (OU) and the quantity of wheat produced increases (OW). The marginal sacrifice necessary to obtain one more unit of wheat having diminished, one substitutes wheat for leisure. There is a pure substitution effect.
2. Figure 17.2 now represents an exchange economy. The individual can obtain wheat (Q_1) by selling tomatoes (Q_2) he produces. Given the existing techniques and the limitation of his available time, the maximum quantity of tomatoes he can produce is OA. If the wheat price decreases from p_1 to p_2 (the price of tomatoes increases), he will sell more tomatoes to get wheat. In Figure 17.2 his sales of tomatoes increase from AV to AU and his consumption of his own tomatoes decreases from OV to OU. His income does not change if it is measured in terms of tomatoes; it increases in terms of wheat. But there is only a process of substitution between both commodities and no income effect.

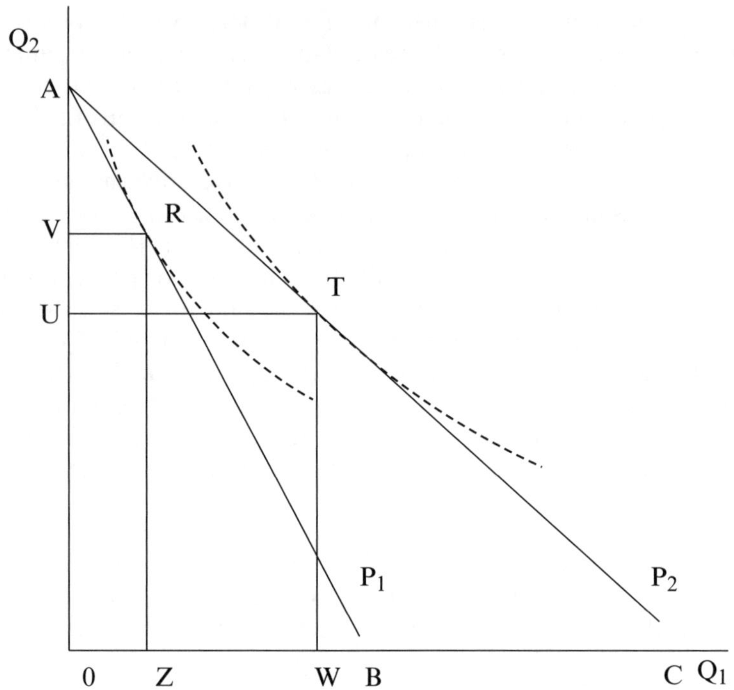

Figure 17.2 Effects of a technological change or a price change

3. Figure 17.1 could be interpreted as representing the *partial* behavior of an individual *only* in his role as a consumer. He is a producer of another commodity, Q_3, which is not represented in the figure, and he demands Q_1 and Q_2. When the budget constraint AB is rotating to the position AC, one implicitly assumes that the relative price decrease of Q_1 in terms of Q_2 does not affect the valuation of Q_3 –the supplied good – in terms of Q_2. The supply of commodity Q_3 in exchange for Q_1 and Q_2 would remain equal to OA (in terms of Q_2), which is debatable. In fact, there is a decrease in the price of Q_1 relatively to Q_3, which ought to affect the supply of Q_3. The new budget constraint is very likely situated between AC and DE (Figure 17.1).[7]

These three interpretations are useful since they make it possible to clarify what precisely is the behavior of the individual who acts. But they may also help in understanding why the traditional distinction between the substitution effect and the income effect is misleading. From a purely formal point of view, one can distinguish, as we have seen, the shift from

R to S and the shift from S to T (Figure 17.1). But these shifts do not correspond to any *actual* human action.

Let us take the first or the second interpretation.[8] It is meaningless to say that point S corresponds to a pure substitution effect (with a constant level of utility), since point D has no meaning for the individual. In fact, he *has* resources equal to OA and there is only a substitution effect, expressed by the rotation of the AB line to AC. Given the time resources he has, substitutions are possible along the budget constraint and these substitutions depend on the relative price between Q_1 and Q_2.

In the third interpretation, one cannot determine the value of the so-called income effect as long as one has not made clear which are the actual substitutions between the quantity of good Q_3, on the one hand, and the quantities of goods Q_1 and Q_2 on the other hand. But this is precisely saying that there is no income effect, and that there are only substitution effects between several possible uses of resources. Let us take the case of an individual who is choosing, at some point of time, a given allocation of his resources, especially as regards his time resources, to obtain a certain basket of goods, among which leisure has to be considered. To accept sacrificing an additional unit of leisure, he necessarily has to get compensation by obtaining a greater quantity of other goods. If ever there is an increase in the market price of time (that is, a decrease in the price of other goods), it creates purely and simply a substitution effect.

The general belief in the existence of an income effect partially stems from an artificial separation between consumption activities and production activities. This distinction is usual in microeconomics: The theory of consumption and the theory of production are founded on different grounds and different behavioral assumptions. In fact one does not supply a good without demanding another good, so that the decision to produce and to supply cannot be separated from the decision to demand and to consume. By cutting, for instance, decisions related to consumption or decisions related to work from other decisions, the traditional theory implicitly maintains as constant certain variables that cannot be maintained as constant. It considers, for instance, the choice between two consumption goods, as if the whole set of activities was not implied. A specific assumption concerning choices made about these other activities is then called the income effect. As we have seen, a change in the relative price between two commodities has consequences which depend not only on the choices made by an individual about these commodities, but about the whole set of possibilities open to him.

In traditional microeconomics the income effect and the substitution effect are presented as similarly general effects. In fact, the substitution effect is the only one to exist. Now, it may appear that something close

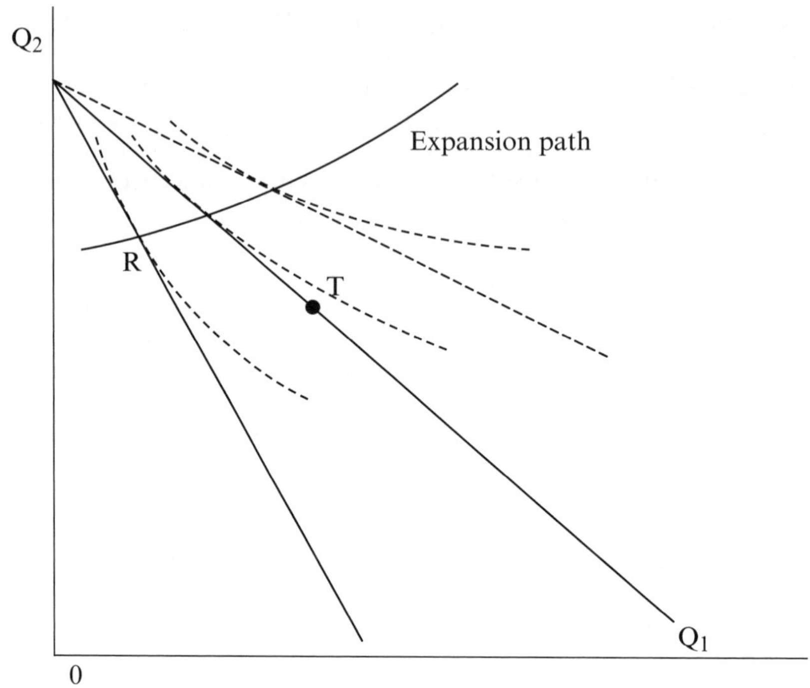

Figure 17.3 A misleading relation between the supply of labor and its price

to the so-called income effect appears under specific assumptions when adjusting from one equilibrium point to another. However, this effect, which describes a specific adjustment path, is only transitory and it does not necessarily exist. This difference between both effects has important consequences. It means, for instance, that the Laffer effect necessarily exists: An individual shifts from an activity that is heavily taxed to other activities. However, the process of adjustment may not be instantaneous, so that one may have the feeling that people react contrary to what the substitution effect would lead to expect. But, this effect, if ever it exists, is necessarily a transitory and secondary phenomenon.

From a formal point of view, one can draw an expansion path so that the quantity of labor is decreasing as long as its price is increasing (Figure 17.3), but this is nothing else than a graphical representation. Now, a graphical assumption does not give any information on the real motives of human behavior. The latter has to be explained by the law of decreasing marginal utility, which is in reality a theory of human choices founded on rational logic. If one believes – as it ought to be – that all reasoning in social sciences has to be coherent with rational logic, it just means that one must get rid of the graphical or mathematical appearances, which are inconsistent with this logic.

APPENDIX IS A BACKWARD-BENDING SUPPLY CURVE POSSIBLE?

As aforementioned, an interesting question can be raised: Is it consistent to admit both that the income effect does not exist and that the supply curve (for instance, for labor) can be locally backward sloping? To try to solve this question, let us take the case of an individual who is going up his supply curve when his real wage increases (Figure 17.4). His supply of labor thus shifts from E to A when his real wage shifts from w_0 to w_1. This increase in supply obviously corresponds to the law of diminishing

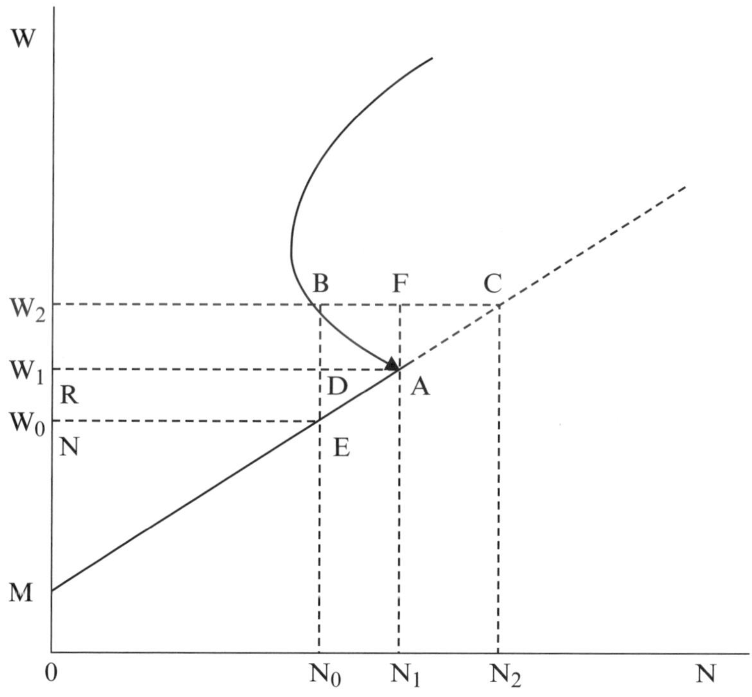

Figure 17.4 The illusion of a backward-bending supply curve

marginal utility. In order to give up one additional unit of leisure, the individual wants a higher real wage as a compensation for his loss of utility. This is exactly the meaning of the supply curve.

However, one has to clarify the distinction between the marginal return and the average return. Let us assume that the supply curve in Figure 17.4 represents the daily supply of labor of the individual. At point A, he works for ten hours for a hourly wage of $1, so his daily income is $10. He considers that it is worthwhile working one more hour only if this additional hour is paid at least $2, which means that he wants an income of at least $12 for 11 hours of work. From his point of view, it is exactly equivalent to get $2 for the marginal hour, the other hours being paid $1, or to get a higher average hourly wage – in our example $1.09 – under the condition that he works 11 hours and not ten. If his job is totally specific – there is no possible substitution with other workers – the price of successive hours can be differentiated and the employer may be ready to pay more for the additional hour.[9]

Now, if we consider a market situation with substitutable workers, such a differentiation of wages according to the number of hours worked within a day is not possible, so that the supply curve of Figure 17.4 represents the amount of work hours offered for any hourly (average) real wage. Let us anyhow consider the behavior of one given worker. Let us assume that he is at point E when the real wage is equal to w_0. The precise meaning of this point is the following. Any wage lower than w_0 would be insufficient to compensate the individual for the disutility of an amount of labor equal to N_0. He needs at least w_0 or more.

However, if the market wage is w_0, he cannot get more than w_0. Now, if the market wage rate increases from w_0 to w_1, the preferred point is A. As there is no wage differentiation, the new wage is paid not only on the marginal hours (N_1–N_0) but even on those hours which were already worked when the real wage was w_0, namely N_0. Point A thus represents the minimum increase in the *average* wage rate, which is necessary for the *marginal* return thus obtained to be considered as a sufficient compensation for the increased disutility of work.

Under the traditional neoclassical approach it would be said that the individual got a surplus equal to MEN and that the increase in the market wage brought him an additional surplus equal to NEAR. In fact, the individual was ready to offer N_0 for a wage equal to w_0. Now, he can obtain w_1 for this amount of work, so that he gets a sort of windfall profit equal to DENR; and he also gets a marginal surplus equal to EDA. For reasons linked to the distinction made above between the average and the marginal wage rate, the existence of this surplus can be disputed: One might say that the increase in the average wage rate (w_1–w_0) is just sufficient to allow the individual to get the minimum marginal wage rate he wants in order to offer additional work time (from N_0 to N_1). Therefore, we cannot quantify something like a surplus. But we can be certain that point A is preferred to point E. For a wage rate equal to w_0 the individual did not want to work more than N_0. An increase in the average wage rate necessarily means an increase in the marginal rate, thus inducing him to work more: He prefers A to D. This is the rationale for the upward-sloping supply curve.

This discussion on the very meaning of the supply curve may help us to decide whether this curve can become backward sloping at some point, for instance at point A. If such a situation exists, it means that if ever the wage rate increases from w_1 to w_2, the supply of labor decreases from N_1 to N_0 (instead of increasing to N_2). This is exactly what is assumed by those who believe in the existence of an income effect: As the individual gets more money for any work hour, he works fewer hours. Is that possible?

Saying that the curve is backward sloping, as represented in Figure 17.4, is saying that point B is preferred to A.[10] As we know, point B is preferred to point D and to point E (the higher the wage rate for a given amount of work, the more satisfied the individual). We also know that D was not preferred to A, but there is no reason for B not to be preferred to A. However, the real question is not knowing whether B is preferred to A, but knowing whether it makes sense saying that B is on the supply curve. We explained above why A is preferred to D (or, at least, not less desired). Exactly the same reasoning has to be made as regards point B: If the wage rate increases from w_1 to w_2, the individual desires a point which is not on the left of point F (for instance, point C). Therefore, although it may be true that B is preferred to A, C is preferred to B. It means that point B is not a point that the individual may *actually* choose.

Another way to look at this problem is the following. As above, the supply curve is nothing but a frontier between points which are not desired (those under the curve) and those that are accepted (those which are on or above the curve). At point E the individual declines all wage rates lower than w_0 and accepts all higher wage rates. At point B, the individual is supposed to decline all wage rates lower than w_2 and to accept all higher wage rates. But it does not make sense to assume both that wage rates higher than w_0 are accepted for an amount of work equal to N_0, and that wages rates under w_2 are declined for the same amount of work.

To summarize, the income effect is supposed to exist because one assumes that the concept of income can be defined in a non-ambiguous way. In fact, this is not true. Whereas it is generally assumed that income can be measured, it has no precise meaning, contrary to the concept of utility, which is precise but does not allow any room for measurement. The present chapter has shown that believing in the income effect is not consistent with the logical theory of utility. In reality the income effect can exist only if one adds a specific assumption. Contrary to the general belief according to which the existence of the income effect is a general principle, it is only a possible consequence of a specific assumption. The substitution effect, consistent with the general theory of utility, is the only general principle.

NOTES

1. Initially published as Salin (1996a).
2. I thank Philippe Lacoude and Frédéric Sautet for their very pertinent comments on a previous version of this text, the idea of which stemmed from a talk with them.
3. The increase in a tax rate decreases the tax base and, beyond a certain tax rate, this effect is sufficiently important for the increase in the tax rate to induce a decrease in tax revenues instead of an increase. It is now usual to label this process as the "Laffer effect." But it had been developed before Arthur Laffer gave it a popular expression. One can find it, for instance, in a refined form in Brennan and Buchanan (1980).
4. Hans-Hermann Hoppe raised an interesting question on a previous version of this chapter: If the income effect does not exist, does it imply that a supply curve cannot be backward sloping? We explain in the Appendix why, in our opinion, it is impossible.
5. Figure 17.1 is extracted from the classical textbook, Henderson and Quandt (1958). But a similar graph can be found in most microeconomics textbooks.
6. Let us use this traditional concept, although it induces the danger of splitting a human being into different, uncoordinated, parts (the consumer, the producer, the taxpayer, and so on).
7. As an example, one may imagine that the budget constraint is rotating around point R.
8. Both interpretations are very close to each other. They imply that, from a given stock of resources – for instance, time resources – an individual can obtain a good either via a technological process of transformation he is doing by himself, or via a process of exchange concerning his labor services or the outcome of his labor.
9. There is always a certain degree of specificity in the employment of a worker. For instance, as transaction costs do exist, an employer will prefer to pay more for extra hours by a worker who is already employed in his firm than hiring an additional worker.
10. If B was not preferred to A, it would just mean that the supply curve cannot go through B.

References

Abel, E. (1981), "Looking Ahead from the Twentieth Century," in R.W. Haigh, G. Gerbner and R.B. Byrne (eds), *Communications in the Twenty-First Century*, New York: John Wiley & Sons, p. 8.

Alvarez, A.S. (2003), "Behavioral and Environmental Correlates of Digital Inequality," *IT&Society*, 1 (5), 7–140.

Bastiat, F. (1848), "Justice et fraternité," *Journal des économistes*, 15 Juin 1848; reprinted in Bastiat, F. (1863), *Œuvres complètes*, vol. IV, Paris: Guillaumin, pp. 298–326.

Bastiat, F. (1863), "Des salaires," *Œuvres complètes*, vol. VI, Paris: Guillaumin (in English: du Huszar, G.B. (ed.) [1964], "Wages," *Economic Harmonies*, Princeton, NJ: Van Nostrand, Chapter XIV, translated by W. Hayden Boyers).

Bhagwati, J. (1958), "Immiserizing Growth: A Geometric Note," *Review of Economic Studies*, 25 (June), 201–5.

Block, W. (1999), "Austrian Theorizing: Recalling the Foundations," *The Quarterly Journal of Austrian Economics*, 2 (4), 21–39.

Brander, J.A. and B.J. Spencer (1984), "Tariff Protection and Imperfect Competition," in H. Kierzkowski, *Monopolistic Competition and International Trade*, Oxford: Clarendon Press, pp. 194–206.

Brennan, G. and J.M. Buchanan (1980), *The Power to Tax*, Cambridge: Cambridge University Press.

Caplan, B. (1999), "The Austrian Search for Realistic Foundations," *Southern Economic Journal*, 65 (4), 823–8.

Coase, R. (1937), "The Nature of the Firm," *Economica*, 4 (16), 386–405.

Coase, R.H. (1960), "The Problem of Social Cost," *Journal of Law and Economics*, 3 (1), 1–44.

Compaine, B. (2001), "Information Gaps: Myth or Reality?" in B. Compaine (ed.), *The Digital Divide*, Cambridge, MA and London: The MIT Press, p. 107.

Dorn, J.A. (ed.) (1997), *The Future of Money in the Information Age*, Washington, DC: Cato Institute.

Dorn, J. (1999), "Interview," in Lepage, H. and P. Wajmann (eds), *Vingt Economistes face à la crise*, Paris: Odile Jacob.

Emerick, N. (2003), *The Real Digital Divide*, FMF monograph no. 36, Johannesburg, South Africa: The Free Market Foundation.

Grossman, G. and E. Helpman (1991), *Innovation and Growth in the Global Economy*, Cambridge, MA: MIT Press.

Hayek, F.A. (1976), *Choice in Currency: A Way to Stop Inflation*, London: Institute of Economic Affairs.

Hayek, F.A. (1978), *Denationalisation of Money – The Argument Refined*, London: Institute of Economic Affairs.

Helpman, E. and P.R. Krugman (1985), *Market Structures and Foreign Trade*, Cambridge, MA: MIT Press.

Helpman, E. and P.R. Krugman (1989), *Trade Policy and Market Structure*, Cambridge, MA: MIT Press.

Henderson, J.M. and R.E. Quandt (1958), *Microeconomic Theory*, New York: McGraw-Hill.

Hoppe, H.H. (1994), "How is Fiat Money Possible? – or, The Devolution of Money and Credit," *Review of Austrian Economics*, 7 (2), 49–74.

Hoppe, H.H., J.G. Hülsmann, and W. Block (1998), "Against Fiduciary Media," *Quarterly Journal of Austrian Economics*, 1 (1), 19–50.

Hülsmann, J.G. (1996), "Free Banking and the Free Bankers," *Review of Austrian Economics*, 9 (1), 3–53.

Kenen, P. (1969), "The Theory of Optimum Currency Areas: An Eclectic View," in R. Mundell and A. Swoboda, *Monetary Problems of the International Economy*, Chicago, IL: The University of Chicago Press, pp. 41–60.

Kennedy, T., B. Wellman and K. Klement (2003), "Gendering the Digital Divide," *IT&Society*, 1 (5), 72–96.

Krugman, P. (1979), "Increasing Returns, Monopolistic Competition, and International Trade," *Journal of International Economics*, 9 (4), 469–79.

Lancaster, K.T. (1966), "A New Approach to Consumer Theory," *Journal of Political Economy*, 74 (April), 132–57.

Lancaster, K.T. (1991), *Modern Consumer Theory*, Aldershot and Brookfield, VT: Edward Elgar.

Lane, G. (2001), "Bastiat, l'aversion pour l'incertitude et la loi de l'association," *Journal des économistes et des études humaines*, 11 (June/September), 415–50.

Lenhart, A. and J.B. Horrigan (2003), "Re-Visualizing the Digital Divide as a Digital Spectrum," *IT&Society*, 1 (5), 23–39.

Liebowitz, S.J. and S.E. Margolis (1999), *Winners, Losers & Microsoft*, Oakland, CA: The Independent Institute.

Lu, M. (2001), "Digital Divide in Developing Countries," *Journal of Global Information Technology Management*, 4 (3), 1–4.

McKinnon, R. (1969), "Private and Official International Money: The

Case of the Dollar," in *Essays in International Finance*, no. 74, Princeton, NJ: International Finance Section.
Mises, L. von (1996), *Human Action: A Treatise on Economics*, 4th edn, Irvington-on-Hudson, NY: Foundation for Economic Education.
Mises, L. von (1998), *Human Action: The Scholar's Edition*, Auburn, AL: The Ludwig von Mises Institute.
Mundell, R.A. (1960), "A Theory of Optimum Currency Areas," *American Economic Review*, 51 (September), 657–65.
Musgrave, P. (1991), "Merits and Demerits of Fiscal Competition," in R. Prud'homme (ed.), *Public Finance with Several Levels of Government, Proceedings of the 46th Congress*, Brussels: IIPF, pp. 281–97.
Oates, W.E. (1972), *Fiscal Federalism*, New York: Harcourt Brace Jovanovich.
OECD (Organisation for Economic Co-operation And Development) (1998), *Harmful Tax Competition*, Paris: OECD Publications.
Rivera-Batiz, L. and P. Romer (1991), "Economic Integration and Endogeneous Growth," *Quarterly Journal of Economics*, 106, 531–56.
Romer, P. (1987), "Growth Based on Increasing Returns Due to Specialization," *American Economic Review*, 77, 56–62.
Rothbard, M. (1956), "Toward a Reconstruction of Utility and Welfare Economics," in M. Sennholz (ed.), *On Freedom and Free Enterprise: Essays in Honor of Ludwig von Mises*, New York: Van Nostrand, p. 227.
Rothbard, M. (1970), *Power and Market*, Arlington, VA: Institute for Humane Studies.
Rothbard, M. (1991), *The Case for a 100 Percent Gold Dollar*, Auburn, AL: Ludwig von Mises Institute.
Rothbard, M. (1993), *Man, Economy and State*, 3rd edn, Auburn, AL: Ludwig von Mises Institute.
Salin, P. (1980), *European Monetary Unity: For Whose Benefit?* Brussels: Institutum Europaeum.
Salin, P. (ed.) (1984), *Currency Competition and Monetary Union*, The Hague: Martinus Nijhoff.
Salin, P. (1989/1991), "The Case Against Tax Harmonization," report prepared for the Conference on Global Disequilibrium, Montréal, McGill University, 17–19 May 1989; also presented at the Annual Meeting of the European Public Choice Society, Beaune, 3–6 April 1991.
Salin, P. (1990a), "Comment on a report by Vito Tanzi and Lans Bovenberg – Is There a Need for Harmonizing Capital Income Taxes within EC Countries?" in H. Siebert (ed.), *Reforming Capital Income Taxation*, Tübingen, Germany: J.C.B. Mohr, Institut für Weltwirtschaft an der Universität Kiel.

Salin, P. (1990b), "The Problems of Tax Harmonization," CIDAS, Conference on A Free Society for Europe, Turin, Italy, 3–5 October.
Salin, P. (1990c), "Macro-Stabilisation and the Market Process," in K. Groenveld, J.A.H. Maks and J. Muysken (eds), *Economic Policy and the Market Process*, Amsterdam: North-Holland Publishing Company.
Salin, P. (1990d), "The Choice of Currency in a Single European Market," *Cato Journal*, 10 (2), 363–76.
Salin, P. (1994), "International Tax Problems: Between Coordination and Competition," *Journal des économistes et des études humaines*, 5 (1), 3–23.
Salin, P. (1995), *La concurrence*, Paris: Presses Universitaires de France.
Salin, P. (1996a), "The Income Effect Does not Exist," *The Review of Austrian Economics*, 1 (9), 95–106.
Salin, P. (1996b), "Cartels as Efficient Productive Structures," *The Review of Austrian Economics*, 9 (2), 79–82.
Salin, P. (1998), "Free Banking and Fractional Reserves: A Comment," *The Quarterly Journal of Austrian Economics*, 1 (3), 61–6.
Salin, P. (2001), "World Regulations and Harmonization," *The Independent Review*, 6 (1), 59–80.
Salin, P. (2002), "The Firm in a Free Society: Following Frédéric Bastiat's Insights," *Journal of Libertarian Studies*, 16 (3), 1–18.
Salin, P. (2007a), *In Defense of the Free Market*, Prague: Liberalni Institut, Bratislava, Konzervativny Institut M.R. Stefanika.
Salin, P. (2007b), "The Case Against 'Tax Harmonization': The OECD and EU Initiatives," in H. H. Gissurarson and T.T. Herbertsson (eds), *Cutting Taxes To Increase Prosperity*, Reykjavik: Bokafélagio Publishing & RSE.
Salin, P. (2010), *Revenir au capitalisme pour éviter les crises*, Paris: Odile Jacob.
Salin, P. (2011a), "Wie viele und welche Währungen benötigt Europa?" in P. Altmiks (ed.), *Die optimale Währung für Europa? Segen und Fluch des Euro*, Munich, Germany: Olzog, pp. 95–116.
Salin, P. (2011b), "De la crise financière à la crise de la dette et de l'euro," *L'Actualité Économique* (Montréal), 87 (4), 503–18.
Salin, P. (2012), "There is no 'Euro crisis'," *The Wall Street Journal*, 18 July.
Salin (2013a), "Entreprise ou marché: où sont les limites?" in M. Gollety (ed.), *L'art, la gestion et l'Etat – Mélanges en l'honneur de Pierre Gregory*, Paris: Editions Eska.
Salin, P. (2013b), "Choosing the Best Policy Mix to Cure Europe's Stagnation," *Cato Journal*, 33 (2), 253–61.
Salin, P. (2014a), *La tyrannie fiscale*, Paris: Odile Jacob.

Salin, P. (2014b), *Concurrence et liberté des échanges*, Nice, France: Libréchange.
Selgin, G. (1988), *The Theory of Free Banking*, Washington, DC: Cato Institute.
Selgin, G. and L. White (1994), "How Would the Invisible Hand Handle Money?" *Journal of Economic Literature*, 32 (4), 1718–49.
Samuelson, P.A. (1969), "The Way of an Economist," in P.A. Samuelson (ed.), *International Economic Relations: Proceedings of the Third Congress of the International Economic Association*, London: Macmillan, pp. 1–11.
Tiebout, C.M. (1956), "A Pure Theory of Local Expenditures," *Journal of Political Economy*, 64 (5), 416–24.
White, L. (1999), *The Theory of Monetary Institutions*, Oxford: Blackwell.

Index

Abel, Ellie 243
agglomeration 69–70
All Saints' Day Manifesto (1975) 177
Apple, Inc. 81, 92
associations 4, 17, 26
  charitable 26
  cultural 26
  members of 5
  voluntary 17
Austrian School 59, 80, 189–91, 195, 198, 264–5, 267, 270, 275–7
  Austrian business cycle theory 160, 170, 190, 194, 197, 200, 204, 214
    concept of 158
  critiques of 265–7
  focus on gold standard 193
  focus on quantity of money 191, 195–6
  use of microeconomics 191
  view of budget deficits 217
austerity policies 212–13, 215, 217–18
  role of savings in adoption of 213–14
  variants of 218

balance of payments 114, 158, 189, 198, 273
  deficit 107
  issues 124–5, 198
  monetarist view of 158–9, 199
Bank of England 221
bankruptcy 24, 173, 200
Basel II Agreement 207
Bastiat, Frédéric 3–6, 11, 17, 78
  Economic Harmonies (1863) 3
Block, Walter 266–7
Brennan, Geoffrey 114
Buchanan, James 114
budget constraints 265–7, 282–5
budget deficits 219
  Austrian school view of 217
  consequences of 216
  Keynesian focus on 157, 215–16
  reduction of 215
Bush, George W.
  administration of 129

capital 23–4, 124, 132, 136, 160, 195
  accumulation of 205, 214
  controls 128
  equity 207–8
  flows of 69
    international 171
    outflow 129
  human 15, 139, 241
  marginal productivity of 199
  taxation of 118–20, 132
capital flight 119–22, 124
capitalism 3, 6, 10, 17, 19, 21, 24–5, 203, 205, 207–8, 211
  firms 12, 14
  organizations 13
Caplan, Bryan 264, 269
  view of Austrian school 264–5
cartels 27, 29, 33–6, 40, 42, 164, 168, 177, 181–2, 200, 234
  as intermediate productive structure 40–41
  as value-producing organization 35–40
  criticisms of 27–8, 30–2, 35, 86–7
  definitions of 40–41, 80
  mergers 41
  monetary 163, 181–2, 224, 230–31, 233
  -monopoly 164, 167
  private 28
  production of coordination gains by 37
  public 86, 164
  theory of 35
  value judgment of 32

cash balances 158, 189–90, 215–16
excess 199
nominal 199, 225–6
purchasing power of 194
real 192–3, 198, 225
central banks 110, 152, 163, 168–9, 175, 177–80, 182, 190–91, 193, 199, 204, 206, 221, 229
European 146
national 154, 224
personnel of 201
single 147, 150, 166–7, 172
centralization 36, 53, 145, 150, 166, 182
of money production 158
of taxation 122
Chicago School 189, 191, 200–201
focus on existing monetary systems 193, 200–201
use of macroeconomics 191–2
China, People's Republic of 205, 214
closed economy 102, 111, 124, 129
moving from 114
taxation system of 117
Coase, Ronald 41, 85
Coase problem 20
collectivism 59, 61
view of individuals 79
commodity flight 121
commodity market 108–9
common currency 38, 178
competitive 177
creation of 175
common markets xiv, 38, 53, 101, 105, 180
concept of 148–9
creation of 52, 122
for currencies 178, 182
communism 128
Compaine, Benjamin 253
comparative advantage 63, 65–6, 68, 74
internal 111
in international trade theory 59–61
competition 30, 52–3, 80, 115–16, 167
definitions of 48
as instrument of change 62
role of diversification in 52
competition theory 244
Austrian 32–3
traditional xiii, 27, 30, 32, 35, 39, 46–7
as basis of European competition law 46
competitive currencies 173–4
constructivism xi, 51, 82, 85
continuous utility function 270
contracts 19, 23, 51, 79, 103, 131, 133, 154, 168, 175, 230, 274
firms as system of 19, 22, 24, 103, 120
freedom 79, 92, 125
labor 15, 23
termination of 15
convertibility guarantees 181
cooperation xi, 4–6, 8, 17, 26, 31, 38, 40–42, 127, 148–9, 165, 185, 243
international 87, 89, 92–3, 96
social 11–12
coordination gains 38, 80, 83
production by cartels 37
corporation 40, 254–5
corporate culture 26
limited 28
unlimited liability 28
credit 36, 165, 170–71, 174, 181, 190, 204, 208, 216, 229
artificial 204–5
expansionary 159
interest on 227
organizations 206–7
currencies/currency 36, 162, 232, 238
choice 170–71
creation of 37–8, 222–4, 232–3
additional unit production 224–5
circulation of existing monetary units 227–8, 234–5
new forms 224, 228, 234
depreciation of 108, 163
exchange rate of 110
fractional reserves 228–30
optimal number of 231
parallel 180
revaluing of 160
currency competition 172–3, 178, 180, 182
role in choice of monetary systems 193, 200

debt crisis 212–19
deflation 157, 171, 174, 226
  concept of 225
  rate of 192
demand curve 279
devaluation
  as policy tool 154
differentiation xii, 11, 13–14, 28, 33, 36, 38–9, 48, 50, 78, 81–2, 172, 178–9, 182, 231, 249, 288
  benefits of 35, 162–3
  of goods 32, 36
    maximum 81
  of roles in firms 3, 7–8, 10
  of taxation systems 127
  optimal degree of 84
digital divide 242–3, 247, 254–7, 260
  concept of 240–41, 249–50
  education 244–6, 248, 250, 252–3
  potential benefits of 243–4, 247
  potential obstacles 244–5
  private endeavours 254–5
  reduction policies 245–6
    compulsory methods 255
    state intervention 253–4
  spreading techniques 247–8
  support for 252
  universal access 256–7
Dorn, James 238

e-business 77, 221
economies of scale 36, 67–9, 73
  diseconomies of scale 38–9
  institutional 38
e-currencies 221–2
  creation of 224
  development of 236–7
    optimal dimension of monetary zones 235
    role of reserves in 236–7
  potential consequences of 231
  web-gold-money (WGM) 232–5
Emerick, Neil 252–3
entrepreneurship 6, 225, 274
Esperanto xvi
Estonia
  use of flat rate tax in 129
ethics 70–73
European Central Bank (ECB) 153, 167–8, 180, 221
  creation of 163
  monetary policy of 175
    purchasing of public bonds 184
European Commission 47–8, 111, 149
  recommendations on taxation policies 106–7, 128
European Court of Justice 91
European Monetary System (EMS) 146, 164, 166
European Union (EU) 44, 47, 53, 85, 91, 122, 136, 141
  integration in 50
  Maastricht Treaty (1992) 146, 148, 166, 168–9, 175–7, 219
    signatories of 168
  member states of 59, 120, 128
  opposition to tax competition in 128
Eurozone 146, 166, 169, 178–9, 219
  Crisis (2009–) 183–5
  economic conditions within 152
  members of 183
  potential collapse of 153
exchange rates 108, 161, 168
  changes in 110, 150
  fixed 150, 154–6, 160, 169, 198, 201
  flexible 156–7, 161–2, 198, 200–201

federalism 86
  fiscal 115, 125
  tax 122
financial crisis 203–212
firms 6–8, 12, 16–17, 20–22
  capitalist 14
  definitions of 11
  internal organization of 39
  organization 7
  as system of contracts 19, 22, 24
  transformation into 6
France 52, 254
  taxation system of 112, 129
free exchange 26, 50, 57–9, 66, 69, 73–4
  benefits of 63, 74
  limiting of 58, 65
  opposition to 58
free markets xii, 33, 63, 86, 109, 180
  shift to 149
free trade 57–8, 66, 68–9, 72, 148, 161
  relationship with growth 74
Friedman, Milton 157, 189, 193, 204, 216

improved variety of quantity theory 195–6

general exchange principle 60, 63–5
exceptions to 71
Germany 173
Deutsche Mark (DM) 169
Fall of Berlin Wall (1989) 53
Global Financial Crisis (2007–9) 203–5
causes of 205–6, 214
governance problems of banks 208
regulations 206–7
US housing policy 206
US subprime mortgage crisis (2007–9) 204
responses to
austerity policies 212–13, 217–18
monetary policy 211
recovery policies 209–10
regulations 211–13
role of savings in 214–15
globalization 58, 62, 73–5, 77–8, 91
definitions of 57, 127
influence of comparative advantage on 58–9
opposition to 58
infant industry issue 63–5, 67, 73
gold 37, 162, 190–91, 197, 199–200, 219, 221, 223–5, 227–8, 232–5
guarantee for currencies 173, 185
prices of 38
property rights in 190
reserves 226, 229, 233
standard 177, 191, 193
stock 190, 230
Great Depression 157
Greece
Sovereign Debt Crisis (2009–) 183–4
gross national product (GNP) 70, 176, 251
growth rates 69–70, 245, 247, 252
decline in 70
potential impact on digital divide 249

harmonization/harmonizing xii–xiii, 52, 79–81, 86–8, 101, 145, 148–50
centralized xiv
international public goods 93–5
norms 91–2
diversity of 93
international 91, 93–4
of production conditions 109, 149
of regulations 90–91, 166
of taxation systems 90, 106, 108–9, 117–18, 120–22, 124–5, 127, 134, 137, 149, 166, 180
process of 49
Hayek, Friedrich xi, xiv, 37, 48, 85, 93, 175, 231
role in development of Austrian business cycle theory 158, 170, 204
theory of competition 115–16, 244
homogenization xiii–xiv, 28, 36, 39, 49, 78, 80, 82–3, 230
in production processes 28, 40
of goods 32
optimal degree of 36, 83–4
profit from 81
world language 82
worldwide 82

Index of Economic Freedom 251
indifference 267
critique of concept 267–8
curves 265
individualism 54, 61
inflation 49, 108, 156, 170, 173, 225–6
concept of 194
hyper-inflation 193–4
money creation as cause of 157
rates of 169, 179, 191, 198, 204
optimal 192
integration xiv–xv, 51–2, 148, 155–6, 182
economic xv, 50–51, 57, 165
European 46, 49–50, 53, 85, 121, 145–8, 162, 182
criticisms of 52–3
linguistic xv–xvi
monetary 146–7, 166, 182
regional political 85, 95
interest rates 169, 204
equilibrium 170
flexibility of 214
fluctuation in 160
real 170–71, 192, 199, 205

International Air Transport Association (IATA) 39
International Monetary Fund (IMF) 165, 216
international tax coordination 115
international trade theory 60, 75, 107
  comparative advantage principle in 59–61
  impact of taxation 104–5
  Ricardian model of 104
investment funds 207
investment goods 158, 190, 194
  demand for 159–60

Kenen, Peter 158
Keynes, John Maynard 204
Keynesianism 156, 158, 198, 209–10, 214–16, 276
  criticisms of 154
  focus on government budget deficits 157, 215–16
  recovery plans 209
  view of causes of unemployment 214

labor 8, 20, 59, 69, 111, 117, 124, 136–7, 279, 286–7
  contracts 15, 23
  market 13, 184, 213, 218
  productivity of 135, 280, 283
  services 15, 22–3, 272–3, 275
  supply of 279–81, 287
Laffer effect 133, 136, 279
  concept of 219
Leviathan state model 114, 122–5, 130, 133, 136, 139, 141
liberalization 62, 70, 121, 182
  international 124
  labor market 184
  opposition to 62–3, 70–71
  trade 77
  unilateral 89
Linux 259
liquidity 37, 171, 204, 210
  supply of 184

macroeconomics xii, 59, 169–70
  use by Chicago School 191–2
market economy 16, 21
market structures
  unstable 35
Marxism 3, 6, 14, 276
McKinnon, Ronald 158
Mexico 106
microeconomics 12, 26, 279, 285
  price change 283–5
    income effect 276, 279, 282, 285–6, 289–90
    substitution effect 279, 282–6
  use by Austrian School 191
Microsoft Corporation 92, 254, 260
  protection of source codes 259–60
von Mises, Ludwig 189–90, 194, 199, 252, 264–5
  regression theorem 194
  role in development of Austrian business cycle theory 158, 170, 204
monetarism 201, 204, 209
  view of balance of payments 158–9, 199
monetary economy 110
monetary policy 152–3, 159, 170, 203, 210–11
  America 169, 203
  convergence of 175
  deflationary 157
  expansionary 198–9, 204–5, 208, 214, 216
  French 169
  German 169
  independent 156, 160
  responses to Global Financial Crisis (2007–9) 211
  single 157
  state interventionism 203, 208–9
monetary stability 160
  international 177
monetary systems 53, 145–6, 149, 167–8, 177–80, 182, 184, 191–3, 200–201, 204, 221–2, 226, 228–9, 234–8
  fractional 230
  non-national 161
  poorly managed 165
  potential denationalization of 231–2
  role of banks in 227
  sterling 221
monetary unification 146–7, 149, 153, 160, 167, 169–70, 174
  European 177

gradual approach to 168
relationship with political unification 147
money 221, 225–6
creation of 36, 41, 80, 162–3, 180, 196, 205, 218, 237
as cause of inflation 157
excessive 201
demand for 225
neutrality of 195
nominal quantity of 197
purchasing power of 159–60, 164, 170, 174, 189–92, 197, 237
quantity theory of 191, 195–7
monopoly 27, 30–32, 36–7, 47, 49, 67–8, 140, 163–4, 167, 173, 182
criticisms of 172
definitions of 47
discriminatory 255
national 163
natural 36, 83
traditional theory of 39
state 49–50, 83
theory of 34–5
Mundell, Robert 157–8, 189, 196, 199–200
role in development of OCA theory 155
view of real cash balances 198
Musgrave, Peggy B.
criticisms of tax competition 116–18
mutual fund 4–5, 17

Napoleonic Code 46
nation states 83–6
dissolution of 85
merging of 84
optimal degree of 84
nationalism 57, 161
neoclassical economists 264, 266, 270, 275
equality 270
equity 267, 269
Networked Readiness Index 250–51
North American Free Trade Agreement (NAFTA)
signatories of 106

oligopoly 30–31
open economy 114
role of tax competition in 132–3
optimum currency areas (OCAs) 152–3, 157–8, 161, 164, 173–4, 178
definitions of 158
theory of 155–6
optimum public good area 115
organization 20–22, 89, 99, 177
capitalist 13
economic 7
hierarchical 9, 13
internal 42
international 94, 141
mutual 5
non-market 20–21
social 19
voluntary 17
Organisation for Economic Co-operation and Development (OECD) 129, 136, 141
Harmful Tax Competition (1998) 128

Phillips curve 216
concept of 157
planned economy 21, 47, 150
politicization
of decisions 52–3, 164
price theory 277
general 198, 200
price index 192, 194–5
production 47, 82, 108–9, 119, 128, 170–71, 273–4
conditions of 101
harmonization of 109, 149
dominant producers 91–2
factors 60, 122, 131, 137, 139, 150, 160, 209, 274, 280
mobile 128, 133, 135–6
returns of 111, 119, 134
foreign 112
money 36, 41, 80, 162–3, 180, 196, 201, 205
national 112
restriction of 33–4
structure 201, 209
unit cost of 24
production processes/systems 11, 33
franchising 23
homogenization in 28, 40

socialist 8
Soviet 19, 32
transformation of 86
profit maximization 14, 34
profit-sharing 15
contradiction of 15–16
mandating of 16
property rights 16, 44–6, 51, 88, 95–6, 228, 246–7, 249
air 123
atmospheric pollution responses 96–7
definitions of 50, 66
ethics of 72–3
universal 72–3
in gold 190
individual 21, 54
intellectual 256–8
private protection of 259–60
legitimate 21–2, 44–5
protection of 50
recognition of 45, 51, 54
sea/water 95–6
protectionism 66–9, 71–2, 89
policies of 69
public goods 140
international 116
issue of harmonization 93–5
purchasing power 156, 171, 173, 176–7, 194–5, 202
generalized 221–2, 236
loss of 111
of money 159–60, 164, 170, 174, 189–92, 197, 222, 237
of people 211
potential 190
purchasing power parity (PPP) 108, 110
pure exchange economy 17, 25–6

Rand, Ayn
concept of 'floating abstractions' 19
Reagan, Ronald 219
regulations
centralized process of 181
criticisms of 213–14
deregulation 180–81, 218
criticisms of 206–7
harmonization of 90–91, 166
responses to Global Financial Crisis (2007–9) 211–12
Revel, Jean-François 241
Ricardo, David 59, 134
model of international trade 104
Rothbard, Murray 30, 33–4
critiques of Austrian school 263–6, 269
critiques of neoclassical analysis 269
view of cartels 40

Samuelson, Paul 61
Sarkozy, Nicolas
French Finance Minister 128
savings 15, 36, 138, 204, 214
artificial 211, 216
circulation of 212
fake 205
role in responses to Global Financial Crisis (2007–9) 214–15
over-taxation of 120–21, 124, 133, 218
returns for 121, 132
voluntary 170, 205, 208–9, 211, 214
self-organization 7–9
single currency 36, 110, 146–8, 151–2, 155, 163–4, 167, 172, 180–81
creation of 149
role in single market 150
single market xiv, 107, 146–8, 171
creation of 171
proposed deregulation of 149–50
role of single currency in 150
social welfare 66, 213
socialism 4–6, 12–13, 17
production 8
sovereignty 34
national 154
role of monetary policy in 147, 152
Soviet Union (USSR) 19, 32
Spain 183
Financial Crisis (2008–14) 183
specialization 5, 7, 9, 67–70, 109, 190
international 59, 89, 106, 108, 111–12, 149
natural 74
potential influence of taxation on 106
super-profit 31–2, 34, 68, 230

supply curve 279–80
Switzerland 129

tariffs 50–52, 87–9, 113, 148, 253
  optimal tariff theory 67–8, 71, 112–13
taxation 71–2, 87, 101–2, 111–12, 119, 123–4, 130, 136–8, 140, 214, 219
  benefit taxes 116–17
  burden of 130–31, 134
  capital income tax 117–18, 138
  centralization 122
  corporate income tax 119, 137
  criticisms of 213
  differentiation of 127
  discriminatory 111–13, 124–5, 132
  ecological taxes 115, 123
  evasion 121, 140
  factor mobility 113, 116
  flat rate of 129
  general expenditure tax 121–2
  harmonization of 90, 106, 108–9, 117–18, 120–22, 124–5, 134, 137, 149, 166, 180
  impact on international trade theory 104–5, 113–14
  income tax 104, 117–21, 131–2, 137, 213, 218
    progressive 111, 113, 128, 138
    proportional 103, 108
  individuals as payers of 103–4, 119–20
  legislation 103
  optimal tax system 114, 129–30, 134
  potential influence on specialization 106
  rates of 59
  tax competition 101, 114, 124–5, 128, 135, 138–9
    criticisms of/opposition to 116–18, 127–9
    factor immobility 133–4, 136–7, 139
    limitations of 139–41
    mobile production factors 134–6, 139
    role in open economy 132–3
  tax coordination 101, 116–18, 122
  tax havens 138
  tax incidence 123
  tax neutrality 102–3
  value-added tax (VAT) 58–9, 103–5, 107–8, 110–12, 119, 131–2, 134, 213
    effects of 105
    fixed rate 110
    flexible rate 110
    non-discriminatory 105
    proportional 108
  zero-tax export system 107
telecommunications xiii, 36–7, 39, 57, 80, 128, 150, 162, 238, 253
theory of exchange 60–61, 72, 270
  general 57, 59
  in international exchange 60
transaction costs 20, 41, 162, 178, 231
  decrease 25, 167, 234–5
transportation 80, 83, 162
  air 238
treasury bonds 173

Ulam, Stanislaw 61
uncertainty 10–11
unemployment
  Keynesian view of causes of 214
United Kingdom (UK) 176, 182
United Nations (UN) 129
  Educational, Scientific and Cultural Organization (UNESCO)
    General Conference (1980)
      Macbride Commission Report 242
United States of America (USA) 83, 106, 122–3, 125, 157, 183–4, 203, 214, 240
  Department of Justice 90, 93, 206
  Federal Home Loan Mortgage Corporation (Freddie Mac) 206
  Federal National Mortgage Association (Fannie Mae) 206
  Federal Reserve System 203–4, 207
  subprime mortgage crisis (2007–9) 204, 206
universality 275
utility theory 277, 279, 290
  neoclassical 269

value 22, 32–3, 39, 64, 71–2, 131, 137, 160, 176, 192, 195, 213, 221–2, 231, 241, 252, 264, 268, 281
  cardinal 272–3
  market 10, 103, 271–2
  negative 226
  nominal 225
  ordinal 272
  of production 35, 37
  reserve of 150, 156
  subjective theory of 59–60, 263, 270–71

wage bill 274
world
  regulations 77–99
  rules, norms and standards 90–93
Wikipedia 240, 244
World Economic Forum
  World Report on Information Technologies (2008) 248–9
World Health Organization (WHO) 90
World Trade Organization (WTO) 87, 89